San Francisco Appetites and Afterthoughts

San Francisco Appetites and Afterthoughts

*In Search of the Good Life
By the Golden Gate*

By Ernest Beyl

GRIZZLY PEAK PRESS
Kensington, CA

For information contact:
Grizzly Peak Press
350 Berkeley Park Boulevard
Kensington, CA 94707
grizzlypeakpress.com

San Francisco Appetites and Afterthoughts
is published by Daniel N. David
and is distributed by Grizzly Peak Press.

Cover Photos Top to Bottom, Left to Right:
Top Row: Ernest Hemingway (photo: Lloyd Arnold), Dungeness
Crab (photo: Fred Hsu), Duke Ellington (photo: Peter Breinig).
Middle Row: Dizzy Gillespie (photo: Rick Carroll), Author's Panama
Hat (photo: Fred Lyon). *Bottom Row:* Maria Callas (photo: Houston
Rogers), Gold Rush Miners in Levi's (photo: Levi Strauss & Co.
Archives), Former San Francisco Mayor Willie Brown, Jr., Charlotte
Shultz, Tony Bennett (photo: Drew Altizer).

Design, layout and typesetting by
Sara B. Brownell • sarabbrownell.com

ISBN Number: 978-0-9839264-9-8
Library of Congress Number: 2016952358

Printed in the United States of America

"The aim of life is to live, and to live means to be aware, joyously, drunkenly, serenely, divinely aware."

~Henry Miller, *Tropic of Cancer*

"Ernie Beyl's *San Francisco Appetites & Afterthoughts* showed me how little I knew about the great City by the Bay, its history, its highlife, and its hidden pleasures. It's the ultimate guide to the city. I highly recommend it."

~Paul Theroux
Novelist and Travel Writer

"Sounds like Ernie Beyl found many Good Lives in San Francisco, and it is a wonder he survived them in this busy boom-town."

~Lawrence Ferlinghetti
Poet, Painter and Publisher

"As long as I've known Ernie—and that's a long time—he's always searched for the Good Life in San Francisco. Obviously he found it. In this perceptive book, a compendium of what he calls his appetites, he writes about everything he loves in his city. Reading about Ernie's appetites jogged my memory of these pleasures."

~Charlotte Shultz
Chief Protocol Officer, San Francisco

"Ernie Beyl is a quintessential San Francisco hipster and as such he possesses an innate "beat" sensibility. He understands what gives San Francisco its flavor. He writes eloquently about the character, and characters, of The City he loves. This collection is Ernie's Perfect Cioppino."

~Randall Kline
SFJAZZ, Founder and Executive Artistic Director

Ernie Beyl's *San Francisco Appetites and Afterthoughts* is an exquisite journey through San Francisco then and now. Culinary, jazz, architecture, the street. All through the unassuming eyes of a reporter and jazz aficionado with an appetite, he beautifully conveys some of San Francisco's most intimate magic. Ernie reveals his personal stories of San Francisco's most seminal moments. For anyone who loves San Francisco, this is a must read.

~Aaron Peskin
District Three, Board of Supervisors, San Francisco

Table of Contents

Introduction

I first met Ernie Beyl in the 1980s, when I was Mayor of San Francisco. During this time, he would occasionally contact my office for assistance on a variety of projects. In 1987, he proposed that the City host "San Francisco Week in Hong Kong," an event in which we hoped to showcase and celebrate the numerous business and cultural ties between the two cities.

Ernie worked tirelessly to put together this event abroad. He arranged for an out-of-service San Francisco cable car to be shipped to Hong Kong, organized a banquet featuring the City's best delicacies, including Dungeness crab and sourdough bread, and planned for the San Francisco Symphony Orchestra to perform in a Hong Kong concert hall. He also coordinated a softball game between a San Francisco team and a team from the Hong Kong Foreign Correspondent's Club. Overall, the event was a success—everyone had a lot of fun and important business agreements were conducted that are still in effect today.

Ernie penned *San Francisco Appetites and Afterthoughts* as a manifestation of his love and passion for our City. He writes that the City is a "kaleidoscope of fragments gathered over many years searching for the good life by the Golden Gate—and finding it."

Ernie's enthusiasm and optimism about San Francisco shine brightly through the pages of this book. It is a great tribute to our City by the Bay.

United States Senator
DIANNE FEINSTEIN

Foreword

I did a stint in Los Angeles in the 1960s before I returned to mother earth—my hometown San Francisco. During my time in the Southland I bought the Jag and did the whole nine yards. Got the obligatory divorce, got the pad in the Hollywood Hills and listened to smooth jazz by Ramsey Lewis. When I finally regained consciousness, I drove Highway One all the way to San Francisco to resume my life. The first person I sought out was a buddy I knew since we were both youngsters. San Francisco had changed. It always changes and not always for the best, as the naysayers like to naysay.

My friend introduced me around to some of his friends. And so it went. My favorite joints were in North Beach—Capp's Corner (an epic loss when it was forced to close) and the Washington Square Bar & Grill. It was the good life. Still is! I guess it could be said that I have an appetite for San Francisco. But not all appetites are about food and wine.

San Francisco Appetites and Afterthoughts is a kaleidoscope of fragments gathered over many years searching for the good life by the Golden Gate—and finding it. It's a hodgepodge of obsessions that focuses on people, places and pleasures. I want to place readers squarely in the middle of the narrative and allow these passions of mine to devolve and swirl about them.

The reader will discover many San Francisco appetites and many afterthoughts about them: music (jazz, blues, boogie woogie, rock 'n' roll), restaurants, saloons, cooking, cookbooks, prose, poetry, photography and photographers, old buildings, old girlfriends, and the quirky bohemian culture of the city.

Here then, are a few of my favorite things. Perhaps some of them are yours as well. And, I hope you remember the John Coltrane 1961 record album "My Favorite Things"—it too is one of my favorite things.

Louis Armstrong.
PHOTO: LIBRARY OF CONGRESS; WIKIMEDIA COMMONS

CHAPTER 1

LOUIS "SATCHMO" ARMSTRONG: THE REAL AMBASSADOR

Louis Armstrong, one of America's greatest performing artists, and one of jazz music's top innovators, once said, "Never play anything the same way twice." And he didn't. It's remarkable that a young black waif from New Orleans became a jazz ambassador as depicted in Dave and Iola Brubeck's jazz musical The Real Ambassadors. The Brubeck musical, which starred Armstrong, dealt with the U.S. Civil Rights Movement and the role of performing artists like Armstrong as representatives of the U.S.

A HISTORY OF JAZZ IN
SAN FRANCISCO

R ight from its rambunctious beginnings, San Francisco had an infatuation with jazz—that compelling American gumbo that rambled from saloons, honky tonks, melodeons, dance halls and brothels, to night clubs and finally to our concert halls.

Not long after gold was discovered at Sutter's Mill in 1848 when San Francisco was a tiny, raw-boned village, miners, merchants, sailors and con men not only patronized girlie shows but also aspired to so-called cultural pursuits. Opera, symphonic music, even ballet of sorts.

And, a little later along the Barbary Coast, entertainment included minstrel shows, ragtime and pop tunes of the time—in short, early jass.

Yes, *jass,* as it was known then, was a precursor to the *jazz* many of us love today.

Jelly Roll Morton, who claimed to have invented this art form, lived and worked in San Francisco for a while between 1917 and 1922. Paul Whiteman, self-styled King of Jazz, played the Fairmont Hotel in 1918. The first talkie movie, Al Jolson's *The Jazz Singer,* was filmed near Union Square in 1927.

The Swing Bands

In the Depression years that followed, and through the 1940s and even into the 1950s, the big swing bands frequently played "two-a-day" vaudeville in Bay Area movie palaces like the Golden Gate Theater and the Orpheum. Sweets Ballroom—big band heaven—thrived in Oakland. Tommy Dorsey, Charlie Barnet, Gene Krupa, Woody Herman, Harry James, Jimmy Lunceford, all found enthusiastic jazz audiences here.

Duke Ellington, a serious musician who knew what he was talking about, once proclaimed jazz as America's true classical music. And to use Ellington's definition, America's true classical music was, and still is, highly appreciated in San Francisco. But it's a tangled story.

The Fillmore and Bop City

Well-known San Francisco jazz clubs had opened, thrived and then disappeared. The Dawn Club opened South of Market in 1940 and was a trad-jazz venue for Dixieland trumpeter Lu Watters; Jimbo's Bop City in the Fillmore district had been around since 1950. Almost all the stars had played there including the deified Charlie Parker. It's long gone.

Jazz was popular in the Fillmore as early as the 1930s and by the 1950s there were more than two dozen night clubs there that presented live music. But an ill-conceived urban renewal plan disrupted the unique urban mix of the neighborhood.

The North Beach Jazz Scene

In the early 1950s the Blackhawk on the edge of the Tenderloin was the city's premier jazz club but it closed in 1963 and the jazz scene moved on. North Beach, with its reputation as a louche entertainment enclave, emerged as the San Francisco jazz epicenter and reigned as such in the fifties, sixties and even into the 1970s.

In those days there were several top North Beach jazz clubs along the one block of Broadway between Columbus and Montgomery:

The Jazz Workshop where Miles Davis, Cannonball Adderley, Gerry Mulligan, Stan Getz, Horace Silver, John Coltrane and Dizzy Gillespie held forth,

Basin Street West where one could be in the royal presence of Duke Ellington and his orchestra,

Sugar Hill that headlined big name blues stars like John Lee Hooker, Lightnin' Sam Hopkins, Big Mama Willie Mae Thornton and T-Bone Walker,

And El Matador with top performers such as Charlie Byrd, Erroll Garner, the Modern Jazz Quartet, George Shearing and Oscar Peterson.

Jazz and the Beats

In 1957 at the Cellar on Green Street, Kenneth Rexroth and Lawrence Ferlinghetti were mixing poetry and jazz, a noble but flawed experiment. Frequently the poetry was very good and so was the jazz. Together it didn't add up. It was not a match made in heaven.

Bill Graham and Chet Helms

Later, in what could have been a mismatch, Bill Graham's Fillmore Auditorium presented not only the top rock 'n' roll acts but many jazz artists too. Chet Helms at the Avalon Ballroom did the same. One night at the Avalon, Charles Lloyd and his superb jazz quartet were on the same bill as Janis Joplin with Big Brother and the Holding Company. No one thought this pairing was the least bit strange.

Keystone Korner

By the seventies the jazz balloon in North Beach was deflating. Then, in 1972, faster than a speeding bullet, a young man named Todd Barkan took over Keystone Korner at 750 Vallejo. Since 1969 the dingy North Beach club had featured rock bands like the Grateful Dead, New Riders of the Purple Sage and Creedence Clearwater Revival. Mike Bloomfield, Elvin Bishop and Boz Scaggs dropped in for sessions.

Under Barkan, Keystone Korner became a jazz club. McCoy Tyner, Bill Evans, Rasheed Roland Kirk, Sonny Rollins, Art Blakey and even "Miles" appeared there.

But Barkan—perhaps not the swiftest with the pocket calculator—was on a collision course with economic reality. In 1983 the club was foundering. There were several fund-raisers including one by Bill Graham at the Fillmore Auditorium. It netted $1,500. Barkan was finished and moved to New York.

The North Beach jazz twilight years were upon us. The Jazz Workshop, Basin Street West, Sugar Hill, El Matador and Keystone Korner had disappeared. However, Jazz at Pearl's on Columbus opened in 1990, showed much promise and demonstrated considerable staying power. But it finally went belly up in 2008—the times they were a-changin'.

Today, SFJAZZ, with its own concert hall building, dominates the jazz scene.

———•••———

CHAPTER 2

CLINT EASTWOOD

"I've been a jazz fan as far back as I can remember. When I was 12 years old living in Oakland, California I discovered a radio program called Dixieland Jubilee, and that was the beginning…I came to Monterey the first time in 1951, when I was in the military…When I got out of the service I kept coming back to the Monterey Peninsula…and when I heard there was going to be a jazz festival in Monterey I came up for that…I came back to the jazz festival over the years and always enjoyed myself…Then in 1970, I was directing my first film, Play Misty for Me, *and I needed an event as a transition in the film…So that's what we filmed…The Monterey Jazz Festival has had so much history that over time its bugs have been worked out and now it's a world-class festival."*

—Clint Eastwood, member of the
Monterey Jazz Festival Board of Directors.

The author with Clint Eastwood at a Monterey Jazz Festival Party.
PHOTO: CRAIG LOVELL; FROM THE AUTHOR'S COLLECTION

TONY BENNETT

Everything in life is timing and lighting. Took Tony Bennett almost forever to make his Monterey Jazz Festival debut. Never got the invite until 2012. Tony was 86 the year he took the stage that Saturday night in September. In full voice and command, Tony eased into the lyric everyone knows. As a full moon began to rise over 5,000 fans in the open-air Main Arena. "I left my heart…" Tony sang and the full house, rising now with the full moon, stood as one to roar, and he saw the moon rise too, and smiled, and sang, "…in San Francisco..." No one there that night will forget the moment. I have seen Tony Bennett in New York and San Francisco but on that cool autumn night a saloon singer out in the open air after dark under a gold, jazzy moon in Monterey made magic.

—Excerpt Gigs & Riffs, *a work in progress*
by Rick Carroll, © *all rights reserved.*

Sheet music for "I Left My Heart In San Francisco" recorded by Tony Bennett in 1962.
PHOTO: AUTHOR'S COLLECTION

JIMMY LYONS AND THE MONTEREY JAZZ FESTIVAL

This back story is a paean to an old friend, Jimmy Lyons. His name may not resonate to some readers unless they have attended the Monterey Jazz Festival. Jimmy was the founder and general manager of this premier jazz event, and my best buddy until he died in 1994. He deserves remembering. He was a giant in San Francisco, a city that has had many giants. And he was responsible for adding an important dimension—a starburst of focus—to my life.

If it weren't for Jimmy Lyons, my Telegraph Hill neighbor many blue moons ago, I would not have enjoyed friendships with Duke Ellington, Dizzy Gillespie, Paul Desmond, John Lewis, Charles Lloyd and other extraordinary jazz artists. Jimmy sharpened my appreciation for jazz and for those who created it.

The Jazz Life Embraced

Here's how all of that happened, how I embraced the jazz life.

Before I met Jimmy I was what might be termed a casual jazz fan. I enjoyed the big swing bands, and the inventiveness of small jazz groups—say, the Modern Jazz Quartet—interested me on an intellectual, albeit finger-snapping level. I attended the first Monterey Jazz Festival in 1958, but more as a social occasion than as a devotee of the music. Then one day in the early 1960s I met Ralph J. Gleason, the incomparable jazz critic (and later rock 'n' roll critic) for the *San Francisco Chronicle*. Gleason and I hit it off. To me he was a god who knew everything there was to know about the dynamics of the hipster life. To Gleason, I was an eager acolyte. Soon he introduced me to Jimmy Lyons and suddenly I had a job as publicity man for the Monterey Jazz Festival.

When Jimmy hired me the first thing he asked me to do was to fire my predecessor, Grover Sales Jr. Jimmy, always non-confrontational,

At the Monterey Jazz Festival (left to right), the author with Jimmy Lyons, founder and general manager.
PHOTO: JERRY STOLL

as I was soon to learn, didn't have the stomach for it. Actually Sales was tiring of the job and really wanted to write about music rather than publicize it—a stance I adopted many years later. But back to Jimmy.

James L. Lyons was born in Beijing, China in 1916 of Presbyterian missionary parents. The family moved to Cleveland in 1922. Early on Jimmy decided on a radio career. He wanted to be a disk jockey and "that's how I got into this strange but wonderful jazz life," he told me once.

Jazz Jubilee and Discapades

After his schooling in the Midwest, and in Southern California where he attended college, Jimmy Lyons became a radio personality in Santa Ana and soon was into jazz. His eagerness caught the attention of big band stylist Stan Kenton, and he became Kenton's remote announcer from a local radio station when the band played nearby in Balboa Beach. Soon Jimmy was leading the good jazz life—playing the music he wanted to hear and hobnobbing with visiting jazz artists.

Then Jimmy was drafted into the army (there was a war on, you will remember). With his radio background, he was assigned to the Armed Forces Radio Network and for three years produced the wildly popular jazz program "Jubilee." Again, he booked the artists he wanted to hear. That's how he met Dizzy Gillespie, Miles Davis, Milt Jackson, Lester Young, Charlie Parker and other iconic jazz names. In the 1940s, out of the army, he moved to San Francisco and became a late-night deejay on KNBC, a strong station heard on the Pacific Coast from Canada to Mexico. Jimmy Lyons was in the jazz catbird seat and his show "Lyon's Den," was an outpost of modern jazz.

A Love Affair with the Monterey Peninsula

Dave Brubeck credited Jimmy with helping to establish his group. One night Jimmy introduced Brubeck to a young alto saxophone player from San Francisco State University named Paul Breitenfeld. The youngster took the name Paul Desmond and became an integral element of the Brubeck sound.

My friend *Chronicle* photographer Peter Breinig, liked to say he played a major role in the creation of the Monterey Jazz Festival. Breinig became a buddy of Jimmy Lyons. One weekend he was going to visit his parents in Monterey. He suggested Jimmy go along for the ride. It was Jimmy's introduction to the Monterey Peninsula. It became a lifetime love affair. Jimmy moved to Big Sur and ran the general store there. On weekends, he drove to Monterey and became a jazz playing disk jockey on a local radio station. Soon he was conferring with Gleason about launching a jazz festival. Today, the Monterey Jazz Festival is the oldest, continuous event of its kind, and arguably the premier jazz festival of the literally hundreds around the world.

Interacting with the Jazz Royalty.

And that's how I caught up to Jimmy and he became my best friend. At first I was amazed at the association. Am I really meeting

Dizzy Gillespie.
PHOTO: COURTESY "RIGHT DOWN FRONT" RON HUDSON JAZZ IMAGES

all of these people?" I asked myself. Having a drink with them? Occasionally smoking a joint with them? Dining with them? Talking about jazz with them? Gradually, I came to accept it. Jimmy Lyons included me in social interaction with the jazz royalty of the time.

We both lived in San Francisco on Telegraph Hill: Jimmy with his wife Laurel, in a small apartment on Alta Street overlooking the Filbert Steps. I, on the Greenwich Steps, a couple of hundred yards away by crow flight. Every morning Jimmy and I greeted the day by stepping out on our decks—with a good sightline between us—and talked to each other by telephone. Sometimes Jimmy would wave a tumbler of Scotch whisky at me by way of greeting. We hung out together incessantly.

Dizzy, Duke and Desmond

When they were in San Francisco many of Jimmy's jazz friends visited his small apartment. I was invited to drop by, and those occasions were priceless to me. One night Dizzy Gillespie—a wise and articulate man who loved to play the jokester—was at Jimmy's. Dizzy said his next stop was Miami for a concert. He added, "It may be your ami, but it ain't my ami."

Duke Ellington came to town. Jimmy told me to rent a nice car, pick up the Duke at the airport and take him to City Hall, where he would receive the keys to the city. I got a white caddy convertible, and took my assistant Vicki Cunningham with me. Duke was delighted. We put the top down. Vicki, a blonde bombshell—as it was okay to say in those days—drove. Duke rode shotgun. I rode in the back.

Paul Desmond was a frequent visitor to the small apartment on Alta. And there Desmond, Jimmy and I drank very cold, straight-up martinis. When Desmond died in 1977, Breinig, a fine pilot with a Piper Cub, flew Jimmy, Paul's ashes, and a shaker of martinis, down over the Big Sur coast. I was invited but couldn't make it. By prearrangement with Desmond, who had been ill for some time, Lyons and Breinig took a sip in honor of their (and my) friend. Then Breinig flew low, banked the airplane and Jimmy threw Desmond and the martinis out the window. The wind was wrong and Desmond and the martinis blew back into the cabin. I still regret not being there.

The Jazz Passion

Over the years I admired and was befriended by many of the greats—Clark Terry, Cal Tjader, Gerry Mulligan, Roy Eldridge, Erroll Garner, Jon Hendricks, Ornette Coleman, John Handy and Charles Lloyd come to mind now, as well as the aforementioned Duke, Dizzy, Desmond and Lewis. There were also several outstanding women jazz artists I became friendly with and whose careers I followed—Sarah Vaughan, Carmen McRae, Etta James, and the San Francisco Bay Area song stylist Mary Stallings who is still with us and singing well these days.

Most of the great jazz artists from the Jimmy Lyons era I was privileged to know as friends are now gone. Of the few who remain, I'm still in touch with John Handy, and Charles Lloyd and I are close friends who meet frequently and enjoy each other's company.

Jazz and the Monterey Jazz Festival were, and still are, all-encompassing passions in my life. When my wife, Joan, became pregnant, we decided that if we had a boy his name would be James. If we had a daughter, her name would be Laurel—after Jimmy's wife (who died a while back).

We had a girl in those pre-ultrasound days. My kids were brought up listening to the music at the festival. Daughter Laurel attended her first Monterey Jazz Festival when she was just five months old. She still attends every year. Son Mike became a concert sound engineer. Son Jeff plays jazz guitar. Nepotism at its finest.

Jimmy Lyons was my best friend. I enjoyed his presence in my life and he enjoyed my presence in his. Jimmy was my conduit to the music and to many of its artists I love to this day.

———•◦•———

CHAPTER 3

HANGTOWN FRY

This intriguingly named dish can still be found in San Francisco on the menus of Tadich Grill and Sam's Grill. Basically it's an omelet with bacon and oysters. But it's the story behind the dish that is worth relating. The Gold Rush town of Placerville up in El Dorado County was known as Hangtown—and that needs no explanation. Frontier justice was harsh. There are two versions of the Hangtown Fry story: The first is that the dish was invented by a prospector who made his poke of gold nuggets. Eggs were very expensive and so were oysters shipped on ice from San Francisco. So that's what this Gold Rush gourmand ordered from his hotel kitchen. The second story is a stopper: A quick-thinking, condemned man in the local hoosegow was asked what he would like for his ritual last meal—an omelet with oysters. Granting his request delayed his hanging—but only for a day.

The bar at Sam's Grill and Seafood Restaurant.
PHOTO: COURTESY OF SAM'S GRILL AND SEAFOOD RESTAURANT

Lunchtime at the Tadich Grill.
PHOTO: CRAIG LEE; COURTESY THE TADICH GRILL

TADICH GRILL: THE ORIGINAL
COLD DAY RESTAURANT

Tadich Grill, the oldest restaurant in San Francisco, was established in 1849. Now in the city's financial district, it began life as a simple waterfront establishment. John Tadich emigrated from Croatia to San Francisco in 1872. He operated what was then called the New World Coffee Saloon. In 1928 he sold it to the Buich family, also from Croatia. The family still owns it today. In the ensuing years the Tadich Grill has become one of the most prominent seafood restaurants in the city. It is still frequently referred to as "The Cold Day Restaurant." The nickname came about in 1882 when a local politician, Alexander Badlam, running for city assessor, stated that it would be a cold day when he was left behind—meaning when he was out of office. Of course, the inevitable happened; he lost the election.

John Briscoe, a San Francisco attorney and poet (an unlikely combination) has written a fine book called *Tadich Grill: The Story of San Francisco's Oldest Restaurant*. We will refrain from quoting some of Briscoe's poetry but here are a few things he pointed out in his book. "Tadich Grill, San Francisco's oldest restaurant, has mirrored its city's history from its founding in 1849, the year of San Francisco's real birth during the gold rush, to its survival of two catastrophic earthquakes. In a way, it has also projected its city's future. It has fed its future mayors when they were young and again years later when they were cutting (over sand dabs) the deals that would decide the city's ever-flamboyant future."

Tadich Grill takes no reservations. There can be a long waiting time for a table. My method—when I have a passion for the Tadich Grill's charcoal-broiled petrale or Hangtown Fry—is to snag a counter seat.

The San Francisco Bank Exchange and Billiard Saloon.
PHOTO: SAN FRANCISCO HISTORY CENTER, SAN FRANCISCO PUBLIC LIBRARY

CHAPTER 4

PISCO PUNCH

San Francisco's rich saloon culture and boozy history dates back to 1579 when Sir Francis Drake sailed into a small bay just north of the Golden Gate with 300 casks of Pisco, a Peruvian brandy. Pisco was available in San Francisco in the 1830s and was in ample supply during the Gold Rush. Later, a popular drink was Pisco Punch. It was well-known in 1853 at the San Francisco Bank Exchange and Billiard Saloon, where the Transamerica Pyramid now stands. Pisco Punch is usually made with Pisco brandy, pineapple juice, sugar, gum Arabic and water.

THE GLORIOUS INSTITUTION
OF THE FREE LUNCH

For one of my birthdays my barber, a thoughtful young woman named Fe Olivar who's been cutting my hair since the days when I had a reasonable amount to cut, gave me a one gallon jar of pickled pigs' feet. What a sensible gift since I have an appetite for pickled pigs' feet.

I dug in. A couple of pickled pigs' feet with a hunk of bread and a bottle of beer made a great lunch. It not only got my digestion going but my muse as well.

When I was kid during the Depression, many working-class bars still provided what was called a free lunch. They were modest but appetizing affairs served all day long for appreciative customers—cheeses, cold cuts like salami, and what we called baloney, occasionally some sliced roast beef or a shank of baked ham, crusty bread, hard-boiled eggs and of course, pickled pigs' feet.

Glorious and Gluttonous

I was told by my father who became a free lunchist in good standing when he first came to the United States in 1913, that astonishing free lunches existed in the best saloons of the time.

My father enjoyed relating mouthwatering stories about this saloon bonanza that was raised to its most glorious and gluttonous form in drinking establishments in New York City, Boston, Philadelphia, Chicago and even way out here in the rawboned wild west of San Francisco. He told tales of free lunches laid out on silver trays and chaffing dishes that included iced oysters and clams, bowls of herring and sour cream, savory hot dishes of beans or spaghetti, a leg of mutton or a huge round of rare beef, and sizzling German and Italian sausages with hot mustard in which to dip them.

All you had to do to partake was to buy one drink—in my father's case this was German beer on tap—and you were good to go—down to the end of the bar and help yourself. Keep in mind free lunches weren't exactly a sign of the barkeep's philanthropy. Eaters drink, but drinkers don't necessarily eat.

Feeding Sumptuously in San Francisco

From the 1870s up to prohibition in 1920 when everything came to a screeching halt saloon-wise, the free lunch was an institution. English writer Rudyard Kipling extolled the Free Lunch in San Francisco in the 1890s. He wrote: *"I came upon a room full of bad salon pictures in which men with hats on the backs of their heads were wolfing down food from a counter. It was the institution of the Free Lunch I had struck. You paid for a drink and got as much as you wanted to eat. For something less than a rupee a day a man can feed himself sumptuously in San Francisco, even though he be a bankrupt."*

Oh to have been in San Francisco in those great days when the free lunch was at its peak. But even in my lifetime I was able to enjoy at least a semblance of that institution.

Breen's Long Bar

When I was a young man there was a wonderful Irish saloon called Breen's on Third Street near Mission. It catered to newspaper types—editors and reporters, typesetters and pressmen. Breen's had a long mahogany bar—my recollection is it was 40 or more feet in length. Acolytes jostled forward and put their elbows on the bar to order a drink. One highball or a schooner of suds on tap allowed you to wander to the end of the bar and load up. There were pickled pigs' feet of course. And I remember once at Breen's there was cracked Dungeness crab in case a claw or two struck your fancy.

Alas, Breen's closed in 1979. I miss the free lunches and think of those times as "the good old days."

The Free Lunch is Gone

I'm afraid the stand-up, saloon dining experience I write about here is a thing of the past but I'm hoping it may return. There's a resurgence of the free lunch at The House of Shields down on New Montgomery and The Comstock Saloon at the confluence of Columbus and Kearny in North Beach. And please understand when I say the free lunch is gone I am not talking about today's shabby bar tricks—a small dish of potato chips, some salty trail-mixy stuff, or the obligatory deep fried zucchini fingers that turn up here and there during so-called happy hour.

Paoli's Tribal Mating Dance
Happy Hour just doesn't cut it as a Free Lunch. An exception I recall fondly was the famed San Francisco watering hole Paoli's, at California and Montgomery. It served a real spread in the early evening when young singles flocked there. Paoli's was a feeding frenzy followed by a tribal mating dance.

A Slice of Baloney
Through my foggy prism of recollection the world was a more generous place when I was a youngster. Not only could you get a proper free lunch in many saloons, but your butcher gave you a slice of baloney to munch on while he was cutting up ox tails for your supper.

In the 1950s I was fortunate to interview Lucius Beebe for the *San Francisco Chronicle*. Beebe was an American writer, dandy and gourmand who died in 1966. He was staying at the old Palace Hotel. I met him in the famed Palace Pied Piper Bar. We stood there looking at the Maxfield Parrish mural behind the bar. We each had a flute of champagne, of course. There were a few "nibblies" in front of us.

"How I miss the days of the old free lunch," Beebe said. Then he uttered his famous, all-purpose quote. He obviously memorized it for just such occasions: "All I want is the best of everything and there's very little left."

CHAPTER 5

THE ANNALS OF SAN FRANCISCO, 1855 —GENERAL EFFECTS OF THE GOLD DISCOVERIES

The vast majority of all the laboring classes in the country had certainly deserted their former pursuits, and had become miners, while a great many others—merchants and their clerks, shopkeepers and their assistants, lawyers, surgeons, officials in every department of the State, of the districts and in the towns, runaway seamen and soldiers, and a great variety of adventurers—likewise began the search for gold.

THE GOLDEN GATE WAS MORE PROMISING THAN BORGER, TEXAS TO THIS PANHANDLE GAL

Throughout its history San Francisco has had more than its share of improbable characters who have added vibrancy and panache to the city. That's because San Francisco is improbable itself—a city founded by a bunch of unsatisfied, adventurous, overachievers in search of gold at the end of the Pacific rainbow.

I'm thinking of such larger-than-life characters as Samuel Brannan (editor of San Francisco's first newspaper), Emperor Norton (off-balance oddball), Levi Strauss (you're probably wearing his jeans right now), Mrs. Abby Fisher (a freed slave who became a prominent San Francisco cook), Sally Stanford (noted madam)....

Joe DiMaggio (homerun hitter), Herb Caen (yes, the columnist), Willie Brown, Jr. (yes, the former mayor), Rose Pak (Chinatown political powerhouse), Lawrence Ferlinghetti (the poet), Carol Doda (the topless queen), Michael McCourt (the Irish bartender), Francis Ford Coppola (the Godfather) and our subject for this chapter, mover and shaker Charlotte Shultz.

Certainly, a mixed bag—all ambitious, all skillful, all winners—even Emperor Norton who crowned himself Emperor of San Francisco and created his own currency.

A Lot of Juice, A Lot of Smarts

Charlotte "Tex" Shultz didn't have to create her own currency, and she's got more "juice" than your local supermarket. Charlotte's "juice" is her magnetism, influence, leverage, and string-pulling power.

A smart gal from a west Texas panhandle town called Borger, Charlotte came to San Francisco in 1963 as Charlotte Smith, a young and nervy blonde bombshell with a lot of smarts. She didn't really know anyone here, but the city by the Golden Gate somehow seemed more promising than Borger, Texas.

The daughter of a couple who ran the general store in the dusty, Texas panhandle town, Charlotte won a local beauty contest when she was five, and announced "I'm going to Hollywood to become a movie star." Later, when her father lost the family business she had to quit college. It didn't stop her. She enrolled in a junior college and later got a scholarship from a sorority and ultimately graduated from two universities, the University of Arkansas with a degree in fashion design, marketing and merchandising, and the University of Texas.

Today, she's San Francisco's chief party-giver—and perhaps, party-goer too—and as City Hall's Chief Protocol Officer, is widely recognized as one of the most important women in the city.

Here's how she happened to grab the brass ring on the San Francisco merry-go-round. But, let's change that to a *gold ring* on the city's social and political merry-go-round.

A Film Festival Gofer

In 1963, after giving Houston, Dallas and Los Angeles a try and a pass, she moved to San Francisco. She recalls now that she used to sit in the ornate lobby of the swanky Fairmont Hotel on Nob Hill and people-watch. She was eager to be part of the scene. Within a few months Charlotte "Tex" Smith was not only part of the scene, she was in many cases, the scene.

I've known Charlotte since she first came to San Francisco. Here's how she came into my life. In those days I had a small PR firm in North Beach. One of my clients was the San Francisco International Film Festival. One day I had a call from Bill Dauer, the boss of the Chamber of Commerce. The chamber ran the film festival then and Dauer said he wanted to send a young woman over to my office to see if I could put her to work. And I did. I liked the long-legged Texan and invited her to work (without salary) as a gofer for the film festival—going for this, going for that. She jumped at it. At first she drove out to the airport to pick up movie stars who were attending the big event. The big blonde was the first contact the Hollywood gentry had with what was to become one of the most important film festivals in the world.

The Go-To Gal

Soon Charlotte was an integral part of the film festival management, organizing its elaborate, star-studded ceremonies and big deal parties. And from there it was onward and upward. She was a shooting star and San Francisco was her firmament. Almost overnight she became the go-to gal, instead of a go-for gal, and a "consider-it-done" asset to one San Francisco mayor after another—eight to date including the present administration's Mayor Edwin Lee.

Charlotte Smith was a volunteer for *then* San Francisco Mayor Jack Shelley who named her his Chief of Protocol. Not long after, at a city hall strategy meeting, she met John Ward (Jack) Mailliard III, a prominent and divorced, fifth generation San Franciscan civic leader. Soon they were dating; then he popped the question. Charlotte became a bride and lived in a San Francisco, Pacific Heights, mansion whose library was wallpapered with swarms of bees. Louis Mailliard, an ancestor of Charlotte's husband, had come to America with Joseph Bonaparte; the older brother of Napoleon Bonaparte I. Family oral history had it that Louis Mailliard was the illegitimate son of Emperor Napoleon. Bees were depicted on Napoleon's coat of arms and symbolized immortality and resurrection. Jack Mailliard's link to French royalty was later debunked by family members. But never mind, Charlotte Mailliard was a royal kind of gal, later to hob nob with royals like England's Queen Elizabeth II.

The Day Queen Elizabeth Left Her Heart in San Francisco

When Dianne Feinstein was mayor, Queen Elizabeth II and her entourage visited San Francisco. Charlotte pulled out all the stops. She organized a high-profile ceremony and party that extended from the marble steps of the City Hall rotunda, to Louise M. Davies Hall where on stage Mary Martin sang her *South Pacific* show-stopper "I'm Gonna

Left to right: former Mayor Willie Brown, Jr., Charlotte Shultz, San Francisco Chief of Protocol, and Tony Bennett.
PHOTO: DREW ALTIZER

Wash that Man Right out of My Hair." And then Tony Bennett did his anthemic "I Left My Heart in San Francisco." (Charlotte has erected a life size, bronze statue of Tony Bennett alongside the entrance to the Fairmont Hotel.)

Then it was on to Trader Vic's in Cosmo Place for lunch. It was the first time the starchy Queen had ever dined in a public restaurant. Later Queen Elizabeth II bestowed on Charlotte the title of Commander of the Royal Victorian Order. That honor was only one of many she has received over the years.

Charlotte didn't need swarms of bees on her wallpaper; she had hit the big time. She became, as *San Francisco Chronicle* columnist Leah Garchik says, "A person who gets things done." The press loved her then and still does. Herb Caen caught her hanging out in North Beach with Francis Ford Coppola and Enrico Banducci and three-dotted it in his column. He told me at the time, "Charlotte is a no BS kind of gal." And these days, an issue of the *Nob Hill Gazette* (which bills itself as "an attitude, not an address) doesn't go by without one or more photos of our gal.

Jack Mailliard died in 1986. Two years later Charlotte married Melvin Swig, owner of the Fairmont Hotel where she once hung out in the lobby and imagined herself as part of the San Francisco scene. When Melvin Swig popped the question he said "What are you going to do with the rest of your life?" When she replied that she didn't know, he said "let me know on Monday." And she did. With Swig, Charlotte became even better known in the city—not just an A-list social figure, but a philanthropist, for example, donating and raising funds for the building of a new San Francisco library.

Charlotte Married the Former Secretary of State

Melvin Swig died in 1993 and remarrying was not on Charlotte's horizon. And that's when former Secretary of State George P. Shultz entered her life. They had met socially and both were widowed. They were married in San Francisco's Grace Cathedral in 1997. It was the social event of the year in the city Charlotte Smith had chosen more than 30 years earlier. Today the couple lives in a Russian Hill penthouse where they entertain guests from all over the world.

Trish Donnally, *Chronicle* fashion editor back in the 1990s, reported that in the penthouse Charlotte has three closets, one with a view of Alcatraz.

Consider it Done!

Party planner Rita Barela recalls another chapter in collected good works of Charlotte: the Black and White Ball, a biennial, black-tie street party benefiting the San Francisco Symphony. "She's real," Rita Barela said once of Charlotte. "She knows you make friends with the janitor and the secretary because they are the ones who make things happen." Once for a Valentine ball she was organizing, she asked a fellow committee member if she had arranged to close one of the city's main arteries so guests could stroll from one party site to another. The committee member replied, "Well, not exactly, but we're working on getting a few policemen." Charlotte said, "You mean you couldn't get the street closed?" "No," was the answer.

"Consider it done," said Charlotte—and it was.

The Day the Bridge Bent and Willie Brown's Fedora Was Tossed into the Winds of the Golden Gate

As San Francisco Mayor Dianne Feinstein's protocol chief Charlotte designed a celebration for the Golden Gate Bridge's 50th anniversary in 1987. It was Charlotte's biggest party event ever—to date that is, until such time when she may throw a book party for this self-effacing author.

The Golden Gate Bridge event attracted approximately one million people. Planned as Bridgewalk 87, it was estimated that when the span opened that morning more than 300,000 surged onto it and another 400,000 to 500,000 gathered to cheer. The *Chronicle's* Carl Nolte who covered Charlotte's event, wrote "Solemn ceremonies scheduled on the bridge were scrapped as the crowd moved forward. Mayor Dianne Feinstein was supposed to throw a wreath from mid-span to honor those who died during the construction during the Great Depression. But the crowd was so big and moved so fast that the wreath disappeared, and Feinstein grabbed a hat (an $800 Fedora) from the head of Assembly Speaker (later San Francisco Mayor) Willie Brown, D-San Francisco, and threw it over the side instead."

Alarmingly, the bridge, which was designed with a convex shape with a notable rise in its center, flattened out. Later bridge officials assured San Franciscans that the bridge was not overstressed.

Well, Charlotte Smith, Mailliard, Swig, Shultz may not really be a shirttail Bonaparte, but the Golden Gate Bridgewalk 87 assured that she is the bee's knees.

———•◦•———

CHAPTER 6

TIE ME KANGAROO DOWN, SPORT

All together now
Tie me kangaroo down, sport
Tie me kangaroo down
Tie me kangaroo down, sport
Tie me kangaroo down
              —Rolf Harris, Australian songwriter

CONFESSIONS OF A DEVIOUS PRESS AGENT

I have always admired well-conceived publicity stunts and those who create them. I once served my time as a Hollywood press agent conceiving stunts to attract the media. I gave that up long ago, but here are some recollections from the old days.

General MacArthur and the Flower Show

An early assignment I got as a reporter for the *San Francisco Chronicle* was to publicize a flower show the newspaper was sponsoring. That will give you a clue as what an indispensable reporter I was. I put together a flower show committee, got a friendly airline on side, and then flew to New York hoping to meet with retired Five Star General of the Army Douglas MacArthur who was holed up in a penthouse in the Waldorf Astoria. I conned my way in to see him, and persuaded him to sign a proclamation declaring my flower show the greatest thing since sliced bread, and I was on my way. It worked out.

On the strength of that caper—adventures like that are always referred to as capers—I later got a job in Hollywood with Steve Hannagan Associates. Hannagan, a flamboyant press agent, was the ex-newspaper guy who put Miami Beach, Sun Valley and the Indianapolis Speedway 500 auto race on the map.

Those of us in the Hannagan organization were referred to as "press agents" because Steve Hannagan thought that to use the more lofty term "public relations experts" was to draw too fine a point on our work.

Mister Pickle and the Jumping Frog

One caper I remember clearly is this: With Hannagan's encouragement I entered a frog named Mister Pickle in the Jumping Frog Contest still held annually in Angel's Camp. So what's this with Mister

33

Pickle? The Hannagan firm had a client called the Pickle Packers of America. And I'm not kidding.

The Pickle Packers of America was the only client requiring knowledge of Mark Twain's 1865 story *The Celebrated Jumping Frog of Calaveras County.*

You will remember the story tells of a bullfrog named Dan'l Webster who can out-jump any other frog in California's gold country. A contest is arranged and a stranger bets forty dollars against the champion. When the stranger is left to care for Dan'l Webster for a time he fills him with buckshot. Of course, Dan'l doesn't get off the ground and the stranger wins the bet.

Angel's Camp, where the story took place, held its first jumping frog contest in 1928. The event continues to this day the third weekend in May.

Mister Pickle Comes in Second

In 1954, hell bent on promoting the Pickle Packers of America whose products were sold in glass jars instead of cans, I entered a frog named Mister Pickle in the Angel's Camp classic. I employed a fulsome young woman who agreed to wear shorts and a Mister Pickle T-shirt and lead our frog on his roadwork before making his official jump. The winning frog that year was a shifty creature named Lucky with a prodigious jump of 16 feet and 10 inches. Mr. Pickle came in second with a jump of 15 feet and 6 inches and achieved fleeting fame for the pickle packers who sponsored him.

The Calaveras County Fair and Jumping Frog Jubilee at Angel's Camp has grown into a major celebration with more than 50,000 attendees annually. It features not only the frog jumping contest that illustrates California Gold Rush history but also a junior livestock auction and literally thousands of county-fair exhibits and products—including home-canned pickles in glass jars.

In 1933 the California Fish and Game Commission became involved in order to regulate and protect the welfare of the California bullfrog. In 1995 the Board of Directors of the 39th District Agricultural Association adopted the "Frog Welfare Policy" that it says "underscores the Fair's commitment to treat the frogs in a humane manner." The current world's record in the Angel's Camp frog jump was set in 1986 by Rosie the Ribeter. She jumped an amazing 21 feet and 5-and-¾ inches. What a frog.

Well, that set me off on a budding career as a press agent. And although those days are long gone, I still love to read about publicity stunts of yore and about those who created them. My observation is that they're not making press agents like that anymore. The world has gotten too serious for that kind of levity.

An Ash Blonde Straight-Up

Hannagan once hired a bunch of tall ash blonde beauties to hang out at fashionable New York City bars and order—what else—a drink called an Ash Blonde, created by his client a booze distiller, and was served straight-up.

There was also a wonderful, highly imaginative guy named Russell Birdwell, who once set about to sell a refrigerator to an Eskimo. Guess who his client was.

A Topless Dancer Straight-Up

And right here in San Francisco, the highly enterprising Davey Rosenberg gave a dancer, Carol Doda, a topless bathing suit and encouraged her to dance on top of a white baby grand piano, at the Condor, a North Beach nightclub. Of course, you know how that turned out.

The Great San Francisco Snail Race

A friend named Kevin Keating once promoted the Great San Francisco Snail Race for one of his restaurant clients. He attempted to get the contestants to travel straight ahead on a simulated race track, but that didn't work. So he drew a big circle with a black marker, put the snails in the circle and the first one to slither across the black marker line was declared the winner. Keating was a friend of *Chronicle* columnist, Stanton Delaplane, who had great appreciation for a good public-

Carol Doda's Condor Club circa 1973.
PHOTO: MICHAEL HOLLEY

ity stunt. He wrote about Keating's snail race of course, but I hooked him on an idea that I still think has legs, but in the last minute—despite Delaplane's encouragement—I chickened out.

Pop Rocks in Dentist Offices

One of my clients at the time was General Foods. And as unlikely as it may seem now, the company was promoting a product called Pop Rocks. These were tiny pieces of fruit flavored, sugary, hard candy that contained carbon dioxide bubbles. After sucking them for a minute or so, they began to pop loudly in the mouth and fizz. My idea was to go around town dropping off packets of Pop Rocks in dentists' offices, but as I said, I chickened out.

Tie Me Kangaroo Down Sport

Years ago I did some publicity for P&O-Orient Lines that ran passenger ships from Australia to the West Coast. The ship Oriana was due to dock in Long Beach with a bunch of Australian tourists. Although my office was in San Francisco I decided to meet the ship and flew to the Southland for my publicity stunt. What I needed was a real kangaroo. There was a zoo in Southern California that provided all kinds of animals to movie studios. So I rented a kangaroo. I envisioned a small kangaroo (a wallaby perhaps). What turned up when the ship came in was about as tall as I am, but probably outweighed me by about 50 pounds. I also hired a comely young woman and put her in a T-shirt and a pair of shorts. She would be the kangaroo's keeper. Actually she was a keeper, the kangaroo was not. My plan was to board the ship and take the girl and the kangaroo up to the bridge for a photo op with Commodore Clifford Edgecombe, Oriana's skipper. My kangaroo was unruly. Only the trainer from the zoo could control it as it jerked around madly at the end of its chain. Commodore Edgecombe looked down on the scene from the wing of the bridge and sent an officer down to me with a note. It said: "Girl okay. Kangaroo not."

Meanwhile, several hundred Aussies lined up on that side of the ship facing the dock and spontaneously burst into song "Tie me kangaroo down, sport, tie me kangaroo down."

No, I'm not making up these stories. And, no they're not making press agents like this anymore.

CHAPTER 7

HENRI CARTIER-BRESSON AND THE DECISIVE MOMENT

"It's an illusion that photos are made with a camera…they are made with the eye, heart and head." That's how one of the world's greatest photographers, Henri Cartier-Bresson, described his art. He referred to his photographs as illustrating what he called the "Decisive Moment."

FRED LYON:
PHOTOGRAPHY THEN AND NOW

I have always admired photographers. At one time I fancied myself one. I had a bunch of Nikons hanging around my neck. I mean real Nikons—the kind that you had to set shutter speed, lens opening, focus manually and watch out for your depth-of-field. And I took a lot of "pics" as photographers used to say. I even sold some: matadors, jazz musicians, travel shots. I had a decided "lean" toward photojournalists and magazines in which their work appeared—*LIFE, Look* and *Collier's.*

Flag Raising on Iwo Jima

Joe Rosenthal—the guy who shot the famous photo of the marines raising the flag on Iwo Jima during World War II—was a friend and colleague when I was a reporter at the *San Francisco Chronicle.*

The Photo Nomad

Later I met and became friendly with photographer David Douglas Duncan, who called himself a "photo nomad" because he was constantly on the move shooting stories on the Korean War for example, and then published a famous book on Pablo Picasso.

God Does the Rest

More recently I came to know and admire Jimo Perini, a North Beach fixture who still shoots black-and-white photo essays with cameras that require 35 millimeter film. He's a rarity and so are his cameras.

One day I ran into Jimo at Caffe Puccini in North Beach and introduced him to my wife. I said "Joanie, this is the famous photographer Jimo."

And in a courtly manner Jimo replied: "I just point the camera and push the button. God does the rest."

But this back story is about my admiration for Fred Lyon, fourth generation San Franciscan and my idea of the consummate photographer. Let me tell you how I met him.

Many years ago when I was reading *LIFE, Look* and *Collier's,* I began noticing a photo credit for a photographer named Fred Lyon. His work was intense and imaginative. It inspired me.

Fred Lyon, General Delivery, Sausalito, California

This was before the days of Google and email but somehow I found out Fred Lyon lived in Sausalito. So I wrote him a letter and I mailed it to "Fred Lyon, General Delivery, Sausalito, California." It was what oldsters called a mash note; today we would call it a fan letter, much like young people do every day to communicate with pop stars or rappers. A few weeks later I got a telephone call. It was Fred Lyon. He invited me to visit him in his studio. And that was how our friendship began.

Since then Fred and I have worked together on stories in Hawaii on the Big Island's King Trail, the Bordeaux wine country of France, on cruise ships and, of course, in San Francisco where we once sated ourselves on tenor saxophonist Sonny Rollins at the old Jazz Workshop on Broadway in North Beach.

Fred Lyon began his professional career at 14 as an apprentice in the Moulin Studio, well-known photo operation founded in San Francisco by Gabriel Moulin in 1909. Later Fred studied at Art Center College in Los Angeles, and during World War II served as a Navy photographer in Washington DC shooting feature stories and covering the White House. By the time he was discharged he had photographed five U.S. Presidents.

Following his Navy discharge he moved to New York City and was soon immersed in the high-pressure, artistic world of fashion. His work at that point was polished to a high degree of photo technique and creativity. He later returned to California and undertook studio and location work in international travel, cuisine, wine, interior design and whatever else caught his fancy. With an established reputation

Fred Lyon self portrait.
PHOTO: COURTESY OF FRED LYON

as a shrewd eye behind the lens, he began getting assignments from top advertising agencies and soon was submitting photo essay ideas to the big New York-based magazines. "I was re-inventing myself as a magazine photographer," he recalls. "Here I was based in San Francisco, one of the most attractive and vibrant cities anywhere. Soon, I began getting those coveted magazine assignments"—*House & Garden, Vogue, Glamour, Mademoiselle, Collier's*—and at the top of the journalistic photo heap —*LIFE* and *Look*. Then, as one of *LIFE's* renowned photo essayists, he was selected to shoot two of that publisher's *Foods of the World* cookbooks on location in Europe. His Viennese and Italian books are now collectors' items.

And it was at about that time I sent my fan letter to Fred Lyon, General Delivery, Sausalito, California.

Living Through the Lens

A couple of years ago a film producer from France, Michael House, did an award-winning documentary—"Living Through the Lens"—on the life and work of Fred Lyon. Others in the Michael House series have been W. Somerset Maugham, Jacques Tati and the famed Parisian photographer, Eugene Atget. Over the years, prominent museums and galleries have mounted showings of Fred Lyon's work— including the San Francisco Museum of Art, the Palace of the Legion of Honor and the Art Institute of Chicago. For one exhibit Fred told the curator "For me photography is a process of discovery rather than contrivance." Another Lyon devotee puts it this way: "Fred anticipates the unexpected."

CHAPTER 8

RICE-A-RONI AND CHOP SUEY

Because of its slogan—"The San Francisco Treat"—Rice-A-Roni is indelibly associated with my city. Good order then, forces me to include it in a list of such San Francisco classics as Hangtown Fry, Celery Victor, Crab Louie, Cioppino and Sourdough. I don't wish to knock this pilaf-like "treat." I have enjoyed it myself occasionally. It was created in the 1930s by Gragnano Products out in the city's Mission District. Rice and vermicelli pasta, both uncooked, are mixed with various chicken soup-like spices, water is added, brought to a boil and the result is fluffed and served. Not bad, but hardly in a class with, say, a Crab Louie, a crusty hunk of sourdough bread, and a glass of sauvignon blanc. But now let's turn to another dubious classic, Chop Suey. I've always thought Chop Suey gets a bum rap. It's Chinese comfort food—the equivalent of my mother's Depression-era "Hobo Stew"—a little of this and a little of that. Much scholarship points the origin of Chop Suey to the Guangdong Province of Southern China where it was served as bits and pieces of this and that—a mixture of nourishing and tasty food stuffs. But I favor the uncorroborated story that Chop Suey was developed during the California Gold Rush in a San Francisco Chinese restaurant. It seems a group of drunken miners showed up late one night demanding to be fed. The hard-pressed cook scraped together what he had available, stirred it in his wok and poured in some soy sauce. His Chop Suey was a success. When I was a kid it was on the menus of most San Francisco Chinatown restaurants. Not now. The Chop Suey days are gone. But not the memory of it—bits and pieces of this and that blended into a satisfying meal.

FROM HINKY DINK'S TO TRADER VIC'S

M ore than eighty years ago an ambitious young knockabout with a wooden leg opened a saloon in a shack on San Pablo Avenue in Oakland. The saloon and the young man both went on to become famous. He became an international celebrity like the celebrity clientele that later favored his restaurants. He created a new and highly popular cuisine and opened a string of restaurants around the world.

The man was Trader Vic who was born in San Francisco in 1902. He was the son of a French-Canadian waiter who worked at various times at the Ritz Old Poodle Dog restaurant and the Hotel St. Francis and later opened a small grocery store in Oakland. His mother was a French woman from the Pyrenees. When Trader Vic—Victor Jules Bergeron, Jr. —was six, a childhood accident left him with tuberculosis of the knee and his left leg was amputated. Not coddled, he was an active youth who was taught not to consider himself handicapped, merely inconvenienced.

In November 1934, he opened his saloon with $800 borrowed from an aunt.

Hinky Dink's

At first the shack accommodated only about 30 blue collar workers from the neighborhood. Prohibition had just been repealed. People were thirsty. The country was in the midst of the Great Depression. Times were hard and Vic served cheap but good French country food. Beer was five cents. He called the new venture Hinky Dink's for the World War I tune "Mademoiselle from Armentieres" that had a line "Hinky-Dinky Parlez-Vous." His father and mother were excellent cooks and Vic learned the basics from them. Soon Hinky Dink's was attracting a hungry San Francisco clientele that was finding its way to Vic's San Pablo Avenue dive.

When it had been open only two years *San Francisco Chronicle* columnist Herb Caen heard about the Oakland sensation. He became a regular and reported "The best restaurant in San Francisco is in Oakland."

In those days Vic, in his mid-thirties, was a gregarious, salty-mouthed, high-spirited scamp. He poured outrageous drinks like a strange concoction of milk, bananas and rum called a Banana Cow. He sang in a gravelly voice and did card tricks. On occasion he came out from behind the bar, gained the attention of his customers and stuck an ice pick in his wooden leg.

Trader Vic's

His penchant for trading meals for goods and services had earned him the nickname "Trader" and he changed the name of the joint to Trader Vic's. One is tempted to add—"the rest is history."

The design theme for Hinky Dink's was funky-rustic. On the walls were snow shoes, deer heads, hunting equipment, newspaper clippings and old photos. Unmatched tables and chairs and a pot-bellied stove set the stage. By 1937 Vic was tiring of funky-rustic. He was about to go Polynesian: shrunken heads, ship models, fishing nets, tiki dolls and tapa cloth. The new cuisine was a Cantonese-Polynesian hybrid. Vic expanded his repertoire of exotic drinks, most based on rum and strong enough to peel paint off the walls if there had been any paint. He had a "Chinese" oven built to his own specifications which he said—with typical chutzpah—dated back to the Han Dynasty. And he developed a secret sauce of soy, ginger and whatever, to coat the meat that would be barbecued in its brick-lined interior.

The "Trader" himself was becoming a legend as a South Seas roustabout. He lost his leg in a shark attack many believed.

Funky and Elegant

Trader Vic's became hot and extraordinarily successful. The completion of the San Francisco-Oakland Bay Bridge in 1936 and the Golden Gate International Exposition on Treasure Island in 1939-1940 brought a new customer base. He opened a Trader Vic's in Seattle. Other locations soon followed.

But it wasn't until 1951 that Vic decided to open in San Francisco. He discussed it with Herb Caen: "Kid, you think I can make it over there?" Caen answered "What's the problem—most of your customers are from San Francisco." Vic found a tin-roofed garage in Cosmo Place, between Taylor and Jones streets. He hired San Francisco architect Gardiner Dailey to design a kind of South Sea Island movie set and told him "When you get through turning this into a restaurant I still want it to look like a shed." Dailey turned out a delicate mix of funky and elegant.

A Shrunken Head

Trader Vic's entryway was lush with tropical plants and led to an opulent, narrow hall. Glass cases ran along both sides with South Seas artifacts, tiki dolls, and yes—a shrunken head. At the far end customers encountered not Trader Vic himself, but Michael Gutierrez with the open reservations book before him. Gutierrez was more than a maître d'. He was keeper of the Trader Vic flame—a former marine with the toughness of a gunnery sergeant and the charm of Cary Grant.

Once past Michael Gutierrez, guests were ushered into one of three dining rooms—the Tiki Room, the Garden Room or the exalted Captain's Cabin with plush, red leather banquettes. It was flanked by a long, polished bar where skilled barmen dispensed those Trader Vic-created rum drinks like the legendary Mai Tai that he created in 1944. This inner sanctum was presided over by maître d' Hans Brandt. If Michael Gutierrez had the charm of Cary Grant, Hans Brandt, with suave leaps and bounds, was the Mikhail Baryshnikov of the Captain's Cabin.

The food was terrific. Barbecued Spareribs, Crab Rangoon, Bongo Bongo Soup (an unctuous puree of oysters and spinach) the Cosmo Salad (sliced artichoke bottoms, mushrooms and celery with a mustard dressing) and Indonesian lamb roast with Javanese sate sauce.

Soon, the tin-roofed shed was receiving international publicity and attracted the affluent social set much like New York's Café Society

Undated photo of Victor Bergeron, Jr. of Trader Vic's.
PHOTO: TIKIROOM.COM

but with raw-boned western élan. In the mid-fifties it was the place to go and the place to be seen. The U.S. government selected it as the Official United Nations Entertainment Center in the Bay Area, making it the restaurant for foreign dignitaries and prominent visitors. U.S. Presidents, movie stars, sports figures, authors, opera stars, locals from old families, debutantes, college students and their dates all flocked to Trader Vic's. In 1983 Queen Elizabeth II dined there when she visited San Francisco. It was the first, and to that time, the only public restaurant the Queen ever visited.

Not a Fathead

Trader Vic, earlier an ebullient, friendly man, began moving from irrepressible to irascible. But the more he exhibited his rough manner or shunned his prominent guests, the more they flocked to his restaurant. Vic had a towering ego that he acknowledged. He said "Ego is good for the soul. But too much ego turns you into a fathead." Most agreed Vic was egotistical but not a fathead. He was prickly, profane, gruff, charming and, at times, even somewhat boyish.

When Vic arrived at Cosmo Place in the morning he stumped through the dining rooms and kitchen greeting everyone like an angry warlord, then disappeared into his small, crowded upstairs office. He usually preferred to have a simple lunch there and called in one of the Chinese cooks and discussed what he might enjoy—perhaps leftover roast lamb with beans or shredded cabbage, lightly fried.

Only occasionally would he descend to sit for a few minutes with a special customer. On those occasions he was fond of pulling his artificial limb from under the table and saying: "Let me tell you something, don't ever get one of these things unless you really need it."

The Parts Wore Out

He developed other interests. He painted and his work found ready collectors and commanded top dollar. He became a sculptor. In 1979 he completed a granite monument that was placed on Angel Island as a tribute to the Chinese and other Asians who journeyed to California to build a new life and between 1910 and 1940 were detained at the Angel Island Immigration Station.

In 1984 Victor Jules Bergeron, Jr. died. Earlier he had lost a lung and had a stroke. "The parts were wearing out," he said.

Trader Vic's on San Francisco's Cosmo Place closed in 1994. The times had changed. Alice Waters had become an international food icon. Her Berkeley restaurant, Chez Panisse, was riding high. Jeremiah Towers signed in with his chic restaurant, Stars and San Francisco society discovered it. The children of San Francisco socialites no longer considered it a rite of passage to have a wallop of rum and tropical fruit juices followed by dinner at Trader Vic's.

Nevertheless, more than a dozen Trader Vic's restaurants still exist in the U.S., Europe, Asia and the Middle East. The mother ship is in the East Bay town of Emeryville where Mai Tais still abound.

CHAPTER 9

THE SAZERAC COCKTAIL

This cocktail was created in New Orleans in the 1850s but later became popular in early San Francisco. These days it is enjoying a resurgence of popularity in many upscale San Francisco bars. A sugar cube is muddled with a few dashes of Peychaud's bitters and a dash or two of Angostura bitters in an old fashioned glass. This is poured into a cocktail shaker and one bar spoon of absinthe or Pernod is added, plus two-and-a-half ounces of Rye whisky. Ice is added to the mixture which is then shaken and strained into an old fashioned glass. Finally the drink is garnished with a lemon peel.

ODE TO THE PANAMA HAT

A s a Panama hat cultist who favors the Charlie Chan model known technically as the Optimo, I've kept a watchful eye on a small shop in San Francisco's outer Richmond.

Paul's Hatworks, a venerable Panama hat shrine, has been in San Francisco since 1918. And through all those years—that is until a few years ago—there have been only three "Pauls"—three skilled, hat-making proprietors.

The first was a Peruvian merchant seaman named Napoleon Marquez who jumped ship here, changed his name to Paul, opened Paul's Hatworks out on Geary and created fine Panama hats for 37 years. Then came Napoleon's godson Kelly Bowling who ran the shop for another 25 years. Then in 1980, Michael Harris became keeper of the Panama hat flame. Harris remained *el jefe* (The Chief) until a few years ago when suddenly the number of "Pauls" jumped by four. Michael Harris retired and something new was in the wind.

And the reason this Optimo-wearing devotee paid close attention to Paul's Hatworks on Geary Boulevard is because the new "Pauls" were four, young San Francisco roommates—Olivia Griffin, Abbie Dwelle, Wendy Hawkins and Kirsten Hove. One would assume the four stylish upstarts would be more familiar with the footwear fashions of Sarah Jessica Parker and her hottie chums than those wonderful gossamer creations known as Panama hats. Wouldn't you? Well, you would be wrong since the four young women who apprenticed under Michael Harris became Panama hat visionaries and are not only fashioning the elegant straw creations but felt fedoras as well.

Panama Hat Hotshots

What follows is an unabashed tribute to the Panama hat. For many zealots—both men and women by the way—there are few uncommonly rare objects in this world that satisfy like a fine Panama hat. They weigh no more than a few ounces and the finest of them have a value exponentially far in excess of their weight.

But don't just take my word for it. Others who have equated Panama hats with the dearest of luxury possessions include Teddy Roosevelt, Franklin D., Churchill, Harry Truman, Humphrey Bogart, Gary Cooper, Sydney Greenstreet, Peter Lorre, Nina Foch, Greta Garbo, Tennessee Williams, Truman Capote, Tom Wolfe, Paul Theroux, Peter Mayle and Willie L. Brown, Jr., just to name a few Panama hat hotshots.

These days, fine Panama hats continue to be found gracing the heads—swelled or otherwise—of statesman, politicians, actors, rock stars, business tycoons, playwrights and assorted writers.

In Peter Mayle's book *Acquired Tastes*, required reading for anyone aspiring to a life of *luxe*, he says that at first he was not a believer in the cult of the Panama hat: "I could have carried my ignorance to the grave if a friend—knowing of my interest in anything preposterously extravagant—hadn't told me about a hat that cost $1,000. But not a solid, indestructible, waterproof, lifetime investment of a hat. This was a mere straw hat. Who would be lunatic enough to pay out four figures for less than three ounces which you hardly know you had on your head."

Teddy Roosevelt and his Panama Hat

But why are they called Panama hats when they actually originated in Ecuador? Because Ecuador was producing fine straw hats as early as 1630. In the late 1800s they were exported and sold in Panamanian ports. Workers on the Panama Canal wore these Ecuadorian straw hats to ward off the tropical sun. A photo shot in 1906 of 26th President Teddy Roosevelt shows him wearing an Ecuadorian-Panama hat while viewing the Canal's excavation.

The Ecuadorian province of Manabi has been historically the center of straw weaving and the town of Montecristi has become famous for the skill of its weavers. It's from Montecristi that Paul's Hatworks acquires the woven, unfinished "bodies."

The Montecristi

Panama hats are woven from the *carludovica palmata*, which despite its frond-like leaves comes from the family of the screw pine, not from palm trees. The fronds are gathered, sorted and dried. Then they are shredded by hand into long thin strands and then sorted again. Finally the weavers take over in the middle of the night when temperature and humidity are the most constant. The weavers are usually young women with delicate but skilled fingers, we are told. They weave almost microscopic cross hatches into tiny, flat rosettes. Over the weeks and months these rosettes become larger and larger. When a hat crown has been woven and shaped the weaver works her way outward, along what will be the brim. But the weaver does not complete the brim and the unfinished "body" remains with hundreds of strands of fiber sticking out from it. Paul's Hatworks purchases these unfinished "bodies" and takes it from there.

There are dozens of styles of Panama hats but Paul's Hatworks customers usually prefer one of four. These are the Optimo or Charlie Chan model (my favorite hat style), the tear drop crown Planter (pointed crown and a wide curled brim), the open Telescope Planter (a round crown) and the Fedora. If Indiana Jones had worn a Panama hat instead of a felt model, the Panama Fedora is the one he would have chosen.

The Conformature

These days when serious customers visit Paul's Hatworks, our lady hat-makers handle them like a violin, a rare Stradivarius—carefully and with dignity. They dazzle their customers as they set an ancient hatter's apparatus called a conformature on their skulls. The conformature is a wood and metal contraption that fits on the head like a loose hat, just on top of the ears. More than 50 flat blades fit tightly against the head—just as a real hat would. One expects the hatter to plug the contraption into a wall socket and fry your brains. But it's from this "form"—hence conformature—that Paul's Hatworks creates the custom-fitted, sublime headgear. The hats are shaped over an ancient steam boiler, and

PHOTO: COURTESY OF FRED LYON

blocked to perfection. The finished product goes for about $300 on up—quite a way up.

Panama hat cultists are a finicky, esoteric breed that believes in the legacy of Montecristi. They have a highly developed sense of just what should crown their skulls and at Paul's Hatworks the legacy continues.

CHAPTER 10

OYSTERS KIRKPATRICK

While New Orleans is the birthplace of Oysters Rockefeller (Antoine's Restaurant), it was in San Francisco that Oysters Kirkpatrick was created—specifically at the Palace Hotel. Chef de cuisine Ernest Arbogast developed the recipe for his boss, Colonel John C. Kirkpatrick, the hotel's general manager in the 1890s. Here's a basic recipe: Open oysters and place on a bed of rock salt. To each oyster add a dash or two of Worcestershire Sauce and some finely chopped green pepper. Top with tomato ketchup, a strip of raw bacon and some grated Parmesan cheese. Bake in a very hot oven for five or six minutes until browned.

IN SEARCH OF THE PERFECT CIOPPINO

One might presume I spend an inordinate amount of time thinking about *cioppino*. And I suppose I do. I think a lot about food in general. But *cioppino* frequently occupies me, as it well should.

On *cioppino* there is some dispute and a bit of mystery. The story behind this succulent, tomato-based fish stew is that it originated in San Francisco—more specifically with Italian fishermen in this city's North Beach neighborhood. There's a considerable weight of publicity to confirm this in cookbooks, websites and from local gourmets and gourmands.

Now, I don't want to be a spoil sport and I bow to no one in my love of San Francisco's North Beach, not to mention its Italian fishing community. Nevertheless I refuse to believe that along the coast of *mare nostrum*, that ancient sea, the Mediterranean, no fisherman ever came up with the grandfather of all *cioppinos*.

The Guiseppe Bazzuro Story

As a long-time and devoted *cioppino* lover I have been doing some serious research and here's a summary.

The San Francisco Chronicle food page said "Local lore has it that this tomato-heavy seafood treat, closely related to *ciuppin*, the fish stew of Genoa, was invented by Guiseppe Bazzuro who turned an abandoned ship into the city's first Italian restaurant in 1850. Genovese fishermen used whatever fish and seafood they had left over. San Francisco *cioppino* in its finest versions, features local Dungeness crab."

Helen Evans Brown in *The West Coast Cookbook* goes with the Guiseppe Bazzuro story and then sensibly adds "What's more, it was supposed to be from an old recipe, well-known in Italy."

Bouillabaisse is Fish Soup, Cioppino is a Fish Stew

American cookery giant James Beard weighed in with an elaborate recipe for *cioppino* that includes Dungeness crab, shrimp, clams, or mussels, or oysters (or all three), sea bass, halibut or other firm-fleshed fish—tomatoes of course. But, he never says it was San Franciscan in origin.

The American Heritage Dictionary describes *cioppino* simply as "A stew made with several kinds of fish and shellfish, tomatoes, and white wine." Then adds: "Italian, perhaps a variant of northwest Italian *ciuppin*." No mention of San Francisco.

My main man on just about anything gustatorial is the incomparable Waverley Root who wrote the authoritative twin volumes, *The Food of France* and *The Food of Italy*. Root never mentions *cioppino*, but traces *brodetto, ciuppin, burrida, cassola, zimini, ghiotto, zuppa de pesce* and, of course, *bouillabaisse,* which he describes as "...the very ancient and very rich fish chowder said to have been invented in Athens and in any case spread throughout the Mediterranean by Greeks...." There we have it, precursors and variations to what in North Beach is called *cioppino.*

And here I'll add my two cents worth. *Bouillabaisse* is a soup, a fish soup or chowder. Cioppino is a fish stew.

The Noble Elixir with Tomatoes

All these noble elixirs include tomatoes in some way or another. Tomatoes were introduced to Europe in the 16th century from across the Atlantic in the New World. So, it figures that a fisherman in a small boat netted a mixed bag of Mediterranean fish and later boiled them up—perhaps even with a bit of seawater—and then threw in a few chopped tomatoes, onions and whatever else was at hand.

Cioppino is Sublime

While planning for this sketch on *cioppino* I did considerable sampling in San Francisco restaurants and even some home cooking to see if I could get it right.

I can testify that admirable *cioppinos* are to be found in and round North Beach. I can give a vote of confidence to those at the North Beach Restaurant, Gigi's *Sotto Mare*, the U.S. Restaurant and A. Sabella's on Fisherman's Wharf. I'm sure there are other establishments in the neighborhood that will offer a fine bowl of *cioppino*, but research is open to individual enterprise.

Perhaps this is more than you ever wanted to know about *cioppino*, but my defense is—*cioppino* is sublime.

———

CHAPTER 11

IT ALL DEPENDS ON YOUR POINT OF VIEW

San Francisco is a city that likes its views. I'm not talking about points of view on city politics, neighborhood gentrification or restaurants. There are plenty of viewpoints on those subjects. San Franciscans are an opinionated bunch. But here I'm talking about views of the Golden Gate Bridge from the Top of the Mark— views from the top of Hyde Street "where little cable cars climb halfway to the stars."—and of course, views from Telegraph Hill north across the bay to Alcatraz, the island and its grim reminder of the maximum-security federal prison that operated there from 1934 to 1963. Yes, that Alcatraz view, day or night, is a knock-out, worth big bucks on the real estate market. Great for having guests over and nursing a few cocktails while the sun goes down. But let's reverse that. While the view of the San Francisco Bay, with Alcatraz in the middle distance, is beautiful—awe inspiring— the view from Alcatraz when it was a federal penitentiary for in-corrigible criminals was equally awe inspiring. But the attitude of the beholder was entirely different—rueful, resentful. It all depends on your point of view.

HARD TIME ON THE ISLAND

L ong before it was a federal prison, Alcatraz, that distinctive, 22-acre island in San Francisco Bay, was used as a camp ground and area for gathering food like birds' eggs and fish, by the Miwoks and the Ohlone, native tribes who settled the area from 10,000 to 20,000 years ago. There is little record of these settlements, but that's what some historians believe. Others assert that these natives may have used Alcatraz for the banishment of wrong-doers. If that conjecture is correct, it is a fascinating prefiguring of how the island was used many centuries later—again as a place of banishment.

La Isla de Los Alcatraces

It wasn't until 1775 that Juan Manuel de Ayala, a Spanish explorer, sailed into San Francisco Bay and began charting it. He named the rocky island *La Isla de Los Alcatraces* (Island of the Pelicans). Over the years the name of the pelican island was anglicized to Alcatraz.

When California became a U.S. possession in 1848 at the end of the war with Mexico over this valuable territory, suddenly Alcatraz became important. The U.S. Army took over Alcatraz and it became the largest military fort west of the Mississippi River. And in 1854 a lighthouse was built on the island's highest point to help guide ships into the bay.

An Army Prison

As early as 1860 the army was using Alcatraz to imprison sol-dier-convicts. Gradually the fortifications there became obsolete and the importance of the military prison grew. In 1907 It was formally designated a military prison. Army prisoners constructed most of the buildings on the island. The last army prisoners and their guards departed in 1933 and the following year Alcatraz became a federal, maximum security penitentiary and remained as such until 1963.

Postcard of Alcatraz.
PHOTO: COLLECTION OF GLENN D. KOCH

The Oppressive View of San Francisco

As a prison Alcatraz was a tough place to do time. The boring, daily routine with endless head counts to make sure everyone was there (13 official counts were made every 24 hours); the work details in the prison laundry. On Sundays prisoners were allowed to play softball. If a batter hit the ball over the wall it was not a homerun but an out. But perhaps the most oppressive thing about Alcatraz was the view of San Francisco (when prisoners were allowed outside and could look at it). There it was—San Francisco—on the prisoner's limited horizon.

Famous Prisoners

Alcatraz had many famous prisoners. Among them were the Chicago mobster Al Capone, George "Machine Gun" Kelly, the first "Public Enemy #1" Alvin Karpis, Mickey Cohen, and "The Birdman of Alcatraz" Robert Stroud.

Missing and Presumed Drowned

Fevered thoughts and planning for escape were ever-present. Did anyone ever escape? Well, that depends on how you define escape. Over the 29 years that the prison operated, 36 men were involved in 14 escape attempts (two prisoners tried to escape twice). Twenty-three were caught, six were shot and killed during their escape attempt, and two drowned. Whether anyone ever succeeded in escaping requires parsing the word escape. Do you define escape as successful if the prisoner got out of the cell house, reached the water of San Francisco Bay, made it to land, or reached land and did not get caught? The National Park Service that operates Alcatraz as a tourist attraction these days, officially says no one ever succeeded in escaping, but to this day there are five prisoners who are listed as "missing and presumed drowned." Did they really drown? Or are they out there somewhere, perhaps reading this book?

—————

CHAPTER 12

A LIBRARY OF SOUP CANS

"I must say I find television very educational. The minute somebody turns it on, I go into the library and read a good book."
—Groucho Marx

"If I don't have a book to read I get nervous and begin reading the labels on soup cans."
—Ernest Beyl

BOOKSTORES FOR THE BOOKISH

Perhaps it's true that you can't tell a book by its cover, but you can certainly tell a city by its bookstores, specifically its small independents. San Francisco, as befits a world-class city with world-class readers, has many fine bookstores large and small—even in this age of the internet. They feed us with intellectual fiber—brain food. Like San Francisco restaurants, they appeal to all tastes and digestions.

The North Beach neighborhood still has a few fine bookstores but it would be good to have even more. You can never have too many bookstores just as you can never have too many dollars with which to buy those books you have always meant to read.

Here in North Beach we have mourned the passing of a few good bookstores that helped feed our book hunger.

Gone but not Forgotten
Remember Thomas Bros. across the street from Clown Alley? It was a gem. It specialized in esoteric maps and travel books and had been at the same location, 550 Jackson Street, since 1920. It was a good place to find Graham Greene's *Journey without Maps,* a street map of London, or an annotated historical map of the Mayan civilization on the Yucatan Peninsula. Why did it finally close? It became a division of Rand McNally and moved to Market Street. The original is missed in the old neighborhood.

Then there was John Carroll: New and Used Books, 633 Vallejo Street. A splendid second-hand bookstore. At John Carroll's you could find books on California history; some by the famous Grabhorn Press. Outside on John Carroll's front porch, so to speak, were bins of paperbacks and hardbacks for a dime to a dollar. I once found a dog-eared copy of *The Charterhouse of Parma* by Stendhal which I should have read years ago since his family name, Beyle, was quite similar to my own.

City Lights Bookstore.
PHOTO: STACEY LEWIS

Too many pages put me off earlier, I suppose. John Carroll too, felt the pressure from the big boys and the internet and he went out of business. He's in Paris now and back in business running a bookshop.

And did you know that for a short time there was a shop called Gourmet Books on Stockton Street? It carried not only cookbooks but also wonderful essays about food like *Between Meals* by the incomparable A.J. Liebling and *American Fried* by Calvin Trillin. Why did it close? Who knows?

Or how about this one? Revolutionary Books, once on Upper Grant Avenue. It closed its doors several years ago and moved to Berkeley. It figures.

We mourn the loss of all of these. But how about the survivors?

Survivors to Nourish Us

City Lights Booksellers and Publishers—Like Shakespeare & Company, Sylvia Beach's Paris bookstore of the twenties that published James Joyce's *Ulysses* and became the focus for the so-called Lost Gen-

Fiction corner at the City Lights Bookstore.
PHOTO: STACEY LEWIS

eration—City Lights, 261 Columbus Avenue, became the focus for the Beat Generation and is probably the most famous bookstore in the U.S. Until recently it was still presided over by its founder Lawrence Ferlinghetti, iconoclastic poet and publisher of Allen Ginsberg's Beat anthem, *Howl.*

William Stout Architectural Books at 804 Montgomery Street, is a great bookstore, whether or not you are into architecture. Profiles of architects and their work. And a few years ago, great paper cutout models of the Eiffel Tower and New York's Chrysler Building. I go there for monographs on architects Frank Gehry or Rem Koolhaas.

The Beat Museum on Broadway—While not a proper bookstore, it nevertheless carries a wide range of Beat books.

Eastwind—This is probably the best Chinese bookstore in the U.S., perhaps the best one outside the People's Republic of China. Located at 1435 Stockton Street, Eastwind comes in two sections—Chinese books in Chinese and Chinese books in English.

Schein & Schein—This fine antique map and print shop is located at 1435 Upper Grant Avenue. While Jimmy and Marti Schein's principal business is in antique maps and prints, the couple also has many rare volumes on early California and the West.

Big Al's: An Adult Bookstore—Well, of course! X-rated bookstores are a fact of life. And given the loopy history of San Francisco, and more specifically, the history of the Barbary Coast and the Latin Quarter (now North Beach), porn books and magazines represent a concept that's here to stay. And, if there is a rating system for adult shops, Big Al's on Broadway rates an A plus. It is the Barnes and Noble of the adult end of the business.

———•·•———

Carmen McRae.
PHOTO: FROM THE AUTHOR'S COLLECTION

CHAPTER 13

DIZZY GILLESPIE AND CARMEN MCRAE

One evening long ago Dizzy Gillespie was appearing at the Jazz Workshop in San Francisco's North Beach. Between sets he jaywalked across Broadway to Sugar Hill where jazz vocalist Carmen McRae was singing. Dizzy stepped up on the small stage and to Carmen's surprise accompanied her obbligato on his strange, up-tilted trumpet as she shaped her version of "I Left My Heart in San Francisco."

THE DIMINUTIVE JAZZ GIANT
ERROLL GARNER

I am thinking about Erroll Garner, the incredible jazz pianist who played the theme song in Clint Eastwood's film *Play Misty for Me.*

I was fortunate enough to know Garner, who died in 1977, and to count him a friend. I met him through Jimmy Lyons, founder and general manager of the Monterey Jazz Festival from its beginning in 1958 through 1992 when he retired.

I met Garner, the diminutive, self-taught piano stylist at the 1970 Monterey Jazz Festival when he performed his composition "Misty" for a sold-out Saturday afternoon concert filmed by Eastwood, who was directing his first movie. I was working as publicist for the Monterey Jazz Festival at the time and Garner and I connected that weekend. I was an enormous admirer of his work and when I told him that, I guess my sincerity came through and he took a liking to me—almost as a mascot. For several years after that, at Christmas, a gift would arrive at my apartment from "Your Buddy, Erroll". The gifts were always beautiful (and expensive) Steuben crystal, animal figurines. One year I got a hippo, another year, a pelican.

Concert by the Sea

I had been turned on to Garner's brilliance as a jazz piano player by a live album, *Concert by the Sea.* In 1955 my friend Jimmy Lyons, then a Monterey Peninsula disk jockey, brought Erroll Garner to Carmel for a concert. The recording of that concert became one of the largest-selling jazz albums of all time. If you're unfamiliar with this landmark recording, do yourself a favor and give it a listen. It's incredible Garner.

My friend Erroll was only five feet four inches tall and when he played he usually sat on a New York telephone book placed on his piano bench. He liked to sing along a bit as he played. Sing is not really the

Erroll Garner circa 1947.
PHOTO: WILLIAM P. GOTTLIEB/IRA AND LEONORE S. GERSHWIN FUND COLLECTION, MUSIC DIVISION, LIBRARY OF CONGRESS; WIKIMEDIA COMMONS

operative word—he liked to growl and hum along with his music. You can hear it on this album. Erroll's piano style was big and two-handed, but his two hands operated completely independently from each other. While his left hand chorded with a metronome-like steadiness, his right hand was all over the place time-wise. Sometimes it raced ahead and sometimes it lagged behind the beat, setting up a tension that could drive you up the wall—but it swung like crazy. Erroll was not a bop or post-bop artist. He was a swing artist who loved pop tunes from the American songbook. You could dance to his music. That is, you could dance to it once Erroll finished the elaborate, all-over-the-keyboard introductions he liked to lay out before he set that left hand swinging, and then teased out the melody with his right hand. He was a powerful and gregarious piano player but off stage he could be a bit shy and not given to small talk.

The Concord Summer Festival

But, that's enough background on this great artist. Now, here's an Erroll Garner anecdote you might enjoy:

In the early 1970s I was doing some publicity work for an East Bay car dealer, Carl Jefferson. Jefferson loved jazz and in 1969 organized the Concord Summer Festival (later to be known as the Concord Jazz Festival) in a grassy town park. Early on Jefferson booked my buddy Erroll Garner.

Before the evening show on which Erroll was to perform, Jefferson, knowing that I had a relationship with the pianist, approached me backstage and asked me a favor. He had planned a post-concert blowout party at his big ranch-style house on the edge of town. Would I gather Erroll after the show and bring him out to the house for the party which would be held on the patio surrounding Jefferson's swimming pool. The mayor would be there along with other city officials and town business leaders and Contra Costa County social types. Jefferson had a baby grand—newly tuned—and wouldn't it be nice if the great Erroll Garner played just a couple of tunes? He left to me the task of advising Erroll all of this.

Erroll Goes to a Party

I drove Erroll to his nearby hotel following the performance. On the way I told him about the party and Jefferson's newly-tuned baby grand. He wasn't exactly thrilled by the idea but he was a gentleman—a heavily sweating gentleman I should add since it was the middle of a hot summer evening and the performance had been—as Erroll's always were—strenuous.

So I parked in front of the hotel and Erroll went to his room for a quick shower and change of clothes. A half hour went by. Then, another half hour. I went into the lobby and telephoned Erroll's room. No answer. I thought we had missed each other passing in the lobby. I went back to the car. No Erroll. Then I thought to look in the hotel cocktail lounge. He was sitting at the bar nursing a big one. He smiled when he saw me and asked if he could buy me a drink. Of course. Then I bought one for Erroll. Then Erroll bought one for me. Erroll had a couple more but I was the designated driver.

We finally got in the car and drove out to Jefferson's house. As I turned into the semi-circular driveway I became dubious. No valet to park cars. In fact no cars in the driveway or along the secluded lane where the Jefferson house was. We parked, got out and approached the big front door and I rang the bell. I could see no lights in the house and heard no party noises. We stood there. Erroll looked really nice. He had on a blue buttoned-down shirt with a silk tie and a cream colored, summer suit. I was dressed okay for a publicist, but a bit rumpled.

I rang the bell again. Then I rang it once more. Finally the door opened. Erroll and I gave our best "hello" smiles. Carl Jefferson stood there in a bathrobe. He did not invite us in.

————•·•————

CHAPTER 14

A SAN FRANCISCO PRIVATE EYE

Dashiell Hammett, the writer of hard-boiled detective novels, lived in San Francisco during the 1920s. He was a private eye for the Pinkerton National Detective Agency and his office was located in the Flood Building on Market Street. He saw the seamy side of San Francisco close up. In his off hours he applied himself to the typewriter. Among his works are The Maltese Falcon, The Thin Man, Red Harvest *and* The Dain Curse. *Hammett once said: "All my characters were based on people I've known personally, or known about." The action of* The Maltese Falcon *and* The Dain Curse *take place in San Francisco. He had a long relationship with playwright Lillian Hellman and died in 1961.*

"I WON'T PLAY THE SAP FOR YOU."

Authors have always loved to write about San Francisco and have set the action of their novels here. A few that come to mind are *McTeague* by Frank Norris, *A Girl of Forty* by Herbert Gold, *The Joy Luck Club* by Amy Tan, *Tales of the City* by Armistead Maupin and my favorite with San Francisco as a backdrop, *The Maltese Falcon* by Dashiell Hammett.

The Maltese Falcon

A murder takes place in an alley off Bush Street, above the Stockton Street tunnel. A character checks into the St. Mark Hotel—a combination of the Mark Hopkins and the Fairmont. Another is told to hock jewelry at a pawn shop at Fifth and Mission, where the *San Francisco Chronicle* is located. Yet another has lunch at the Palace Hotel. A bad guy goes to a play at the Geary Theater. A taxicab takes a woman to the Ferry Building. Alcatraz foghorns blow.

John's Grill

And notably, two detectives, one from the San Francisco Police Department, the other a private eye, have lunch at John's Grill on Ellis Street. The private eye asks the waiter to hurry his order of …"chops, baked potato and sliced tomatoes." The brief passage that takes place in John's Grill has, over the years since the book was first published in 1929, become a masterful marketing tool for the still-existing restaurant that was opened in 1908. The second floor features a museum of Dashiell Hammett and *The Maltese Falcon* memorabilia—including an impressive casting of the black falcon that plays a major role in the book. And on the menu one will find "Sam Spade Lamb Chops."

Still photo from The Maltese Falcon *starring Humphrey Bogart.*
PHOTO: ©WARNER BROS.

If They Hang You I'll Always Remember You

The best line from the book about the hard-boiled detective Sam Spade is, "I won't play the sap for you." Sam is speaking to the beautiful Brigid O'Shaughnessy, a devious counterbalance for the tough detective.

A few moments earlier in the complicated murder mystery, with Brigid standing very close to Sam and inviting him to kiss her, he utters these unforgettable lines: "I'm going to send you over. The chances are you'll get off with life. That means you'll be out again in twenty years. You're an angel. I'll wait for you." (He clears his throat and then he says) "If they hang you I'll always remember you."

Humphrey Bogart, Mary Astor, Sydney Greenstreet, and Peter Lorre

I'm sorry if I spoiled this by revealing the book's ending. I'm assuming you are of literary bent if you're reading this book of mine. And that you have probably read *The Maltese Falcon* or seen the classic 1941 movie directed by John Huston and starring Humphrey Bogart as Sam Spade, Mary Astor as Brigid O'Shaughnessy, Sydney Greenstreet as the "Fatman" Casper Gutman, and Peter Lorre as the repulsive Joel Cairo.

It's time for you to read *The Maltese Falcon* once again. And time to go to John's Grill for the chops, baked potato, and sliced tomatoes.

———•◦•———

John and Laura Mattos
PHOTO: COURTESY JOHN MATTOS

CHAPTER 15

LAURA IS HOWLED

Much has been written about Allen Ginsberg and his iconic Beat poem Howl. *Ginsberg first read it aloud at the Six Gallery on Fillmore Street, October 7, 1955. This addendum has been added courtesy of John Mattos, renowned San Francisco graphic designer. John's wife Laura—herself an accomplished editor and art gallery owner—died in 2015. Laura was a bit of a Beat and here's the story: Both John and Laura were born in Modesto, California and went to high school there during the Beat years. They were in the same grade and the same English class. One day the assignment was to read a poem aloud. Laura stood and read a blistering stanza from* Howl. *When she finished, the teacher said "Not only are you out of this class, but you are out of this school." Laura got up, grabbed her copy of* Howl *and walked out. She never did get a high school diploma, but she went on to gain an English degree at the University of California in Berkeley. Along the way she and John Mattos were reunited and married.*

THE POETIC LIFE OF SAN FRANCISCO

One sun-spackled day in San Francisco a casually-dressed young man was standing purposively at the corner of Columbus Avenue and Broadway selling poems. For only a dollar he would recite one of his poems then give a copy to the purchaser. How intelligent. How sensible. How (in that overworked phrase) "very San Francisco." Living in a city where one can buy a poem on a street corner is almost, but not quite, as good as creating one.

To undertake a poetic history of San Francisco, in prose no less, is fraught with pitfalls: who to include; who to omit. And the ability to quote here from more than a handful of poets is limited.

One of the earliest San Francisco poems was written by a comedic gold miner in 1849 who, after slipping in the deep mud at the corner of Clay and Kearny Streets, scrawled this poetic traffic warning:

> *This street is impassable*
> *Not even jackassable*

Was this indeed a poem? Of course! Who is to say that poems must always deal with lofty subjects?

Through the years there have been many poets in San Francisco—pranksters, rhymesters, sonneteers, balladeers, rhapsodists, discontents, malcontents, misfits, storytellers, zealots, wake-up-call tacticians, shock and awe messengers, social climbers and pompous asses. At times it has been difficult to tell one from the other.

The Gold Rush and Beyond

Early San Francisco spawned poets at the drop of a rhyming couplet. A devil-may-care, bohemian lifestyle made it almost mandatory that young men and women of artistic temperament give it a try. Bret Harte, Samuel Clemens, Ina Coolbrith, Jack London, Ambrose Bierce, George Sterling, Robert Louis Stevenson, Charles Warren Stoddard, Mary Austin, Joaquin Miller and many others wrote poetry. Some of it quite good. Some mediocre. Some dreadful. The point is they wrote it. The muse was upon them.

Consider American actress and poet Adah Isaacs Menken (1835-1868). Wildly popular in wildly literary early San Francisco, Adah took the free-swinging, art-seeking city by storm as *Mazeppa*, the Lord Byron stem-winder. In her version, a tartar youth (played by Adah) is stripped by captors and, as a climax, rides off stage on horseback wearing only flesh colored tights with her long black hair streaming and concealing. On opening night at Macguire's Opera House she charmed Bret Harte, Joaquin Miller, and Charles Warren Stoddard, San Francisco's first known gay poet. San Francisco loved Adah and she, in turn, loved San Francisco, or at least various prominent San Franciscans. Later she took *Mazeppa* to Paris and London. Her best recalled poem, flamboyant and autobiographical, is *Infelicia,* which she dedicated to her good friend Charles Dickens. A lengthy and turgid work, it ends like this:

> *Where is the promise of my years*
> *Once written on my brow?*
> *Ere errors agonies and fears*
> *Brought with them all that speaks in tears*
> *Ere I had sunk beneath my peers*
> *Where sleeps that promise now?*

She died in London in poverty and forgotten by her early admirers.

The Saga of Black Bart PO8

Not as rhapsodic as many other poets of the time, but a poet nevertheless, was Charles Boles (1829-1870), a dapper easterner who began holding up Wells Fargo stages in Northern California in the

1870s. A short man, Boles placed a derby hat on his head to give him a certain ranginess, covered himself with a large flour sack with eye holes cut out and stood in the middle of the roadway with a shotgun. When the stagecoach stopped, Boles called out "Throw down the box," in a deep, stagy voice. After the stagecoach had driven away in haste, Boles rifled the box and left behind one of his poems. Here's an example:

> *So here I've stood while wind and rain*
> *Have set the trees a sobbin'*
> *And risked my life for that damned box*
> *That wasn't worth the robbin'*

He signed his poems Black Bart, PO8.

Black Bart was finally apprehended and sent to San Quentin but, a model prisoner, he was released in four-and-a-half years and disappeared.

George Sterling and his Cool, Grey City of Love

But the poet who seemed to capture a young San Francisco best was George Sterling (1869-1901). Struggling to be the most bohemian in a city of struggling, would-be bohemians, Sterling, a former seminarian born on Long Island, came to Northern California only to become a real estate salesman. He wrote poetry while riding the ferryboat on his way to San Francisco to pursue commerce. Ambrose Bierce (1842-1914?), a journalist and occasional poet himself, befriended Sterling, as did a young Jack London (1876-1916) recently out of Oakland High School. And by the way, the question mark following Bierce's born-and-died statistics is not a typo. He went to Mexico to join Pancho Villa's revolutionary army in 1914 but disappeared. It is assumed by many that he was shot by a revolutionary firing squad that year. A surviving snippet of Bierce's poetry reads:

When mountains were stained as with wine
By the dawning of Time, and as wine
Were the seas.

Sterling and his friends wandered bohemian San Francisco looking for wine, women and song. They found all three without difficulty. Sterling is seldom read these days but is remembered for a few lines in his work *The City by the Sea—San Francisco*.

At the end of our streets is sunrise;
At the end of our streets are spars;
At the end of our streets is sunset;
At the end of our streets the stars.

Confused and alcoholic, or vice versa, Sterling sadly took his own life by poison in his room in San Francisco's Bohemian Club.

The Poets of Angel Island

Chinese began immigrating to San Francisco in large numbers soon after gold was discovered in California in 1848. They were badly treated although they helped build the transcontinental railroad and the Napa-Sonoma vineyards and labored in the state's light industries. Angel Island, the California State Park in San Francisco Bay, was used as an immigration detention site from 1910 to 1940 for Chinese (as well as other minorities) who journeyed from their motherland to build a new life in California. They were awaiting the outcome of health examinations and final disposition of their quest for immigration.

Long after the old Chinese detention barracks had been closed a park ranger found Chinese characters inscribed on the walls. In their frustration, the detainees, many of whom spent months and even years there, carved personal poems on the walls. More than 135 have been recorded. The poems are written in the Chinese classical style and provide a vivid reminder of a sad chapter in Chinese-American history. Here is an example:

> *My parents are old; my family is poor.*
> *Cold weather comes; hot weather goes.*
> *Heartless white devils,*
> *Sadness and anger fill my heart.*

Nearby Voices: Stanford, Carmel, and Big Sur

While perhaps not included in our self-imposed physical boundaries on this poetic history of San Francisco, poets only a few miles to the south were important voices and had considerable influence on their counterparts in the city. Most notable was Robinson Jeffers (1887-1962), whose poetic epics *Roan Stallion, Tamar, Solstice* and *Hungerfield*, with the rugged California coast as a jarring background, still resound. Consider these lines ending *Hungerfield* which he dedicated to his wife Una:

> *Here is the poem dearest; you will never read it nor hear it.*
> *You were more beautiful than a hawk flying;*
> *You were faithful and a lion heart*
> *Like this rough hero Hungerfield.*
> *But the ashes have fallen*
> *And the flame has gone up; nothing remains.*
> *You are earth and air; you are in the beauty of the ocean*
> *And the great streaming triumphs of sundown;*
> *You are alive and well in the tender young grass rejoicing*
> *When soft rain falls all night,*
> *And little rosy-fleeced clouds float on the dawn.*
> *—I shall be with you presently.*

Yvor Winters (1900-1968), a professor of English at Stanford University, wrote a poem in 1942 called *To A Military Rifle* with lines that resonate strongly today:

The times come round again;
The private life is small;
And individual men
Are counted not at all.
Now life is general,
And the bewildered muse,
Thinking what she has done,
Confronts the daily news.

Also south of San Francisco in the rugged coastal country known as Big Sur, Henry Miller (1891-1980) was writing poetry and prose and painting delicate watercolors. While in residence on Big Sur's Partington Ridge, 1000 feet above the Pacific, he attracted a never-ending parade of acolytes who drove him to distraction and made him the unwilling center of an unfocused and unrealized arts colony. Later he commented: "Artists never thrive in colonies. Ants do."

San Francisco's Poetry Renaissance

Kenneth Rexroth (1905-1982) led what is now termed San Francisco's Poetic Renaissance and by most accounts must be considered a towering Northern California poet of our time. Erudite, outspoken and highly influential, Rexroth vented his considerable poetic fury at war and the evanescent nature of a life unfulfilled. Overlooked for some time, his collected works have been republished.

How many went to work for Time *?*
How many died of prefrontal
lobotomies in the Communist Party?
How many on the advice of
their psychoanalysts, decide
A business career was best after all?

Although Rexroth was present at the dawn of the counterculture Beat Generation movement and served as its drumbeater and catalyst, he did not consider himself a part of it. In the introduction to a volume of his complete works, Sam Hamill recounts that when asked if Rexroth considered himself a Beat poet, he replied "An entomologist is not a bug."

The Ascent of Lawrence Ferlinghetti

City Lights, Lawrence Ferlinghetti's landmark San Francisco bookstore, became a kind of clubhouse for writers of the Beat Generation in the 1950s. Today, it is a magnet for baby boomer visitors to the city and also for their offspring who read Ferlinghetti and Beat writers like Jack Kerouac, Allen Ginsberg and others for college courses. Ferlinghetti is widely recognized as this country's greatest living poet. This is also the man—not actually a Beat poet by the way—who published Ginsberg's epic *Howl*, which became a Beat anthem. The poem was deemed obscene by the San Francisco Police Department. Ferlinghetti vigorously defended his right to publish it. After a much-publicized trial the court ruled in favor of Ferlinghetti.

Former San Francisco Mayor Joseph L. Alioto (1917-1998), who liked to think of himself as a poet, wrote "Ferlinghetti Howls and Beats the Rap":

> *So Howl Lorenzo, Howl night and day*
> *To knock the dry-balled Censor out of play*
> *And leave the First Amendment to decide*
> *What people want to honor or deride.*

These days Lawrence Ferlinghetti, poet, painter, pamphleteer, publisher and bookstore proprietor and former San Francisco Poet Laureate, strides through the streets of North Beach like a colossus and continues to rail at big government, big business, civil rights abuses, and this country's pugnacious war stance, as he always has. He walks tall and straight, his pale blue eyes mesmerizing. Ferlinghetti is highly conscious of his standing as a poet and activist. What makes him an important figure, a celebrity actually, is not just his poetry. It is also his unshakable belief in the importance of the poetic voice and his confidence that poetry is capable of transforming the world. He is an intellectual guerrilla. In *A Coney Island of the Mind* published in 1958 he writes about a setting whereby the poet moves from passive to active.

> *Who may cause the lips*
> *Of those who are asleep*
> *To speak*

And in the same poem he tackles just what it means to be a poet:

> *Constantly risking absurdity and death*
> *Whenever he performs above the heads of his audience*
> *The poet like an acrobat climbs on rime*
> *To a high wire of his own making*

The Beats

It is tempting to quote many of the so-called Beat poets since the movement of the 1950s had such energy and spawned a literary upheaval that galvanized intellectually restless youth as well as the establishment; especially the establishment media. But in the interest of maintaining solid relations with one's editor, we will list a bunch of Beats and quote only a few. The Beat generation produced not only the giants of the movement, Allen Ginsberg and Jack Kerouac, but a knapsack-full of other fine poets including Gregory Corso, Gary Snyder, Michael McClure, William Burroughs Jr., Philip Lamantia, Philip Whelan, Jack Micheline, Bob Kaufman, Diane DiPrima, Alan Watts, Josephine Miles, Brother Antonius, Jack Spicer, Robert Duncan and James Broughton.

It was Rexroth who in 1955 organized the history-making gathering at San Francisco's Six Gallery where Ginsberg first shouted his Walt Whitmanesque *Howl* while Kerouac cheered him on. We will quote only this riveting scrap:

I saw the best minds of my generation destroyed by madness,
Starving hysterical naked,
dragging themselves through the negro streets at dawn
Looking for an angry fix,
angelheaded hipsters burning for the ancient heavenly
connection to the starry dynamo in the machinery of the night,

After Ferlinghetti published *Howl* the Beat Movement was never the same. Poetry had gone big time. San Francisco became ground zero for a new literary movement.

The outspoken and the outcasts were published and publicized. Some entered the mainstream; some did not. Here are a few samples. Consider these lines by widely-published Diane DiPrima:

Alas
I believe
I might have become
A great writer
but
the chairs
in the library
were too hard

Or, let's affect a transition to the hippies who followed the Beats with this by Gregory Corso from *Variations on a Generation*:

In 1950 these poets gave a name to a generation, calling it
the Beat Generation; they did not know when they created that
stupid name what the vast extent of the future demand would be.

Rock Poets

Although popular music—rock 'n' roll music for example—has seen almost legendary poetic artistry—Paul Simon, Patti Smith, Leonard Cohen, and our Nobel Laureate Bob Dylan come to mind—the lyrics

Joan Baez and Bob Dylan, Civil Rights March on Washington, D.C., 1963.
PHOTO: WIKIMEDIA COMMONS

of the San Francisco rock bands did not leave poetry lovers in ecstasy. Nevertheless, perhaps two diametrically opposed examples should be mentioned. The apex of rock 'n' roll as anti-Vietnam political theater was created by Joe McDonald who in 1965 wrote a tune for his band, Country Joe and Fish, called *I-Feel-Like-I'm-Fixin'-to-Die Rag*. It is not too far a stretch to suggest that Country Joe MacDonald and other popular artists of the time were prominent in bringing down the White House of Lyndon Johnson and crystallizing the mood of dissent that eventually ended the Vietnam War. While many San Francisco rock bands expressed anti-war sentiments in their work, many also zeroed in on the swirling drug culture. Jefferson Airplane vocalist Grace Slick is credited with this bit of San Francisco rock 'n' roll poesy:

> *One pill makes you larger*
> *And one pill makes you small,*
> *And the ones that mother gives you*
> *Don't do anything at all.*

Lawrence Ferlinghetti at City Lights Bookstore.
PHOTO: STACEY LEWIS

San Francisco Poetry Today

But what of recent poets and poetry in San Francisco? It is tempting to follow the standard line that poets and their poetry are drifting in the slack water and have little if any marked influence on our lives. Yet, there are poets everywhere in San Francisco. They come out of the woodwork. Remember the young man at the beginning of this essay selling his poems on the street corner? The City of San Francisco, which this writer maintains takes its poetry and its poets seriously, has also had a series of Poets Laureate and pays them homage—Lawrence Ferlinghetti, Janice Mirikitani, Devorah Major and Jack Hirschman, for example. (The concept of the Poet Laureate dates back to 15th Century England when poet Ben Jonson was given a pension.) Another local group has mounted a campaign to establish an International Poetry Museum in San Francisco. And, of course, Ferlinghetti's internationally-recognized City Lights offers frequent readings and other events.

It has become almost axiomatic that those who give a damn about poetry, rate poets as being "major" or "minor" like ballplayers, politicians and socialites. But, who is really keeping score? Poetry should inform, advise, delight, infuriate, incite, entertain—or all of the above. That is why the wag at the San Francisco mud hole and Black Bart PO8 are included in this sketchy account along with such poets as Robinson Jeffers, Kenneth Rexroth and Lawrence Ferlinghetti.

———•••———

San Francisco sourdough bread.
PHOTO: ERNEST BEYL

CHAPTER 16

THE SOURDOUGH SAGA

Bagels are fine. English muffins have their charm. Warm tortillas have doting fans as do steamed pork buns. Even foamy, white, commercial bread has devotees and responds well to tuna salad. But it's the iconic San Francisco sourdough that turns on residents of this bread-wise city. It began with the Gold Rush in 1849. Many believe the miners brought sourdough "starter" or "mother" north from Mexico. While panning for gold they had to do things for themselves, even making their own bread. Some say miners carried their "mother" under their saddles to keep it warm and "alive." Others tell they kept "mother" in their armpits. "Mother" was just a bit of yesterday's bread dough—flour, water, salt, and wild yeast. But not all 49ers were miners. In 1849 a French immigrant, Louis Isadore Boudin, opened a bakery in San Francisco. Boudin's is still going strong and is the mother ship of sourdough bakeries. It says its "mother" dates back to the original 1849 supply, but the baker no longer keeps the "mother" in his armpit.

ERNIE'S RESTAURANT:
GONE BUT NOT FORGOTTEN

One day I walked down the gentle slope of Montgomery Street between Pacific and Jackson on my way to score a hamburger at Clown Alley and felt the tug of nostalgia for gourmet splendors past.

There was the old brick, three-story building that once housed the greatest restaurant in the city. It was named Ernie's and in its prime its acclaim went far beyond San Francisco. But it had a humble beginning.

Ernie's, 847 Montgomery, opened in 1934 by an Italian cook, Ernie Carlesso, as Il Trovatore Café—a North Beach saloon with spaghetti. Five years later he renamed it Ernie's and sold a share of the business to waiter Amrogilo Gotti. Together they bought the classic brick building that had once housed the old Frisco Dance Hall, a notorious Barbary Coast landmark. Carlesso died in 1946 and Gotti retired a year later. At that point Gotti's two sons, Victor and Roland, who worked there as busboys, took over the joint.

In a few years they had turned Ernie's from a simple *trattoria* with red checkered table cloths into a top drawer establishment— arguably one of the most famous restaurants in the world. Victor and Roland tore the old place apart and recast it in the San Francisco Victorian mode—maroon silk brocade walls, deep burgundy carpets, crystal chandeliers, discreet banquettes and tables with starched white linen, fine china, glassware and cutlery, deft waiters in tuxedos presided over by the shrewd and elegant Gotti brothers. It was a Victorian stage setting of a high style, of fancy French cuisine accompanied by the best wines the brothers could locate. It had a good run but the landmark establishment finally closed its doors in 1995. The Gotti brothers went on to perfect their golf game and lead happy lives. Neither is with us anymore.

In a Hitchcock Film

Ernie's Restaurant enjoyed international acclaim. It was reviewed glowingly by big slick magazines like *Holiday*. Food critics, not only here, but in New York, and in other so-called gourmet capitals, awarded it stars, toques, and forks. Socialites, columnists, politicians, movie stars and international luminaries flocked to Ernie's. Frank Sinatra, Alfred Hitchcock, Barbra Streisand, Walter Cronkite, Marilyn Monroe, and Cary Grant, dropped in regularly. Hitchcock included Ernie's in his San Francisco-based film, *Vertigo* with Kim Novak and Jimmy Stewart, but scenes presumably in the restaurant were actually shot on a Hollywood sound stage. Roland Gotti went south to play the bartender. While perhaps not in the same league as the cable cars and Coit Tower, Ernie's Restaurant was a major tourist attraction.

Locally it was a rite of passage that young men-about-town took their dates to Ernie's—especially when things were getting serious.

Even I went there—after all it was named Ernie's Restaurant—when I could scrape together the requisite cash.

Ernie's was on My Beat

All of this was in the early 1950s when I was a dispensable reporter for the *San Francisco Chronicle*, earning, as I recall, $135.00 a week. And, as a dispensable reporter, Scott Newhall, who at that time was editor of a *Chronicle* Sunday section, *This World*, called me into his office one day and declared me editor of an annual *Chronicle* endeavor called *Gourmet*, a tabloid insert on San Francisco restaurants. I was skinny and Newhall said "You do like to eat, don't you?" My job was to eat my way around town and write about it. Not bad for a dispensable reporter. Ernie's Restaurant was on my beat, as they say in the newspaper game. And I took full advantage of it.

But let me end this short memoir with how my dining experiences at famed Ernie's Restaurant almost landed me in the slammer.

In my capacity as a newly-minted food writer I "covered" Ernie's and wrote glowingly about it. And that began a brief and spurious career as the dandy Lucius Beebe of North Beach.

A Brass "E" from Ernie's Restaurant.
PHOTO: ERNEST BEYL

One late evening I dined at Ernie's with a young woman of short acquaintance. The evening began with several martinis at the famed mahogany bar that had come around the Horn on a sailing ship. Later, with our Veal Oscar (fresh asparagus tips on sautéed veal, topped by Dungeness crab legs and napped with Béarnaise sauce), we enjoyed a fine bottle of California Cabernet Sauvignon. Then it was a Cognac—or perhaps two.

We finally left just at closing time. In fact we were last out the door. The waiters and busboys were getting a bit edgy but the Gotti brothers smiled us graciously into the street. Lights were going out within the hallowed restaurant.

Now, those of us who were around in those days will remember that the façade of Ernie's Restaurant featured a series of wrought-iron flower boxes fronted by a spaced series of decorative brass "E"s. Very handsome—and very desirable for a guy whose name is Ernie.

Yes, I did. I tried to rip one of those "E"s from the flower box. A cruising black-and-white slowed and stopped. Somehow I convinced the officer that I was just leaning on the flower box, clearing my head and waiting for a cab. Roland Gotti came out and confirmed that I was only a danger to myself, and the police car left.

The next time I made a reservation at Ernie's there was a flat package waiting at my table. I opened it and found a large brass "E" just like those outside. The Gotti brothers had a lot of class.

———•◦•———

CHAPTER 17

WILLIAM SAROYAN

William Saroyan, who knew a thing or two about San Francisco saloons, immortalized "Izzy's," local barkeep Izzy Gomez's establishment in "The Time of Your Life." When Saroyan won the Pulitzer Prize in 1939 for his San Francisco speakeasy drama, he refused to accept it saying—business shouldn't judge art.

William Saroyan.
PHOTO: LIBRARY OF CONGRESS PRINTS AND PHOTOGRAPHS DIVISION; WIKIMEDIA COMMONS

DRINKING ESTABLISHMENTS
FOR THE DRINKING ESTABLISHMENT

A re the good, old-fashioned saloons that many of us have known and loved a dying social institution? A few years ago to pursue the question we asked Michael McCourt, celebrated San Francisco bartender, to enlighten us.

"Saloons are us," he stated with conviction from behind the plank. "Us," he continued with the bluff assurance only an Irish bartender can muster, "are the keepers of the flame. Saloons are drinking establishments for what's left of the drinking establishment. They are places to go to find out who has died."

He added "Nowadays, people are dying who never died before."

Obviously, the question requires further exploration.

There are those of us—a hard core of saloonists—who fervently hope that saloons are not a dying institution and, in fact, sense a resurgence of the San Francisco saloon culture.

Vox Saloonibus Populi

But, before tackling the issue head on, let's take a close look at saloons and explore the role they have played in the social fabric of cities everywhere—and in San Francisco in particular.

So, just what constitutes a proper saloon culture? We're not talking about your fancy cocktail lounge culture. That exists as well. We are talking here about your friendly, comfortable and comforting, neighborhood saloons.

Based on *vox saloonibus populi*, the following points define the saloon experience.

A good saloon provides shelter from an encroaching world.

A good saloon is a second home.

A good saloon will lend you money (cab fare maybe), take your messages, or tell callers you are not there (even if you are), and serve as your post office.

In a good saloon the bartender not only knows your name but your beverage of choice.

It is important that saloonists, both men and women, actually sit at the bar whether brooding in solitude or anxious for conversation—not at some tiny table off in a corner.

Finally, a good saloon is like a good private club. It cossets its members and provides them with camaraderie and a sense of well-being.

Saloons in San Francisco History

San Francisco has always been a good saloon town. A saloon culture existed here right from the town's boozy beginnings.

We once asked Ed Moose—barkeep, restaurateur, sports fan, student of politics, ardent conversationalist—just why that is so.

"There has always been an openness about San Francisco with lots of cross cultural exchange between social groups. There is a democracy of spirit here. The working class and social class mix freely. Where? In saloons, of course," Moose stated.

Even before the tiny frontier village was officially named San Francisco in 1847, *Yerba Buena*, the sleepy Mexican outpost on the Bay with only about 400 hardy residents, had a few elemental drinking establishments called *cantinas*. But soon after gold was discovered at Sutter's Mill in 1848, miners, merchants, adventurers, clerks, entrepreneurs, gamblers and just plain ruffians, flocked to this western boomtown and by the end of 1849 the population had swelled to 25,000. Most of the customers seemed to be thirsty and were looking for a decent meal and some companionship. That's when saloons sprang up to provide the necessary social ambience. Shortly, there was whisky, gambling, conversation, music, and even prostitution—call them your five basic "mood" groups.

Enterprising saloon keepers threw up leaky tents or rough wooden shacks and went into the bar business. As arriving vessels were abandoned at anchor or in the shore side mud by their crews who headed for the gold fields, some were dragged to higher ground and turned into saloons and boarding houses.

The Bella Union: Plain Talk and Beautiful Girls

In 1852 the restless population of San Francisco was about 50,000 and saloons took on an even greater social importance. Soon, they ranged from simple beer or whisky joints to elaborate melodeons or concert saloons that featured "freedom from constrained etiquette," as one advertised. Perhaps the most popular of these establishments was the Bella Union, a barroom and variety house that opened in 1849 at Washington and Kearny streets. It was destroyed several times by massive fires that raged in San Francisco's largely wooden structures. The Bella Union distributed a "dodger" or leaflet that promised "Plain Talk and Beautiful Girls." Then it cautioned "If you don't want to risk both optics, shut one eye."

The Barbary Coast

In the 1850s San Francisco's infamous Barbary Coast added vice and danger to the turbulent San Francisco scene. Pacific Avenue (then Pacific Street) between Sansome and Montgomery streets, was the locus for the Barbary Coast. But the saloons, gambling joints, dancehalls and brothels spread out to the surrounding area. The Barbary Coast was originally known as Sydney Town because it was largely populated by convicts who had escaped from Australian prisons and had found their way to San Francisco. Later it was renamed by sailors who likened it to the pirate's lair in North Africa known as the Barbary Coast.

Many of San Francisco's Barbary Coast saloons were "crimp joints," rough barrooms where unsuspecting sailors were drugged and then "Shanghaied"—literally kidnapped—for unbelievably hard service lasting many months, or even years, on ships, frequently bound for the Orient. In 1880 one rough character called Shanghai Kelly operated a saloon and boarding house on Pacific Street between Drumm and

Davis streets. Many sailors who had just arrived in San Francisco from East Coast ports after passage around South America's Cape Horn, awakened the following day, dulled by monumental hangovers, only to find themselves outbound on another vessel. Today a retro saloon called Shanghai Kelly's on the corner of Polk Street and Broadway continues the legend but without the rough stuff.

The First San Francisco Saloons

It was on the Barbary Coast that an enterprising Irish bartender named Michael Finn spiked customers' drinks. He earned immortality in the phrase "to slip someone a Mickey."

It wasn't until 1917 that the Barbary Coast faded away after the Red Light Abatement Act closed the dancehalls. Today, what was the Barbary Coast is a fashionable and genteel enclave known as the Jackson Square Historical District.

Beer slaked the thirst of early San Franciscans as well as whisky. As early as 1851 gold miner John Wieland opened San Francisco's first brewery. By 1856 there were 15 breweries. In 1861 an Alsatian named Ferdinand E. Wagner opened Wagner's Beer Hall. It is still operating today—logically enough as The Saloon. It is the oldest continuously operating saloon in San Francisco and is still at the original site; the corner of Grant Avenue and Fresno Street.

By 1862 there were more than 1,000 saloons in San Francisco. More than 300 were grocery saloons. Homeward bound working stiffs frequently stopped off at such establishments for a sack of flour or some other staple. There, among the foodstuffs, they found a plank suspended between two barrels where they could wet their whistles with beer, grappa or some other combustible. A well-known grocery saloon of the time was Meyer's at Brannan and Beale streets.

Unlike the simple grocery saloons, there were many elaborate barrooms where the largely male population could mingle with the opposite sex and even do a bit of dancing. In 1896 near Union Square there was a saloon in the Dance Hall of the Native Sons of California building at 420 Mason Street. The all-wooden building was destroyed in the fire and quake of 1906.

As the city built and prospered, saloons sprang up along the streetcar lines that ran out into working class neighborhoods that were beginning to crop up at the edge of the western sand dunes.

San Francisco's catastrophic earthquake and fire in 1906, wiped out many saloons, but it didn't take long for them to be resurrected.

The Speakeasies

Then, along came the 18th Amendment to the Constitution in 1920 and Prohibition was launched. It was finally repealed with the 21st Amendment in December 1933. But let's not debate the Prohibition issue. It did however generate a fascinating period in U.S. history—nowhere more so than in San Francisco. The fact is that during Prohibition the operation of saloons hardly stumbled. They simply became speakeasies (patronized by both men and women) and served illicit alcohol of all types. Poet Kenneth Rexroth wrote about San Francisco during Prohibition. "...Prohibition simply didn't exist. There were several bars along Market Street where a perfect stranger could walk in and get a full whiskey glass of respectable moonshine or grappa for 25 cents." There were popular speakeasies all over the city, especially in North Beach and the Tenderloin.

The classic San Francisco speakeasy was Izzy Gomez's which operated at 848 Pacific Avenue. Izzy Gomez, a portly, handsome man who always wore a black fedora, not only served booze but also thick steaks and other restoratives. Izzy attracted an eclectic group of regulars, including the Mexican muralist Diego Rivera when he was in town.

Just as there is a Shanghai Kelly's saloon today, there is also an Izzy's Steak and Chop House on Steiner Street.

Some Classic San Francisco Saloons

During and after Prohibition there were many saloons clustered around the newspaper offices in the city. The original *San Francisco*

Examiner was located then at Third and Market Streets. Breen's, Jerry and Johnny's, and the House of Shields were popular with the *Examiner* news staff and printers. Over at Fifth and Mission streets, *San Francisco Chronicle* staffers hung out at Hanno's in an alley behind the plant. Later when the *Examiner* moved to Fifth Street, near Mission, the M & M became the saloon of choice.

Saloons come and go just as their habitués do. Those wishing to pursue their own research and qualify as a master San Francisco saloonist may wish to check out a few of these:

Red's Place in Chinatown, a fixture at the same location on Jackson Street since 1937; Perry's, the popular Union Street saloon opened by Perry Butler, a transplanted New Yorker, in 1970 (the late *Chronicle* columnist Charles McCabe wrote that Perry's was "Mr. Butler's seminary for drinkers."); the Buena Vista, the bar where *Chronicle* columnist Stanton Delaplane introduced Irish Coffee; Vesuvio's, a Beat Generation joint still operating; Spec's at 12 Adler Place, in a tiny North Beach alley now called Saroyan Place; Gino and Carlo; LaRocca's Corner; and the aforementioned Saloon. Sports bars, which can be said to be a saloon sub-classification, are popular. And by the way, Fern Bars, now not the fashion, weren't a sub-classification of true saloons, although companionship frequently can, and does, exist between men and women in saloons.

It is good to remember and to embrace the memories of bartenders past and present: Certainly the aforementioned—now departed—Michael McCourt was the MVP of San Francisco bartenders. The highly literate Neil Riofski, of whom it was said kept a copy of the Unabridged Oxford English Dictionary at hand for emergencies; Bobby McCambridge and Bobby Frugoli; the late, sad-faced Sean Mooney of Mooney's Irish Pub (or are all Irish bartenders sad-faced?); Dennis O'Connor; Seamus Coyle; Cyril Boyce; Michael English; Cookie Picetti; Shanty Malone; Allen McVeigh. These are just a few.

So, is the saloon culture dying in San Francisco? Those who may believe this point to the fact that people don't drink as much as they once did. Certainly health concerns are paramount. Nevertheless, the saloon culture is not totally dependent on drinking. Even former drinkers still frequent saloons, sit at the bar and sip soda water. Like many good things saloons have waxed and waned over the years. At present the saloon culture is healthy in San Francisco.

The late Glenn Dorenbush, perhaps the quintessential San Francisco saloonist, spoke for many of us when he said fervently "God, I love saloons."

CHAPTER 18

CRAB LOUIE

The Old Poodle Dog, a French restaurant that dated its San Francisco founding back to 1849, is said to have created the Dungeness Crab Louie in 1908. The chef was Louis Coutard and the salad and dressing were named for him. Another old San Francisco establishment, Solari's, had a Crab Louie on the menu in 1914. Today Crab Louie is ubiquitous in San Francisco restaurants. Louie Dressing— something like Thousand Island Dressing—is usually mayonnaise, chili sauce (or ketchup), pickle relish, and a dash of Worcestershire Sauce.

BRACHYURA DECAPODA: CRAB BY ANY OTHER NAME WOULD TASTE AS SWEET

The other day I got to musing about crab. The Dungeness crab season had just opened. San Franciscans know about these things. I submit to you that November 15 was one of the most important dates on this year's calendar. I was ready for it. I put in my order at Swan Oyster Depot for a few big ones—cracked and ready to go. I had been in training for crab season all summer—doing some field work with crab from up around Oregon someplace. Good but not great. Then the boom fell. Toxic algae had poisoned the water from Santa Barbara north to somewhere in Washington. And Dungeness crab was off limits. But, as of this writing, Dungeness crab is back on the okay list. We devotees are in luck.

There are literally thousands of species and subspecies of crab. And we have dined on them with gusto as far back as prehistoric times.

Crabs are forbidding creatures, exoskeletal—all spines and claws and hard carapaces. One wonders how that first gourmet decided they were edible. Perhaps he or she had already encountered an oyster, squeezed a bit of lemon juice on it and slurped it down. After that, crab was a cinch.

As you may have surmised, crab is my thing. I never met a crab I didn't like—well, maybe a few. Here are some personal observations.

Alaska King Crab

This is that giant crab from Alaska. In this case bigger is not better. But I suppose King Crab—*Paralithodes camtschaticus*—is better than no crab at all. Meat comes from the legs and claws, and doesn't have much flavor—at least for me. King Crab is frequently steamed and dipped in melted butter, perhaps the only sensible way to devour this giant. King Crab flounders—to use a fishy metaphor.

Chesapeake Bay Blue Crab

Its Latin name—*Callinectes sapidus*—means beautiful swimmer. And by the way there's a classic book on Blue Crab called *Beautiful Swimmers*, by William W. Warner. Devotees usually have east coast, Chesapeake Bay Blue Crab one of two ways—either steamed in beer spiced with Old Bay seasoning—or, shell-and-all, when the crabs are molting and sloughing off their old hard skeletons and beginning to grow new ones. The flavor of the steamed crab is somewhat nutty and "crabby," if you will. The flavor of the molting, shell-and-all, crab, is nil as far as I'm concerned. I don't understand the big deal about soft shell crab. Enlighten me.

Peekytoe Crab

What a ridiculous name for a noble crustacean. Peekytoe—what's that all about? Actually they are small Atlantic Rock Crab (*Cancer irroratus*) that were a throwaway by-product of Maine lobster fishermen until about 1997—that's when Rod Mitchell, proprietor of a seafood wholesaler in Portland, Maine decided to call them by their slang name. Peekytoe or "picked toe" came from their sharp pointed claw. What do they taste like?—lightly sweet and briny.

Stone Crab

Stone Crab from Florida, specifically from the iconic Miami Beach restaurant Joe's Stone Crab founded in 1913, is marvelous with a mustard-mayonnaise sauce. Its Latin name is *Menippe mercenaria*. If there was no such thing as Dungeness Crab, Stone Crab would be my favorite. Only the claws are eaten. They're large—about the size of the palm of your hand—and have a nutty and salty taste. Crab fishermen twist off one claw for the market and throw the crab back in the water where they promptly grow another one. Thank you Mother Nature.

Shanghai Hairy Crab

So-called Hairy Crabs are a delicacy in Asia. They are also known as the Chinese Mitten Crab, in Latin, *Eriocheir sinensis*. Hairy Crabs are not really hairy; fuzzy would be a better adjective. But you don't eat the fuzz. Usually steamed, most Shanghai restaurants require you to tear the beast apart with your own claws. When I visited Shanghai a few years ago I found that they were messy to eat and much ado about very little. I tried them in several restaurants and each time discerned a whiff of frequently worn athletic socks—not unpleasant I should add. Lest you lose faith with your crab-centric author, let's just say the flavor of the Hairy Crab was musky like a proper athletic sock should be.

Australian Mud Crab

The Australian Mud Crab (*Scylla serrata*) rates a mention here. When I tried them in Sydney, steamed and served with mayonnaise, I thought they had a faint aroma of ammonia, and that put me off. Maybe that's why they are also frequently served in Australia in a "chilli" sauce. I tried that too but they're not as good as the Chilli Crab served in the food stalls of Singapore where they use those Mud Crabs that have probably crawled all the way from Australia.

European Edible Crab

This versatile crab (*Cancer pagurus*), also called Brown Crab because of its color, is found mostly in European markets and restaurants. As are some of its brethren, it is sweet and briny. European Edible Crab is prominent in crab bisque, bouillabaisse and in Crabe Mexicaine.

One of Ernest Hemingway's favorite Paris restaurants was the legendary seafood house Prunier that dates back to 1872. One of his favorite dinners there—he writes about it in *A Moveable Feast*—was Oysters (either *portugaises* or *marennes*), Crabe Mexicaine and a bottle or two of cold Sancerre. Crabe Mexicaine is a complicated affair. Crab meat—European Edible Crab—surrounded by mushrooms and chopped red bell pepper, topped with fish *fumet* (fish stock), fish *veloute* (lots of butter and flour to make a *roux*, then thinned with *fumet*), and white wine sauce, with tomato sauce decorating the edge of the plate. It's then popped under the broiler for a few minutes. If you're not hungry now, you never will be.

Dungeness Crab

Ah, but Dungeness Crab—*Metacarcinus magister*—Incredible! The aristocrat! Simply the best crab in the world, it's named after the port of Dungeness in the state of Washington. But what is it about this sideways-crawling beauty that makes it so special? Well, for one, it does not smell like athletic socks, new or used, or ammonia. Dungeness Crab tastes slightly sea-salty and the word funky comes to mind. Funky in a nice way. And it's not necessary to mask its glory with a lot of sauce. It's best cracked and cold with you picking the meat from the claws, legs and bodies and dipping it in a bit of homemade mayonnaise.

If you insist on complicating your Dungeness Crab life try it (when you can) as Crab Cioppino, Crab Ciacucco (cioppino with a hot peppery attitude), Crab Louie, the Palace Court Salad with crab legs, or as Shanghai-style Crab Soup Dumplings, at the Bund Shanghai Restaurant in Chinatown.

Well, that's it—I'm all crabbed out.

CHAPTER 19

WHAT MAKES CURRY, CURRY?

Curry is a sauce served over meat, fish or vegetables, and usually with steamed rice. Curry powder is ground from a wide variety of dried leaves, roots, twigs, berries, seeds and such. Some of these are listed below in alphabetical order.

Asafetida—*A smelly resin found in Kashmir. An acquired taste.*
Cardamom—*In pods or seeds, and is highly aromatic.*
Cayenne—*Made from dried red chilies and is frequently called red chili powder.*
Chilies—*Fresh green chilies and very hot.*
Cinnamon—*Comes in sticks of bark, or in powder form.*
Cloves—*Used either as whole cloves or in powder form.*
Coconut—*Fresh or grated.*
Coriander—*An herb whose leaves are used for intense flavor.*
Cumin—*A spicy seed, sometimes ground to a powder.*
Curry Leaves—*Yes, there is a curry tree. It grows in India and Sri Lanka. No, it does not taste or smell like curry, more like sage, some say like mugwort.*
Fennel—*These seeds have a licorice-like flavor.*
Garam Masala—*Usually a mixture of spices, cardamom, cinnamon, cumin, peppercorns and nutmeg.*
Ginger—*The spicy root is used fresh, slivered or mashed, and in powder form.*
Nigella—*A spicy seed with an earthy aroma, good with vegetable and fish dishes.*
Mustard—*This pungent seed is also used as an oil in Bengal and Kashmir.*
Nutmeg—*Adds a mild, spicy flavor to many curries.*
Saffron—*These threads are the stigma of crocuses that grow in India. They add a distinctive yellow color to Indian food.*
Sesame—*Seeds that add a nutty component to many Indian foods.*
Turmeric—*A spice that, along with saffron, adds a yellow color to curries and other food.*
Vark—*This is real silver tissue paper, used as an attractive garnish for elaborate Indian dishes.*

AN ANCIENT INDIAN
CULINARY MYSTIQUE

I have an enduring appetite for curry. Here's how that came about. Many years ago I sailed on the P&O passenger ship Himalaya as press officer. My job was to seek out interesting passengers for the press to write about when we hit port. And as a free-lance writer I was also looking for a good story myself. I found it aboard the Himalaya. My story was the ship's glorious curry. In those days the galleys of ships of the Peninsular and Oriental Steam Navigation Company were staffed by Indians, usually from the state of Goa, the one-time Portuguese province on the Indian subcontinent's southwest coast. In the kitchens of the grand old Himalaya there was one Goanese worker that attract-ed me. He was the curry cook and his assignment was to prepare the various Indian curries for the crew. Passengers found curry on their menus once a week or so, but the ship's British staff and Punjabi and Goanese crew found curry on their plates in the mess hall everyday. I was considered crew and so got my fill of all things curry.

The Unmistakable Sniff of Curry

One day at sea I wandered into the galley and sought out the curry cook. "What is curry powder?" I asked him. He decided to show me.

On a long worktable he laid out small piles of dried leaves, roots, twigs, berries, seeds, and such. Cardamom, caraway, anise, ginger, gar-lic, chilies, fenugreek, cloves, cinnamon, turmeric, coriander, fennel, mace, poppy seeds, cumin, mustard seeds, black peppercorns, bay leaf, saffron, sometimes asafetida—maybe more. I can't remember. Then, seemingly at random, he took a pinch of this and a pinch of that and dropped them in a large stone mortar. And with a mammoth pestle he pulverized the lot of it. It was the magic of the curry cult—a group of which I am now a member in good standing. When my new-found Goanese friend was finished, he allowed me to peek into the mortar. A

113

vaguely yellow-orange powder greeted me and I sniffed the magnificent, unmistakable sniff of curry.

A Pseudo Kind of Curry That Tastes Curryish

To many of us—probably most of us—curry powder is the stuff that comes from the supermarket in a small jar about the size of a toilet paper spool, or in a small rectangular tin can. And that's fine. When prepared with that powder, a pseudo kind of curry tastes curryish.

To some few of us curry is something else again—home ground curry powder, pulverized in a mortar. Magic powder! Your clothes will smell of it. You entire house will be redolent with that remarkable smell.

A Curry to Make You Scream for Mercy

The curry concept dates back more than 4,000 years on the Indian subcontinent. Archeologists figured it out from studying shards of pottery and from forensic dental tests. The word curry probably comes from a Tamil Indian word *Kaari,* which originally referred to a meat or vegetable dish eaten with rice. It was a kind of spicy stew. Cookery in India has long been considered a gift of the gods—and it is. Historians believe the spicy food concept began logically in a hot climate and with a people that used its indigenous spices for flavor. The spicy curries were a good foil for the hot weather, and in a country where refrigeration was non-existent, the spices worked as a food preservative.

Curry can be mild or it can be as hot as a blast furnace. In India curry was not prepared as a fiery gravy over rice until after Columbus mistakenly took the New World for the Spice Islands and sent chilies back to Europe. From there the hot capsicum pods made their way to India and Southeast Asia.

I recall once on a visit to Malaysia's capital Kuala Lumpur, I cockily uttered the word "hot" when my turbaned waiter asked how I wanted my curry. Fortunately he had placed me in a special air-conditioned dining room away from the local customers. After the first bite of my lamb curry over rice, I screamed for mercy—and water.

Brits Love Curry and it Loves Them

Perhaps the greatest devourers of curry outside of India and Southeast Asia are the British. Today, there are thousands of curry houses in Great Britain, and the UK even celebrates a national curry week. (It's in October in case you want to pop over to London to attend.) The British love of curry dates back to the British Raj, in the 19th and 20th centuries when colonial India was dominated by British civil servants and the military. The Brits ate what their colonial Indian household servants provided them—and that was curry, in all its forms, and with all of its accompanying condiments, usually referred to *sambals.* In the galley office aboard the Himalaya there was a notice posted that listed more than 20 varieties of *sambals* including chopped onions and tomatoes, raisins, dried banana, ground coconut, cucumber, mangoes, limes, hard-boiled eggs, and a variety of chutneys.

San Franciscans Love Curry and it Loves Them

And, of course, curry is big in food-savvy San Francisco. There are some fine Indian restaurants here and some of them are noted for their curry dishes. A few that come to mind are Dosa, on Fillmore (another is on Valencia), which features classic South Indian dishes; Udupi Palace on Valencia is another serving South Indian fare; Amber India, downtown, is upscale and has a wide variety of Indian dishes of various styles; and Lahore Karahi in the Tenderloin has wonderful curry offerings.

And that's the story of the curry cult. When writing this story I suggested to my editor that the printer sift some good curry powder between the pages of this paper for realism. But that idea never gained traction.

CHAPTER 20

CLARK TERRY AT DOC RICKETTS'S LAB

When Clark Terry, the incomparable jazz fluegelhorn player, came to town he would occasionally drop into Jimmy Lyons's small San Francisco apartment on Telegraph Hill and Jimmy would invite me over for drinks and conversation. Gradually I got to know Clark well through my association with the Monterey Jazz Festival where I was publicist. He was always gracious with his time and a lot of fun to be around. In those days Jimmy Lyons, in his role as general manager of the festival, booked Clark frequently and he was always a hit with the audience. Also in those days, Jimmy used the guitar player Mundell Lowe as his musical director. Although Jimmy ran the festival with an iron hand, it was easier for him to defer to Mundell on some matters of programming. Also, for a few years back then, Jimmy booked a vocalist named Betty Bennett who at one time had been married to Andre Previn. Betty and Mundell were together a lot at the festival and they fell in love. Since they met at the Monterey Jazz Festival they decided to get married there and that's how Doc Ricketts's Lab comes into the story. You will recall that Doc Ricketts, a close friend of John Steinbeck, operated a marine biological laboratory on Cannery Row. After Ricketts was killed in an auto-train crash right up the road from his lab, various members of the board of directors of the Monterey Jazz Festival, all local citizens, took over the lab and maintained it as a private club where they held boozy, steak dinners—sometimes with a jazz trio or quartet in residence. One member of the board was a local judge and the idea was for him to marry Betty and Mundell in the rear of the lab on an outdoor deck one fine fall day during that year's festival. My recollection is that there were only about a dozen guests invited. I was one. We gathered in the afternoon sun at the edge of Monterey Bay and the judge performed the ceremony. At the conclusion, Mundell kissed the bride and suddenly we heard a fluegelhorn playing softly "When I Fall in Love." It was Clark Terry.

Clark Terry at the Monterey Jazz Festival
PHOTO: RIGHT DOWN FRONT, RON HUDSON JAZZ IMAGES

THE NIFTY CAT STRIKES WEST

In 1966, in an almost accidental fashion, I produced a record album in San Francisco with the great Roy Eldridge, my favorite jazz trumpet artist. The album was called "The Nifty Cat Strikes West." Ah 1966. Those were the days. I was so immersed in jazz that it no longer satisfied me to just sit in smoky nightclubs like the Jazz Workshop in North Beach, open my ears and snap my fingers on the second and fourth beats. I was itchy to be involved, itchy to be part of the jazz scene. "The Nifty Cat Strikes West"—I still have a few copies of the 33 rpm LP—is an example of scratching the itch. Here's how it happened.

Big Bands and the Movie Palaces

When I was a youngster, junior high school age, jazz was already a dominant force in my life. Tall for my age, I was sneaking into local ballrooms to hear my idols—Jimmy Lunceford, Duke Ellington, Harry James, Count Basie, Charlie Barnet, Artie Shaw. At the same time I discovered two-a-day vaudeville in local movie palaces. It was the tail end of the big band era and they played on stage between films. There were three movie theaters in the San Francisco Bay Area that featured vaudeville along with first run movies—the Golden Gate in San Francisco and the Orpheum and the T & D across the bay in Oakland. My favorite was the Golden Gate, an imposing, 1930s, multi-story structure at the corner of Golden Gate Avenue and Taylor Street. It's still there but now it features road shows of New York musicals.

Krupa at the Golden Gate

One day in January 1943 I learned that Gene Krupa and his band were to appear there. Krupa had an enormous reputation as a jazz drummer and I heard that his band featured a hot trumpet player named Roy Eldridge. I cut school to attend and got there early. When

Left to right: Roy Eldridge on trumpet, Grover Mitchell on trombone, Eric Dixon on saxophone
PHOTO: ERNEST BEYL

the doors opened for the first show of the day I rushed in and found a seat down in front near the stage. Then I suffered through the movie—whatever it was—and waited for Krupa.

When the movie was over I sat expectantly in the dark for a few minutes. Suddenly a spotlight showed a large illuminated circle on the closed red velvet curtain. Then, softly at first, I heard the boom of the bass drum, then tom toms, then loud cymbals, snare drum rolls and the snap of rim shots—all of this before the curtain parted. Finally it swung back to reveal the band. Harsh, bright reflections glanced off the brass instruments.

Gritty Eldridge Hooked Me

Handsome and boyish, Krupa smiled and dominated the scene. But I was mesmerized by the short, compact trumpet player, Roy Eldridge. No musical experience since that time has grabbed me like Roy Eldridge's sharp and biting trumpet attack. But even more compelling to me was the tone that came from that brass bell. It was not clarion

Roy Eldridge in 1946.
PHOTO: LIBRARY OF CONGRESS; WIKIMEDIA COMMONS

clear as I was prepared to believe trumpets should sound. The Eldridge trumpet sound grated. It slid out with a gritty insinuation. It sounded like rasping threads of spittle were vibrating in the trumpeter's horn. It sounded dirty—as in gritty. I was hooked.

Let Me off Uptown

When the show was over I walked around to the stage door where the musicians actually came out into the daylight—into real air. My archangel Gabriel walked out onto the sidewalk, signed an autograph for me and made a few offhand, reasonably pleasant comments. He wasn't exactly warm and cuddly, jazz musicians just aren't. Then he walked up the street and into Original Joe's. Even a gritty archangel like Roy Eldridge must eat.

Krupa Busted in San Francisco

On the way home I stopped at a music shop and bought a Gene Krupa record. It featured Roy Eldridge on trumpet with Anita O'Day on vocals. The hit number on the record was "Let Me off Uptown" and Eldridge and O'Day both sang on it, kicking the lyrics back and forth between them. When I got home I placed the record on my family's monster Zenith and cranked up the sound. Roy Eldridge, nicknamed "Little Jazz," from Pittsburgh, Pennsylvania, was my man.

The next day San Francisco newspapers reported that Krupa had been arrested. The charges were contributing to the delinquency of a minor and possession. The story said Krupa had asked his underage valet and "gofer" to retrieve an envelope of some mysterious substance from his St. Francis Hotel room. That didn't go over well at home.

Roy Eldridge and Count Basie

Fast forward to 1966. By now I have become publicist for the Monterey Jazz Festival. I still have that jazz itch and I am itching to scratch it, to become even more involved. One day Dr. Herb Wong, then a disk jockey for KJAZZ in Alameda, called me: "Is Roy Eldridge still your main man?" Indeed he was.

At that time Eldridge was playing with Count Basie and his Orchestra and touring the West Coast. After a week at Basin Street West in North Beach, Basie himself had taken off for the East and a few of his key sidemen were hanging around San Francisco.

Herb and I rounded them up for a studio date and one day we all met at Leo De Gar Kulka's Golden State Recorders, South of Market Street. It was the Basie Orchestra in miniature—a sextet—Grover Mitchell on trombone, Eric Dixon on tenor saxophone, Norman Kennon on bass, Louis Bellson on drums, and Roy Eldridge on trumpet. We commandeered local pianist Bill Bell for the Basie role. The session began about 11 a.m. and stretched late into the afternoon.

Not knowing anything about producing a record album, I thought that was a long time. I discovered later that cutting a record sometimes takes days, weeks maybe, even months (and in the case of some artists, years). But these jazz pros knew what they were doing. Motion was not wasted, nor was there a lot time for small talk. They knew what they were there to accomplish, and they accomplished it in swinging order.

Warming up with Ellington

They warmed up with a couple of Duke Ellington tunes. Three eventually made it on to the album—"I'm Beginning to see the Light," "Things Ain't what They Used to be," and "Satin Doll."

Jazz critics frequently cited Roy Eldridge's "competitive nature." Jazz artists can be competitive like professional athletes. They rejoice in what they term "cutting sessions"—trying to blow the other guys off the stage. It seems to go with the territory.

That afternoon Eldridge, while full of camaraderie with his fellow Basie buddies, showed his competitive nature. After playing a slow, achingly beautiful and somewhat sardonic solo on "Willow Weep for Me," he loosened up still more with a few belts from a bottle of bourbon that sat on the floor next to his chair. Then the incomparable timekeeper Bellson kicked it off with some chink a-chink a-chinks on his ride cymbal.

Blue 'n' Boogie Sizzles

Eldridge let all of us know what was in his mind and played sizzling lines on "Blue 'n' Boogie" by John Burks "Dizzy" Gillespie. Dizzy, an astounding trumpet artist, readily acknowledged he was influenced by Eldridge. Jazz writer Leonard Feather, a friend whom I admired, put it this way: "He (Roy Eldridge) was as vital a figure in the development of trumpet jazz during the 1930s as Louis Armstrong had been in the 1920s, as Gillespie was to be in the 1940s, or Miles Davis in the 1950s." Feather wrote that in 1960. Wynton Marsalis, later to become an important continuation of the jazz trumpet pantheon, was born in 1961.

The Impresario Strikes West

The New York record company, Master Jazz Recordings, bought the master tape of my album "The Nifty Cat Strikes West" and issued it. There are copies still around for collectors. I see them listed on the internet. After Herb Wong and I paid off the Roy Eldridge Sextet, the recording studio and other expenses (bourbon), I netted about $200. I was an impresario. I had produced an album with Roy Eldridge, one of the greatest jazz trumpet artists of all time.

Roy Eldridge died in 1989. He was 78. I still play "The Nifty Cat Strikes West" once in a while to rev up my engine. As I said, I had an itch and I scratched it.

CHAPTER 21

FLO ALLEN

Flo Allen was a model in San Francisco's North Beach. She was also the hostess at a Beat Generation hangout called The Old Spaghetti Factory. While Flo modeled with her clothes on, she was also famous for modeling in the nude. She is said to have done so for Man Ray, the American surrealist photographer who spent most of his career as an expatriate in France.

Lawrence Ferlingetti and Florence Allen in an issue of Life magazine, 1957.
PHOTO: AUTHOR'S COLLECTION

IN PURSUIT OF NORTH BEACH

I'm on a rant as I write this. So I hope you won't mind if I rattle on a bit. Here are some of my Appetites and Afterthoughts about North Beach in the old days. A kind of torch song for this classic neighborhood, now fast disappearing before our tired eyes.

"It was the best of times. It was the worst of times." —to harken back to Dickens's *Tale of Two Cities.* Let's call this the *Tale of Two Neighborhoods*—one past and one present. Things have changed. And while some things change for the better. Others change for the worst. And frankly, I miss those old days.

First, let's make this perfectly clear, Yes, we still have a few enduring symbols of North Beach—like ancient bugs caught in amber, to be examined in the light of day. Consider these:

The Saloon, Liguria Bakery, City Lights Booksellers and Publishers, Molinari Delicatessen, Biordi Art Imports, Little City Market, North Beach Restaurant and Mario's Bohemian Cigar Store and Café.

Gone but not Forgotten

But, now consider this: What we've lost over the years is mind blowing.

Capp's Corner comes to mind—Yes, there was a gasping attempt to reopen it, but that didn't work. But it should never have closed in the first place. The neighborhood is diminished without Capp's Corner.

The Jazz Workshop—Changing times on Broadway and the advent of rock 'n' roll did in this wonderful old jazz club.

Enrico's Sidewalk Cafe—Enrico Banducci, once considered the "Mayor of North Beach," went bust.

The hungry i—See Enrico Banducci above. When you go bust, you go bust.

Enrico Banducci with the author.
PHOTO: PETER BRENIG

Vanessi's—Does anyone out there remember Vanessi's on Broadway? Sitting at the counter watching the showmen cooks prepare my meal in those hot pans was a near religious experience.

Carol Doda, A Class Act

And would you believe that Broadway was once a street that featured fine restaurants like Vanessi's, Swiss Louie's and New Joe's, and jazz clubs like the Jazz Workshop, El Matador, Sugar Hill, and Basin Street West—instead of dark, sleaze-ball skin joints where the clientele wear their caps in their laps rather than on their heads? I'm excluding the Condor here with Carol Doda coming down from the ceiling on a white, baby grand—that was a classy act.

Washington Square Bar & Grill—Several iterations of wannabes have tried to revive it but have never made it work.

La Felce—This was my favorite North Beach restaurant. The food was simple, but incredibly good. Can any of you remember the olive oil-dressed pinto beans served with minced onion and parsley? La Felce closed several years ago, but I still remember those beans.

Today, the ubiquitous symbol of North Beach is the pizza parlor. I wonder just how many pizza parlors constitute too many pizza parlors.

The Old Apothecary Shops

In the old days we had three drugstores bordering Washington Square. We called them apothecaries.

At one time we had three Italian delicatessens in North Beach and enough business for all three. Now there is only Molinari that dates its founding back to 1896. In my time there was also Panelli Bros. that closed after 82 years, and the Florence Ravioli Factory, 58 years on Stockton Street before a big rent increase drove the brothers out.

There were four meat markets—now there is only the Little City Market, operated by Ron Spinali and his son Michael. Still going strong after more than 60 years. Now that's endurance.

Grocery Stores—The history of grocery stores in North Beach is checkered, as it is in other San Francisco neighborhoods. Many were, and still are, delivery systems for half-pint flasks of booze. Not real grocery stores.

For Blue Collar Workers

There was an Army-Navy store on Stockton where you could buy fishing tackle, first aid kits, canteens and jackknives. What a great idea.

Also on Stockton, in the space presently occupied by the restaurant Park Tavern, there was a store that sold elaborate overstuffed furniture that looked like it was designed for (or by) Benito Mussolini.

And, of course, hip readers will remember the Pagoda Palace—now a hole in the ground.

Let's talk hardware stores. My favorite was Figoni Hardware on Upper Grant Avenue. Of course, I can't complain too much about its loss, since artist Kevin Brown moved in and named his gallery Live Worms from a sign he found when he cleaned out the place. Figoni Hardware sold live worms for fishing bait.

And there was a working man's clothing store a few blocks away on Upper Grant that sold Oshkosh and Can't Bust 'Em shirts and overalls for the longshoremen and other blue collar workers who shopped there.

The Old Salami Factory

There were also several bakeries in North Beach, and I liked having a choice. There was Danilo's, and one across the street but I can't remember its name. Still operating are Victoria Pastry Company, and Stella's Pasticceria e Cafe, where the legendary sacripantina cake is still baked.

Then there is the incomparable Liguria Bakery (still the home of the quintessential focaccia bread), and finally the Italian French Baking Company which closed a while back.

There was a salami factory on Green Street (Columbus Salami, as I recall). You could smell the drying salami all over the neighborhood.

But Upper Grant Avenue still has a few shops that make sense to us old-timers. ARIA, Schein & Schein, and Live Worms, come to mind.

So what happened here? The old Italians died off. Some of their offspring sold out and moved to the suburbs Then rising rents, changing tastes and sometimes shoddy products simply got the better of us.

The Old Spaghetti Factory

These days, when I get in a funk—as I am while writing this—I like to remember a place that, to me, symbolized everything magical about North Beach. It was the Old Spaghetti Factory that closed in 1985. Do you remember it? The Old Spaghetti Factory, a wonderful metaphor for the old North Beach, was on Green Street, just up the hill a bit from Grant Avenue. That was the place where a magnificent, brown-skinned, Rubenesque woman named Flo Allen held court when she wasn't doing nude modeling. If you were truly cool (cool was the operative state for which we all strived in those days), Flo would greet you as a spaghetti-fancier with a kiss on both cheeks, pour you a glass of red wine, and make you wait for a while in one of the many old spring-sprung sofas that dotted the large room. The Beats hung out there as they did on Upper Grant Avenue. And by the way, I miss the Beats. Today North Beach has only ersatz, lower case beats and wannabe hippies.

There was a feeling of belonging at the Old Spaghetti Factory—a feeling of North Beach comradeship. I don't get that feeling much anymore.

As I said earlier in this rant, things are changing. And change can be bad. But, then again it can be good. "If we want things to stay as they are, things will have to change." That's a quote from a wonderful novel, *The Leopard*, by Giuseppe di Lampedusa, about a Sicilian society threatened by the possibility of change.

CHAPTER 22

SACRIPANTINA

Stella's Pastry & Cafe in North Beach—originally called Stella's Pasticceria e Café ("confectionary" in Italian)—serves an ethereal layer cake that is the Sophia Loren of all Italian desserts. It's called sacripantina, which translates roughly into "holy bread." Sacripantina is a round sponge cake of several layers with zabaglione, Marsala and rum, and a dash of maraschino cherry juice for finesse. The Santucci family that founded the bakery many years ago guarded the recipe which has since been trademarked by the State of California. The story goes that the recipe was brought to San Francisco from a bakery in Genoa. It was the only one in Genoa (or perhaps in all of Italy) that made this incredible cake. It seems that the wife of a Genovese nobleman wanted to present her husband with a new dessert to gain his increased ardor (an engaging idea that makes sense), so she created a special cake for him. The nobleman took one bite and cried out "Sacripantina!"

I DREAM OF CAKE

I happen to like cake, the fancier the better. That's why I miss Shinmin Li's cake shop on Upper Grant Avenue.

When Shinmin Li was a young girl in China her mother did not allow her to eat sweets so she sometimes dreamed of cake. Not just simple cakes but huge, elaborately decorated cakes with layer after layer mounting before her and swirls of icing forming flowers, birds and exotic creatures. When she was eight her family immigrated to the United States from Guangdong Province. Later she graduated from the School of Visual Arts in New York and then studied at Le Cordon Bleu in Sydney, Australia and became a *Patisserie Supérieur.*

Shinmin settled in San Francisco and began working as a baker in the upscale Aqua restaurant. Several years ago her dreams of cake came full circle and she opened I Dream of Cake, using a commercial kitchen. Then she moved to North Beach and opened a chic shop at 1351 Grant Avenue.

Now closed, it was open by appointment only. Shinmin's creations were displayed here like rare jewels gleaming under pinpoint display lights and had price tags from $350 to $2000 or more depending on the cake and other factors like packing and shipping.

Highly creative, Shinmin was alert to contemporary cultural signals in fashion and industrial design and applied this to her work. Hence her range of sculptural cakes included a 2005 Porsche GT, a stiletto heel ladies shoe, a Gucci handbag, a three-story Victorian house, and, of course, spectacular, multi-layered wedding cakes. Among customers were novelist Danielle Steele (tan alligator handbag cake for her birthday); Stephen Jenkins, lead singer for Third Eye Blind (an electric guitar cake); Chuck Williams of Williams Sonoma (pots and pans cake); and Olympic Gold Medal skier Johnny Mosley (a Gold medal cake).

Shinmin Li.
PHOTO: ERNEST BEYL

The unique cakes Shinmin created were for weddings, birthdays, anniversaries, holiday parties, Bar Mitzvahs and other special events.

Once, for a Manhattan wedding, she flew to New York with her cake as carry-on luggage. Fortunately it was a light flight and the cake rode in the seat beside her with its own seat belt.

I had an appetite for Shinmin Li's cakes. Too bad, but now it's an appetite I can't satisfy.

CHAPTER 23

ANNIE LEIBOVITZ

"My favorite animal is steak," said Annie Leibovitz, the famed photographer whose first job was with the publication Rolling Stone.

HOMAGE TO THE HAMBURGER

I was a late-comer to the hamburger. Now I am its greatest champion. As a kid I was devoted to the hot dog. In those days the most sublime form of the *genus* hot dog was to be found at Casper's in Oakland. The foot-long hot dogs in a steamed bun were laced with wedges of raw onion, tomato, bright yellow mustard, and sweet pickle relish. We called them garbage rolls. I still yearn for them.

As I became more sophisticated in matters gastronomic I moved on to the hamburger. What is it really about the hamburger? What a remarkable and utterly satisfying thing it is. The beef patty, dark and juicy. The onion, raw or grilled. The mustard. The slice of tomato. The leaf of lettuce. Dill pickle or sweet pickle relish. All housed between two opposing sections of white, toasted sesame-seeded bun. And a slice of cheese, and you're close to the five basic food groups. Well, I've eaten my fair share of hamburgers. And I suppose if it came right down to a decision on what to eat on any given day, hamburgers (plural) and perhaps spaghetti would rate at the top with me.

There are those who believe the quintessential North Beach hamburger was served at the long-gone Vanessi's on Broadway. Indeed it was a fine burger. Huge and beefy, on a slab of hollowed-out sourdough roll that tore the roof of your mouth asunder as juice dripped down into your sleeves.

One Day I Had Three Clown Alley Burgers
Today, the successor to the Vanessi burgers is to be found in the North Beach establishment, Original Joe's.

But let's move into this homage to the hamburger with Clown Alley, 42 Columbus Avenue, since it provided an important chapter in the hamburger annals of San Francisco. It opened in 1962 and closed

35 years later in 1996 after serving perhaps a million 1/3-pound, flame-broiled burgers on toasted sesame-seeded buns.

Clown Alley was the dream of San Francisco legend Enrico Banducci, proprietor of the hungry i, the San Francisco club where new comics and other nightclub acts honed their skills. Woody Allen, Jonathan Winters, Mort Sahl, Bill Cosby, Lenny Bruce, Dick Gregory, Barbra Streisand, and Diana Ross all played the hungry i early in their careers. Most credited Enrico for their start. Entrepreneur Alfred Pailhe was a partner of "Bandooch" in those days and through a now-hazy business arrangement, wound up with the hamburger joint. Clown Alley attracted an eclectic crowd: North Beach neighbors, cops, taxi drivers, night people, and "acts" from the hungry i. Barbra Streisand dropped by. From around the corner on Montgomery Street, lawyer Melvin Belli came by frequently with his two racing greyhounds and fed them burger scraps.

In the old days, I felt so good about Clown Alley burgers that sometimes I had two. There was one occasion when I actually had three. But, of course, on that day I didn't have fries or a vanilla milkshake.

Rejoicing in North Beach

Alfred Pailhe died in 1988, and his son Bill Pailhe kept the place going until 1997. Then, much to my sorrow, he closed it. Then, just as suddenly as it closed, Clown Alley came back to life in 1998. Bill Paihle gave the old place a new coat of paint, put up a few clown posters and re-created Clown Alley right down to the flame-broiler and the free-standing buffet of condiments. There was rejoicing in North Beach and throughout the city. So Clown Alley was again for a while hamburger heaven as decreed long ago by the Supreme Gourmet Upstairs.

But it wasn't to last. Clown Alley, that gourmet palace, closed for good in 2002.

CHAPTER 24

FOCCACIA

Foccacia, that unleavened flatbread so popular in San Francisco's North Beach, dates back to the Etruscans prior to the Roman Empire. It was the Romans who named it— panis focacius—panis simply means bread, focacius is the Latin word for fireplace. It was used widely to feed slaves during the Roman Empire. Today it's seasoned with olive oil and salt and sometimes has various toppings, including tomato sauce, onions, even raisins for a sweet version.

THE LIGURIA BAKERY

It can be said with some surety that the tasty flatbread North Beach Italians call focaccia is one of the reasons I live in San Francisco. Others are campari, cappuccino, sacripantina and salami. Each is a metaphor for the astonishingly satisfying North Beach life. Focaccia is foremost. It long ago captured my attention. And, when I think of focaccia, as I often do, I think of the Liguria Bakery. One day I stepped into the hole-in-the-wall bakery operated by the Soracco family for almost 100 years, for a slice and a chat. I had been invited by the Soraccos—father George, mother Josephine, daughter Mary and sons Michael and Daniel—to spend a bit of time discussing my passion for focaccia. I came away with several slices for my lunch under a tree in Washington Square, but also with a tale of an immigrant family of bakers from Genoa, the port city of the province of Liguria in northwest Italy. It was grandfather Ambrogio and his brother Joseph who led the Soraccos to San Francisco back in 1910. Within a year the two had opened the Liguria Bakery on Grant Avenue. In 1915 they moved it, along with the original brick-lined oven, to its present location, 1700 Stockton at the corner of Filbert. In those days the Soraccos made not only focaccia—it sold then for about 25 cents a sheet—but also sourdough loaves, biscotti, panatone and grissini. At various times the Soraccos also sold eggs, butter, milk and blocks of ice. They provided a delivery service to nearby houses and restaurants by horse-drawn carriage. Gradually, focaccia dominated the business and the Liguria became a one product operation. The old, brick-lined, then wood-burning, oven was converted to gas but that's about the only substantial change on the premises. A simple counter, an ancient cash register (no longer used), a roll-top desk, empty shelves from the days when other products were sold, a roll of white paper and spool of cotton string to wrap and tie the 8- by 10-inch sheets of focaccia. In a tilt toward the modern are a few framed and autographed photos of customers—Lily Tomlin, Adam

West, Francis Ford Coppola, and another focaccia devotee Darth Vadar. Also, in a wonderful flashback to an earlier and simpler time, in chipped gold lettering on the large window, facing the sidewalk is a sign reading:

LIGURIA BAKERY
Soracco & Co.
Tel: GARFIELD 1 3786

When I visited, father George and sons Michael and Daniel commenced baking at about 5 a.m. Although they were secretive (and who wouldn't be) about the exact ingredients and methods they employ, it will reveal nothing to report that flour, yeast, water, canola and olive oil and "some spices," they say, go into the making of this exquisite flatbread. "But no preservatives," they added. The dough is kneaded and left to rise slightly. Then it is rolled and placed into flat pans and laced with olive oil and coarse salt. The pans are slid into the oven on flat paddles with long handles attached. The oven is heated the night before to about 800 to 900 degrees Fahrenheit and the sheets of focaccia are baked for ten to fifteen minutes.

Mother Josephine and daughter Mary are still front-of-the-house and greet customers, wrap focaccia and take care of the cash. No checks.

There are five varieties of focaccia sold in sheets of the customer's choice. An ancient 7-Up promotional sign offers the following: Pizza (with tomato sauce topping), Raisin (sprinkled with raisins), Onion (chopped green onions), Plain (just the coarse salt), and Garlic.

For those with a passion for Liguria's focaccia, it is a good idea to get down to Stockton and Filbert early. Sometimes you may have to stand in a line that stretches out onto the sidewalk. Posted hours are 8 a.m. to 2 p.m. Monday through Friday; 7 a.m. to 2 p.m. on Saturday, and 7 a.m. to noon on Sunday. But when Liguria sells out, that's it. The "CLOSED" sign goes up on the door and the day is over.

As I said, focaccia is one of the reasons I live in San Francisco.

CHAPTER 25

GRAPPA

Grappa—usually 80 or 100 proof and distilled from grape skins, pulp and seeds—is a popular drink in San Francisco's North Beach. So, when I get a yen for grappa, which is often, I get myself to the North Beach Restaurant, grappa headquarters. I find a snifter of grappa makes the perfect wind-up to a fine meal. But at North Beach Restaurant, one of the neighborhood's finest places to dine, one doesn't just order a grappa after dinner. One asks for the grappa menu. For it is here at the bar that one can peruse almost 20 grappas of different styles and flavors. All are served in warm brandy snifters. These grappas range from about $10 an ounce upward. One grappa at North Beach Restaurant goes for $4,500.00 for a ten-liter bottle. It's Grappa Del Refosco Da Peduncolo Rosso, *distilled by the Refosco family in northeast Italy and is said to be a fruity grappa with an intense aroma and flavor. I haven't had occasion to acquire that ten-liter bottle.*

UNIONE SPORTIVA AND
THE ORIGINAL U.S. RESTAURANT

There was rejoicing in the streets of North Beach when the Original U.S. Restaurant re-opened after an alarming and disheartening episode when it was forced to close at its previous site. The reopening was a major event in the neighborhood. It represented one uptick on a slippery slope that has seen restaurant closings that have demoralized many of us.

For those unfamiliar with this venerable North Beach establishment, let me add a bit of history. It opened in 1919 and the U.S. stood for *Unione Sportiva*—a union of neighborhood Italian athletic clubs. This is the third iteration of the restaurant since that time. In modern times, so to speak, it has been owned and operated by Gaspare Giudice, from Sicily, who makes a fine and knowledgeable host, and Benjamin Ruiz is executive chef—not from Sicily but a Mexican with a Sicilian attitude. Additional investors in the new operation are Alberto Cipollina, who ran the original place for many years, and Mario Alioto, marketing boss for the San Francisco Giants.

Old Photos Add Historic Charm

A few years ago I reviewed the U.S. Restaurant for *Northside San Francisco* and gave it a favorable rating. So I thought it was time to reassess this neighborhood standby in its new location, 414 Columbus Avenue, formerly the site of the now-defunct Colosseo.

Old-timers in North Beach will remember the site as the home of the old Nebbia Bakery. Sensibly, Gaspare and his associates uncovered the original mural from the dining room ceiling—wonderful cherubs with loaves of bread in hand—but got rid of the gaudy wall murals of Roman gladiators on the streets of Rome that were added by Colosseo. Now the pale blue walls that match the ceiling are covered with historic black-and-white photos from the restaurant's past. Terra cotta tile floors complete the seasoned look of the place and there's a wine bar at the rear laid out for counter dining.

Calamari Fritti

The new U.S. Restaurant seems like old times to me: roast shoulder of lamb and lima beans on Tuesday was, and still is, one of my favorites. The lamb is roasted with a blizzard of rosemary that perfumes it nicely. It's crackly on the outside and a bit pink in the inside. The lima beans are slightly al dente. I usually add a bit of olive oil and also ask the kitchen to cover them with chopped, raw red onion. A few other outstanding daily specials are stewed tripe on Tuesday. Tripe may not be everyone's favorite, but if done with care, as U.S. Restaurant does it, cooked for hours in a rich and spicy tomato sauce, it is superb. On Friday the calamari fritti is a good choice with a peppery, white flour batter coating, It's deep fried very quickly and the calamari is crunchy and not oily as it sometimes is at other restaurants. And one of the specials on Saturday is calves liver and onions, nicely accomplished, sautéed baby liver with a topping of grilled onions.

Some Excellent Pizzas

Besides the specialties mentioned above, the lunch menu includes omelets any style, a series of sandwiches including some Sicilian-style offerings, and all served with salad or fries. There's a soup of the day. I like to begin with *pastina en brodo*, a rich chicken broth with those tiny bits of pasta swimming around. And there are ten or more pasta dishes, all with red sauces executed well by the kitchen, and quite lusty. There are also some excellent pizzas. My favorite is the Sicilian Trapanese with fresh tomatoes, mozzarella and Sicilian sausage.

At lunch U.S. Restaurant is decidedly informal. There's the scurrying friendliness of the servers who initially place a basket of crusty bread on your table along with a small bowl of cold cannellini beans, dressed with olive oil, wine vinegar, chopped onion and bit of celery. It's a complimentary appetizer and a good way to start your meal.

Sicilian Specialties

Evenings U.S. Restaurant becomes a bit more formal with white tablecloths and a more extensive menu—all Italian, but with many Sicilian specialties that remind Gaspare of his homeland. There's a sizable dinner menu with offerings—*antipasti, insalada, pasta, pesce, carne, contorni* (side orders), and a variety of those pizzas.

One thing I do miss at U.S. Restaurant is sitting at the counter in the old place and watching the cooks sling those hot pans back and forth as they prepared my meal. These days the kitchen is out of sight and when I mentioned this to Gaspare he invited me back there to watch Benjamin prepare my *linguine con vongole.* In a large, hot pan he lavished some olive oil and a spoonful of minced garlic. A minute or two later he tossed in a couple of dozen Manila clams from Washington state and poured in about a cup or a bit more of white wine. After giving the whole thing a good shake, he placed another large pan, upside down over the one on the stove, and turned the heat to high. After about five minutes he uncovered the pan, made sure all the clams had opened, added a dash or two of salt and pepper and red pepper flakes, and a sprinkling of Italian parsley. After a few more shakes of the pan he drained some linguine and added it to the pan. A few more shakes and he served the *linguine con vongole* in a hot bowl and I followed my waitperson, Renee, out to my table in the dining room. It was a wonderful meal—simple, but elegant at the same time.

The wine list is modest and built around Italian and California vintage offerings. The house red is adequate. There's also a selection of beers.

CHAPTER 26

THE INSATIABLE GAEL GREENE

Let's honor a gutsy voluptuary named Gael Greene who once wrote the following sentence, which alone is enough to make her a heroine in this book: "Great food is like sex—the more you have the more you want." Gael Greene is the famously sensual restaurant critic and food writer, whose blog, The Insatiable Critic, and newsletter, Forkplay, is required reading for me—and perhaps for you too. Here are a few biographical highlights on this remarkable woman's lusty career. In 1968 editor Clay Felker founded a magazine called New York—*still published today—that was destined to become one of the most influential periodicals ever created. Think quirkier than* The New Yorker *which it resembled in those days.* New York's *early writing stable included Tom Wolfe, Jimmy Breslin, Gay Talese, Gloria Steinem and Woody Allen. Within a few months of the magazine's founding and shaky beginnings, Felker offered Gael Greene (formerly a* New York Post *reporter) the restaurant critic job. She has said she was taken by surprise. She was a high paid magazine freelancer and did not think of herself as a food writer. But she couldn't resist the idea of eating on someone else's dime and became one of the most influential restaurant critics in the country. Never understating or adopting a buttoned-down opinion, she trashed New York's sacrosanct "21" Club as boring and described the Colony as "Forrest Lawn." Her barbed dissection of Elaine's, the hangout of the literati, remains a great read. And she celebrated some of Manhattan's beloved institutions like Lutece and Café Chauveron, and later, Le Bernadin, but also found words to salute a midtown snack bar. Then in 2008, on* New York *magazine's 40th anniversary and in her own 40th year at the magazine, she was suddenly fired. At the time, Glenn Collins, referring to her as the "priestess of radicchio," wrote in the* New York Times, *"But even among those who might have seen it coming, many were taken aback at the expulsion of the sensualist who influenced the way a generation of New Yorkers ate, and who served as a lusty narrator of restaurant life in New York for decades." Now that I've got you hooked on Gael Greene let's fill in the blank spots in her career. After graduation from University of Michigan and stints at the* Detroit Free press, *she joined the news service* United Press *as a*

Gail Greene.
PHOTO: DAN WYNN

reporter. *When they refused to assign her to cover Elvis Presley between concerts at the local stadium she did it on her own time. Then when she happened to be the only woman in his suite between shows, she couldn't resist as he led her toward his bed. She later claimed she didn't remember much but she distinctly recalled him asking her to call room service on the way out and order him a fried egg sandwich. She likes to think it was a sign that she was meant to write about food. Later, she wrote a couple of novels, one of them the bestselling* Blue Skies, No Candy. *Let's just say it was a hot read. In 2006 she published her memoir,* Insatiable. The New York Times *said it was "Frank and funny… a gustatory napkin-ripper." Syndicated columnist Liz Smith wrote a cover blurb—"Gael Greene is the best food writer since the late M.F.K. Fisher." A great comparison since Fisher too was a sensualist and wrote about food in a lusty manner. Obviously a woman of appetite, Gael Greene peppered her memoir with miscellaneous seductions—including Clint Eastwood and Burt Reynolds who never denied the encounters.*

THE HAPHAZARD GOURMET

Many of the great food writers have written about the sublime French bean dish, cassoulet. Waverley Root, A. J. Liebling, James Beard, Craig Claiborne, Georges-Auguste Escoffier and my friend Richard Gehman all loved cassoulet. They had their own favorite recipes, and wrote about cassoulet endearingly. But who was my friend Richard Gehman and what did he have to do with cassoulet?

Richard Gehman was the author of several novels, an off-Broadway musical, biographies of Frank Sinatra, Humphrey Bogart, Jerry Lewis, Hugh Hefner, and literally thousands of magazine pieces. He also wrote several cookbooks—one called *The Haphazard Gourmet* which he assuredly was. He was married five times, including a stint with Academy Award-winning actress Estelle Parsons and had nine children.

In 1963 *Newsweek* did a piece on Gehman and said he was half god and half goat. A workaholic as well as an alcoholic, he frequently had three or four major magazine articles in various publications appearing in the same month. His obituary in the Lancaster, Pennsylvania *New Era* (he was born in Lancaster) reported that he kept 11 typewriters in his study, each with a different manuscript on which he worked as it suited him.

Richard Gehman lived hard. He died in 1972 when he was 51. I still think of him frequently. Mostly, I think of Richard when I get hungry for cassoulet. When he was still with us, Richard and I communicated constantly by mail and by telephone. He lived In New York City and I lived in San Francisco. We exchanged stories, anecdotes and ideas about food; and about our so-called love lives. These love lives (so-called) we frequently equated with good food and drink. We also exchanged recipes and on occasion we cooked together when he was in San Francisco or I journeyed to New York. When we cooked

together it was usually for small groups of young women with whom we were attempting to ingratiate ourselves.

Richard and I had a lot of fun together. We shared a love of jazz and boyish pranks although we weren't boys. For example, we sometimes played the game of jacks in various bars. The loser bought the drinks. We both also enjoyed good scotch, good wine and good food, and we liked to "double date," as we described it in those days.

One day in 1963 I wrote Dick a letter and requested his recipe for cassoulet. In the letter, I told Dick that I planned a small dinner party in my apartment and that its success depended on the success of the cassoulet I hoped to prepare. It would be a major event. I had recently met an attractive young woman in a San Francisco coffeehouse and I had it in mind to invite her to share in the cassoulet shopping, cooking, and eating. I reasoned that I would undoubtedly get to know her well during the time it took to do all of that. In any case, I sent a letter off to my friend and in a few days I received this reply.

"My Dear Comrade:

You have asked for my recipe for cassoulet. Undoubtedly a seduction depends on it. First however, a few words about this noble dish. There are basically three kinds of cassoulet—Castelnaudary, Carcassonne and Toulouse. All are in the French Region of Languedoc. The original dish appears to have come from Castelnaudary. It contains beans, of course, fresh pork, some ham, and some bacon rinds. In Carcassonne they add some mutton and partridge, if it is in season. In Toulouse, and I lean toward Toulouse in my admiration for cassoulet, they add some good sausage and some preserved duck, and perhaps a bit of preserved goose if it is available.

That grand textbook Larousse Gastronomique *has a charming anecdote by Anatole France, the French novelist, poet and critic, about a woman of his acquaintance, a certain Madame Clemence, who operated a Paris restaurant. Anatole, who obviously researched Madame Clemence's cassoulet as well as he prob-*

Richard Gehman.
PHOTO: ERNEST BEYL

ably did Madame Clemence, said the lady had the same cassoulet
on the stove for 20 years. She just added to the pot over the years.
Quite a lady, but please don't try that.

You will find that my version of this noble dish ranges far and
wide within the acceptable parameters.

And here is Richard Gehman's recipe for cassoulet in his own
words.

Cassoulet a la Richard Gehman

First, buy yourself a good-sized earthenware casserole. You
will need it if you are going to pretend to be a cook. Next, get two
packages of either Navy Beans or Great Northern Beans. Soak
them overnight in water to cover. Sometimes it's fun to vary the
appearance of this dish by using red kidney beans, one package,
along with one package of whites.

Okay, do this in the morning. This dish ought to simmer all
day long while you dip lavishly into the cooking wine. Put the
beans in a stock you make with a couple of ham hocks and put
them on the stove to simmer gently.

Let them simmer about two hours, accompanied by one whole
onion stuck with a couple of cloves. Add a bay leaf, some parsley
and a couple of stalks of celery, leaves and all. You may want to
put in some oregano. Just a pinch, please. Or thyme. Or both. Just
a pinch. Salt and pepper moderately.

Meanwhile, get one cut-up chicken and fry it in olive oil
until it is nice and brown. Then set the brown chicken pieces aside
somewhere.

At the same time get at least two pounds of link sausages, the
best you can find. Parboil them in water for about ten minutes. Pour
away the water and set aside.

Now, take that great big casserole you have just sensibly
bought and take a hunk of butter and grease the sumbitch—
Inside naturally.

Now spoon a layer of your simmered beans over the bottom of the casserole.

Next lay some chicken over that, and put some of the sausages there to cuddle up to the chicken meat. Put a layer of beans over that. Cover all the meat with beans.

Now take some pepperoni that you have cleverly purchased in advance and have sliced into coins, and lay that in.

Another layer of beans.

Put in the rest of the chicken and sausage.

Another layer of beans.

By the way, I like to use lamb in this which is a lot of trouble, but you might as well go for it if you want to get the reputation (totally spurious, of course) of being a great cook. Get some shoulder or breast of lamb, fry it in oil with the chicken, or separately, very gently, until it too is brown all over. Did it occur to you that the lamb should probably be cut into chunks (like stew meat) by your butcher and that it ought to be lean? Probably not.

Recently, I've lost 20 pounds on a diet and this is making me so hungry I'm half out of my mind.

Anyhow, the lamb and chicken should go into the casserole together if you are of the mind that you should use lamb as well. I would really advise it.

Well, moving right along here, keep alternating layers of all that stuff until you've reached the top and run out of beans and meat—chicken, lamb, sausage, pepperoni and whatever else you wish, but please no beef.

If you have simmered the beans with ham hocks little hunks go on in also in various layers.

On top put about half a pound of bacon laid out in strips (raw, bacon, please).

Now, take the water you have cooked the beans in and pour it into the casserole. Add about a cup of dry white wine. Cover it.

Put all of this into the oven—the whole shmear, and turn it up to 300 degrees and let it go that way for about an hour. Watch it carefully. Make sure the heat doesn't dry it out. You ought to look at it every 15 minutes or so. If it seems to be drying out—that is, if you can't see liquid bubbling at the sides, add another bit of wine and bean-simmered juice.

I don't know about you and this dish, Ernesto. You are obviously no cook, and I hate to trust you with it. The bacon on top must be dry at the end and crisp, but there must be fluid bubbling beneath it.

Anyhow, after you have let it go for an hour at 300 degrees, turn the oven down to 250 and then you can let it go for two hours more (not absolutely necessary; it can go for two hours more, or one hour.)

Now, there are two extra added attractions to this.

Take one or two great ripe tomatoes and slice them and put them on top of the casserole just before you serve it. Or make croutons and put them on top of it just before you are going to serve. But no more than 15 minutes before.

If you can get an honest-to-god goose instead of chicken or even a duck, that's better. But I wouldn't trust you with that. It's tough enough for a real cook.

You serve this with salad and…my god I wish I had some now. I haven't had a single good thing to eat for five weeks and I'm starving.

Dick Gehman did come to San Francisco and stayed in my Telegraph Hill apartment with me. We created a magnificent cassoulet for an appreciative—but limited—audience but I have mislaid my notes on that event.

CHAPTER 27

MARK TWAIN

"When I build a fire under a person…I do not do it merely because of the enjoyment I get out of seeing him fry, but because he is worth the trouble. It is then a compliment, a distinction; let him give thanks and keep quiet. I do not fry the small, the commonplace."

—Mark Twain

SAN FRANCISCO PROSE:
A LOOK BACKWARD AND FORWARD

In the coffeehouses all over the city—but especially in North Beach—you will see them sitting before their cappuccinos and espressos, laptops open on the tiny tables. They are mostly young men and women who glance curiously and thoughtfully at the passing scene. They are waiting for the muse to present herself between coffee sips. They tap out extended lines of prose or poetry in fits-and-starts. All are writers. Some published. Most not. But never mind. The scent of creation still wafts through North Beach like the perfume of garlic and red wine. It always has. It's irresistible.

San Francisco has a long history of providing inspiration and succor to writers. And almost from its start the Latin Quarter, that later would become famed as North Beach, coddled them. They were attracted because of the area's lively and rakish, bohemian culture.

Paradoxically, we submit that it has not been necessary to actually live in North Beach to be a North Beach Writer (the caps on the word "Writer" seem appropriate). The fact is, some North Beach Writers have lived in North Beach, others have not. What has always been necessary though is a certain attitude, a philosophical, nonconformist set of mind, and an appreciation of the neighborhood and its laid back, Mediterranean ambience.

Nor is the distinction made here between writers of prose and writers of poetry. Writers of prose sometimes do write poetry. Similarly, poets do sometimes resort to prose. And, a writer need not write about North Beach to be a North Beach Writer. However, some have and some do.

Samuel Langhorne Clemens
Right from the beginning San Francisco's *literati* was attracted to its Latin Quarter, spreading out from the slopes of Telegraph Hill.

Perhaps the most famous of these writers was Samuel Langhorne Clemens, known as Mark Twain, the river pilot and newspaper correspondent turned author who served briefly in 1864 on San Francisco's *Daily Morning Call.*

San Francisco poet Ina Coolbrith, a contemporary of Clemens, founded the influential literary magazine *Overland Monthly* that published many San Francisco writers of the time. She lived on Russian Hill but wandered the city's compelling Latin Quarter with friends including Clemens and Bret Harte, the school teacher who wrote *The Luck of Roaring Camp* and *The Outcasts of Poker Flat.* Later Coolbrith became librarian of the Oakland Public Library and suggested books for the youngster Jack London to read. At one point she was also librarian of the then youthful, and then bohemian, Bohemian Club.

Robert Louis Stevenson

Robert Louis Stevenson came to Northern California in 1879. It was here that he wrote *Silverado Squatters,* personal recollections of his time in the hills above Napa Valley. He too prowled the Latin Quarter and enjoyed visiting the studio of bohemian artist Jules Tavernier at 728 Montgomery Street and lived for a while in a boarding house on Bush Street with his wife Fanny Osbourne.

George Sterling

Perhaps the greatest bohemian of them all, and in retrospect highly qualified to be called a North Beach Writer, was the poet George Sterling. From 1901 onward he maintained a studio in the Montgomery Block (where the Transamerica Pyramid now sits) for convivial, alcohol-induced conversation and (it is said) extra-marital encounters. A former seminarian, Sterling began his sojourn in California in the East Bay as a real estate salesman. He wrote poetry on the ferryboat on his way to San Francisco in pursuit of commerce. Soon Ambrose Bierce, who wrote for William Randolph Hearst's *Examiner,* befriended Sterling and guided him in what was then said to be the pursuit of "John Barleycorn." Jack London also befriended the would-be poet, and wandered bohemian San Francisco with him. Sterling later became famous writing about the "Cool, Grey City of Love, the City of Saint Francis," but sadly he took his own life by poison in his quarters at the Bohemian Club.

William Saroyan

Sometime later William Saroyan found the pleasures of North Beach to his liking. Herb Caen once called the Armenian-American from Fresno, "a crazy young writer who would have starved to death if it weren't for his kindly friends." Saroyan's play, *The Time of Your Life*, was awarded a Pulitzer Prize which he refused believing that commerce should not taint art.

Barnaby Conrad

Barnaby Conrad, once part of the North Beach scene, published a novel in 1952, *Matador*, based on the life of bullfighter Manolete. It became an immense success and in 1953 Conrad spun off his bullfighting *aficion* by opening a handsome club, El Matador on Broadway in the heart of North Beach. Conrad lived on Telegraph Hill, then on Bay Street. Later, after much success with his writing and his nightclub, he moved out on Pacific Avenue, and still later to Belvedere. Though, before his death he resided in Southern California, his literary roots were in North Beach.

Allen Ginsberg's *Howl*

Perhaps the concept of North Beach Writers was best illustrated by the Beats—the 1950s group that included Jack Kerouac, Allen Ginsberg, Gregory Corso and Bob Kaufman, to name a few. The Beats merged with a group that Kenneth Rexroth, poet and counterculture spokesman, identified as the San Francisco Renaissance Poets, the most well-known of whom was, and still is, Lawrence Ferlinghetti, proprietor of City Lights Booksellers and Publishers.

On a history-making evening, October 7, 1955, five poets—Allen Ginsberg, Michael McClure, Gary Snyder, Philip Whelan, and Philip

Allen Ginsberg, American poet.
PHOTO: MICHIEL HENDRYCKX; WIKIMEDIA COMMONS

Lamantia appeared at the Six Gallery and read their poetry. Ginsberg read *Howl*, which was soon to become the Beat anthem. Kerouac was there cheering him. Later that night Ferlinghetti sent Ginsberg a telegram offering to publish *Howl*, which he did. *Howl*, number four in the City Lights Pocket Poets Series, was printed in England and when it came into San Francisco, U.S. Customs and Immigration officials seized it. Ferlinghetti and Shigeyoshi Murao, the manager of City Lights, were promptly arrested by San Francisco police. The ACLU posted bail, Ferlinghetti vigorously defended the poem, as did noted San Francisco defense attorney Jake Erlich, and after a much-publicized trial, Judge Clayton Horn ruled in favor of Ferlinghetti.

The Beat Life

Those were heady days. Poetry was being read aloud in North Beach joints like the Cellar where it was recited to the accompaniment of live, improvised jazz. Kenneth Rexroth said, "If we can get poetry out into the life of the country, it can be creative. Homer or the guy who wrote *Beowulf* was show business. We simply want to make poetry a part of show business." And they did. Upper Grant Avenue became the haven for what Herb Caen termed "Beatniks." Small clubs and coffeehouses sprang to life like the Co-Existence Bagel Shop, The Place, The Coffee Gallery, 12 Adler Place, Vesuvio's, and The Anxious Asp. They attracted disaffected students, "suits" out of uniform from the world of business and commerce and eastern magazine editors who spread the fame of the "Beats" and of San Francisco's North Beach.

Richard Brautigan

Richard Brautigan came to San Francisco in 1955, associated with the Beats and after considerable success as a writer, took his own life in Bolinas in 1984. He once wrote "The act of dying is like hitch-hiking into a strange town late at night where it is cold and raining, and you are alone again." An habitué of North Beach, Brautigan had a rapid rise to fame with young people who found his *Trout Fishing in America, The Confederate General from Big Sur,* and other books suited their yearning lifestyle. Also a poet, Brautigan wrote eight poems that were printed on seed packets, packaged and sold under the title *Please Plant This Book.*

McCabe and Delaplane

San Francisco reporters and columnists have occasionally made the cut as North Beach Writers. The late *San Francisco Chronicle* columnists Charles McCabe and Stanton Delaplane come to mind. McCabe, who lived on Telegraph Hill, roamed North Beach and turned out acerbic columns that deplored San Francisco's loss of blue-collar jobs and what he termed the surrender to a tourist economy. The impeccable prose stylist, Delaplane, also lived on Telegraph Hill and wrote about North Beach during a highly productive period of his life. This, from his last column of short, stop-and-go sentences, April 19, 1988, was titled "The Best News Came from North Beach."

"I walked in North Beach to sharpen my wits. The best cops drew North Beach. The restaurants spread a good table for them—as they did for reporters. Delicatessens sold 27 kinds of sausage—each one better than the last. A vinegar

shop sold 50 flavors. There was a store where I bought fresh pasta. A French bread bakery where we stopped at four in the morning for a hot crusty loaf. The days were full of sun."

Maupin and Shilts

A special place should be reserved for writer Armistead Maupin, whose serialized slice of city life appeared in the *San Francisco Chronicle* for many years. They later appeared in book form and the work made Maupin an international celebrity. So too, we must remember another *Chronicle* writer (free-lance), Randy Shilts, a pioneering gay journalist, who in 1981 covered what was called the Gay Beat by the newspaper. Shilts wrote three highly-acclaimed books—*The Mayor of Castro Street: The Life and Times of Harvey Milk, And the Band Played On: Politics, People and the AIDS Epidemic,* and *Conduct Unbecoming: Gays and Lesbians in the U.S. Military from Vietnam to the Persian Gulf.* He died of AIDS in 1994 at the age of 42.

But who are the North Beach Writers of today? While the area still hosts fine writers too numerous to list here, certainly, the two foremost and most enduring are Lawrence Ferlinghetti and Herbert Gold.

Lawrence Ferlinghetti

These days, poet, painter, pamphlet scribe, publisher and bookstore owner, Ferlinghetti, still strides through the streets of North Beach like a colossus. Now 97, he walks tall and straight, his pale blue eyes fixed on another orbit. Ferlinghetti became entwined inexorably with the Beat movement, although he always seemed somewhat separated from it. Adjacent to it, perhaps, as he pursued his own uncompromising independence with what he terms "oral poetry" such as his riveting *A Coney Island of the Mind.* Ferlinghetti's bookstore City Lights on Columbus Avenue a few doors from Broadway, now has landmark status. Like Shakespeare & Company, Sylvia Beach's Paris bookstore that published James Joyce's *Ulysses* and became a focus for the Lost Generation, City Lights became the focus for the Beat Generation and is probably the most famous bookstore in the United States.

Still a populist spokesman, he may be the most famed poet of our time, but he is not now in the glare of publicity as he once was.

Herbert Gold

Perhaps the quintessential North Beach Writer of prose today, and he can frequently be found in Caffe Puccini and other North Beach coffeehouses, is Herbert Gold, a longtime resident of nearby Russian Hill. "North Beach is my village," he says. However, in a recent interview, Gold said "If you write about North Beach writers you must approach it as an archeologist sifting through memories. There are only a few of us left."

Herb Gold ran away from home as a teenager and headed west to San Francisco where he stayed for a time in North Beach. He realized that San Francisco and his hometown, Cleveland, were dissimilar and he filed away the San Francisco experience for the future. Later, in 1957, he visited the city, staying for a while with his Columbia University friend Allen Ginsberg. Gold moved to San Francisco permanently in 1960. He has written more than 20 novels to date, the last one with the intriguing title *When a Psychopath Falls in Love.*

Critics agree that Gold was able to straddle the worlds of both the Beats and the Establishment. In 1954 he brought out a picaresque novel, *The Man Who Was Not With It*, that captured the same rootless, disaffection explored by Kerouac in *On the Road*, published the same year. Gold's novel *Fathers*, was praised by critic Larry Smith as "...a book as skillful and rich as Ivan Turgenev's *Fathers and Sons*"—not insignificant praise.

Herb Gold has been critically acclaimed for his novels, short stories and essays since the late 50s. He is a compelling storyteller and is a keen observer of contemporary life. He is able to capture brilliantly the emotional patterns of a time and a place. Several of his books are positioned in San Francisco, with passages set in North Beach, that have a total ring of truth, *A Girl of Forty* and *She Took My Arm As If She Loved Me*, for example.

Through the years, North Beach has seen both flood and ebb tides as a haven for writers. During the 1800s San Francisco's intellectual ferment, coupled with its dashing and bawdy Latin Quarter, saw many writers drawing inspiration from the City by the Bay. Certainly an exciting period was the 1950s when the Beats made North Beach famous. Today the coffeehouses of North Beach and elsewhere in the city are still attracting those with literary inclinations. There are certainly writers drawing inspiration and sustenance not only from the spirits of those who have gone before, but from the spirit of the city itself.

Perhaps Herb Gold is right when he says those searching for San Francisco writers today must approach the task as an archeologist sifting through memories. But what a pleasure to sift through those memories.

———•◦•———

John Handy.
PHOTO: COURTESY OF "RIGHT DOWN FRONT" RON HUDSON JAZZ IMAGES

CHAPTER 28

JOHN HANDY AND HIS SPANISH LADY

My friend John Handy is a jazz saxophonist of much merit. He has played with many of the giants, Charles Mingus, for example, and he has led his own small groups in the San Francisco area for many years. In 1965 he had an enormously successful album on Columbia called "Spanish Lady." It was a tour de force that lasted nearly an hour and was considered revolutionary at the time. I knew that John Handy wanted to play the Monterey Jazz Festival and perform "Spanish Lady," a composition he had written earlier that was attracting considerable attention in San Francisco. Here's how that live recording came about. The trick was getting Jimmy Lyons, founder and general manager of the festival, out to hear the Handy group which was performing in a Divisadero Street bar called the Both/And. Jimmy was notoriously sedentary. His idea of a good evening was a few drinks in his apartment on Telegraph Hill and then maybe a walk down to Vanessi's for an early dinner.

One evening I took Jimmy and his wife Laurel out to dinner—saying nothing about going to the Both/And afterward. When we left the restaurant and got in my car I simply headed for Divisadero. I parked right in front of the place and Jimmy knew I had him. We walked in and were instantly recognized by the owners who—like a scene out of Goodfellas—whipped a small cocktail table and three chairs out of the darkness and plunked us right down in front of the stage. Handy was midway in a spirited rendition of "Spanish Lady." When he spied us in the audience, he raised his hand and literally stopped the music. When the place became quiet he gave the downbeat and started "Spanish Lady" over again. At the conclusion, Handy walked down off the bandstand and approached our table. Jimmy asked him to sit down and an extra chair was brought. Then Jimmy said "Okay, okay, you're on the Saturday afternoon show at Monterey." And that's how it happened.

AHMAD JAMAL REVISITED

A few years ago I wrote a review of a performance at the Monterey Jazz Festival by pianist Ahmad Jamal. I stated that Jamal, who had always been one of my favorite jazz artists, had disappointed me. The Ahmad Jamal light but percussive style I loved back in the 1950s for its incredible soft-loud dynamics with extended vamps that created tension almost to the breaking point, had changed, but to me—not for the better.

The Ahmad Jamal sound I experienced at Monterey was dense with big, two-handed chords that crashed into what I deemed to be a thick, soupy, and overwhelming percussive thunder. It smothered me, I said.

A Miles Davis Favorite

So what went wrong with me last year at the Monterey Jazz Festival?

Well, allow me to present a little jazz history courtesy of another jazz legend Miles Davis. The moody jazz trumpet artist once said "… he (Ahmad Jamal) knocked me out with his concept of space, his lightness of touch, his understatement, and the way he phrased notes, and chords and passages."

Miles referred to Jamal's "melodic understatement."   I think it would be fair to say that to Miles Davis, Ahmad's Jamal's silences—the blank spaces that created tension—were as important as the notes he played. Jamal also had (and still has) a highly refined sense of dynamics—short, heavy, staccato chords frequently alternating with soft, ear-straining, single notes.

Later, I thought about my comments in that review and regretted them. In one sentence I stated that Ahmad Jamal had lost it. But now I realize that I had lost it. I was stuck in what was a debilitating time warp—1958. That's when Ahmad Jamal, then just 28, came out with his now classic album *But Not for Me: Live at the Pershing*. (The Pershing Lounge in Chicago).

I decided to give Jamal another chance. Or rather Randall Kline, founder and executive artistic director for SFJAZZ, decided to give me another chance. "Try Jamal again," he suggested. And I did.

I Got the Message

The occasion was an Ahmad Jamal Quartet appearance in Herbst Theatre, an elegant Beaux Arts hall seating only 900 or so. The concert was sold out. I was conscious that the average age of the well-dressed audience members was about 50. That meant some of them, as I did, had probably purchased *But Not for Me* when it was issued, while others learned to love it through their parents or older friends.

The rangy and handsome Jamal was supported by James Cammack on the string bass, Herlin Riley on a standard drum kit and Manolo Badrena who played timbales, conga and bongo drums, and other assorted scratch, tinkle, and whistle-makers. Their back-up to Jamal's confident and aggressive offerings was brilliant. I got the message, which I didn't earlier at the Monterey Jazz Festival. The tone of the evening was crisp and crystal clear with jagged, swinging, frequently Latin-infused rhythms.

A Nuanced and Audacious Jamal

Jamal offered us an array of standards—among them "Autumn Rain," "Blue Moon," and his memorable "Poinciana" from the *But Not for Me* album. Listening to this 2011 Ahmad Jamal Quartet I came to the conclusion that what I was hearing was not really the same Ahmad Jamal who had first turned me on in 1958 but a new, more nuanced and audacious Jamal who over the years built on Broadway and movie show tunes and then deconstructed them masterfully—sometimes almost beyond recognition. Yes, Jamal still utilizes those extended vamps, three or four single note patterns that go on until your teeth ache. But then an explosion of drum patterns interrupts and sets off, *Poinciana* for example, in an entirely new direction.

Jamal is Highly Accessible

Jamal still exercises that spare delicacy he was noted for when he led his trio with Israel Crosby on string bass and Vernell Fournier on drums, and produced albums like *But Not for Me* or *All of You,* (live at the Alhambra Lounge, also in Chicago). But these days the timekeeping is more fractured, yet precise. And the melody, if you can discern and identify it, comes in Jamal's heavy staccato, two-handed chords that shift the trajectory in unexpected ways.

While Jamal today is highly accessible to the appreciative listener, his music demands more from his audience now than it did when I first heard him many years ago. That's good to my way of thinking and hearing. Ahmad Jamal gave me another chance to expand my musical horizons—with a little help from Randall Kline at SFJAZZ.

Readers can make their own re-assessment of Ahmad Jamal with recordings—*A Quiet Time* and *Poinciana Revisited.*

———•••———

CHAPTER 29

THE YEAR RONNIE LOTT GAVE 'EM THE FINGER

Ronnie Lott was the San Francisco 49'ers star cornerback and safety from 1981 through 1990. He was famous for the bone-jarring tackles he inflicted on opponents. An All-American from USC, Lott was a First Round, NFL Draft pick in 1981. In his first season as a 49er he helped his team win Super Bowl XVI. Playing safety in 1985 his left pinky finger was crushed and needed bone graft surgery to repair it. But such surgery wouldn't give him enough time to recuperate before the 1986 football season began. So, Lott had the tip of that finger surgically amputated and after recovering quickly he was ready to go.

THE SUPER BOWL CITY THAT WAS

In February of 2016 I attended a memorial service for Hadley Roff, a one-time journalist who went on to serve as troubleshooter and confidante to four San Francisco mayors. It was one of those events at which "everyone was there"—current Mayor Ed Lee, former mayors Willie Brown, Jr., Frank Jordan, Lt. Governor of California Gavin Newsom, and the principal speaker for the Hadley Roff memorial, U.S. Senator Dianne Feinstein.

Hadley Roff had worked for Senator Feinstein as deputy mayor of San Francisco at a crucial time in the city's history. In November 1978, Dianne Feinstein, then president of the board of supervisors, was named mayor when then Mayor George Moscone and board of supervisors member Harvey Milk were assassinated in City Hall— by yet another supervisor, Dan White. The city was in chaos. That same month came news of the Jonestown Massacre in which more than 900 members of the so-called People's Temple in San Francisco died in a bizarre, cult-suicide in Jonestown, Guyana. On top of that was the devastating AIDS epidemic, and an ever-increasing homeless population.

At Hadley Roff's memorial service Senator Feinstein recalled those terrible times. " The city was falling apart," she said. "But Hadley brought us together with his cool demeanor and his wise counsel. He didn't panic. In my staff meetings he was a voice of reason and led us through hard times by suggesting courses of action that made sense." Then changing her tone for a moment Senator Feinstein said, "In fact many years later at a luncheon he ripped open his shirt and revealed a T-shirt that had the inscription 'I Survived the Mayor's Staff Meetings.'—and he did, and so did I."

Hadley Roff was also a fierce football fan—a San Francisco 49ers fan, and attended most games.

Senator Feinstein explained that a few years later San Francisco was still in a funk. It was a rough time. But in January of 1982 the 49ers won their first Super Bowl. Joe Montana, Ronnie Lott, Dwight Clark, and of course, Coach Bill Walsh, were heroes. There was reason to be proud of San Francisco again. Thus is the power of hometown sports.

Senator Feinstein concluded: "There was going to be a victory parade. I was in a car with Eddie DeBartolo and Bill Walsh, and I wondered, in a city still grieving from the wounds of those recent catastrophic days, how many San Francisco citizens would come to our celebration. We turned a corner, and then I knew. More than one million people came out for the parade. And I knew San Francisco was getting well and had discovered something it could be joyous about. And I knew that football had accomplished that."

Vintage postcard of the Cliff House and Seal Rocks circa 1930s.
PHOTO: COLLECTION OF GLENN D. KOCH

CHAPTER 30

THE CLIFF HOUSE AND THE CLAM CHOWDER

In the 1930s when I was a boy in San Francisco, my father and I went by streetcar out to Land's End at Point Lobos where he shared his passion for mid-winter swimming by taking me to Sutro Baths, a massive, glass-enclosed Victorian amusement center. We paddled around in one of several heated salt water tanks. After our swim we went to the adjacent Cliff House restaurant and stared out at the fog-bound Pacific while enjoying steaming bowls of clam chowder. I can still taste that clam chowder.

Sutro Baths.
PHOTO: COLLECTION OF GLENN D. KOCH

TAKING A PLUNGE AT SUTRO BATHS

Both the Cliff House, which opened in 1863, and Sutro Baths, in 1881, were creations of Adolph Sutro, wealthy Comstock Lode mining engineer and later San Francisco mayor. The first Cliff House was destroyed by fire in 1894 and Sutro rebuilt it as a Victorian chateau. It survived San Francisco's catastrophic 1906 earthquake and fire only to burn to the ground again the following year. Then, in 1909 it was rebuilt in a simple, neo-classic manner and became a San Francisco landmark. Sutro Baths finally burned down in 1966 and is now a stark ruin.

My father and I frequently swam at Sutro Baths but stopped going there in 1937 after its conversion to an ice skating rink, but we continued to go to the Cliff House for clam chowder.

I was reminded of this boyhood pleasure when the Cliff House underwent its fourth restoration and reopened several years ago. The new Cliff House is now two restaurants. One is Sutro's in a dramatic new wing with panoramic ocean views—Seal Rocks just offshore, and the Sutro Baths ruins nearby. The other is the Bistro, which is reminiscent of the original Cliff House where I dined as a boy. These days I go there for the clam chowder and to recall those boyhood outings with my father.

San Francisco Chronicle columnist Herb Caen in his office.
PHOTO: NANCY WONG

CHAPTER 31

THE POWER LUNCH

These days in San Francisco, the power lunch, as important as the boardroom for big decisions, could be anywhere from the sandwich stand beneath City Hall's grand staircase, to a Vietnamese noodle soup joint in the Tenderloin. But back in the good old days, it was at Jack's on Sacramento. Jack's, founded in 1864, was decidedly San Francisco French, with mutton chops, Filet of Sole Marguery and Chicken Mascotte (sautéed chicken with mushrooms, hearts of artichoke in a sherry and brown stock reduction). Jack's was, until it closed in 2002, a hangout for San Francisco power brokers. Long-gone financier Lou Lurie had his own table there—the one under the stairway leading to red-curtained salons on the floor above. Chronicle columnist Herb Caen was a regular at Jack's. The cooking and the service were impeccable—especially if you were a top drawer power broker. Bardelli's over on O'Farrell was another luncheon gathering spot for the business and political elite. Once, two former San Francisco mayors and the then-incumbent mayor were seen there at lunch—but at different tables. They were George Christopher, John Shelley, and Joseph Alioto.

SAM'S GRILL AND SEAFOOD RESTAURANT

A while back Sam's Grill, that historic fixture of San Francisco downtown dining at 374 Bush Street, was on life support. Then it closed and remained dark for several months and we were all worried. But suddenly, it came back to life when a small group of Sam's loyalists took it over, negotiated a new lease for the 147-year-old seafood restaurant, touched up the paint here and there and reopened to loud rejoicing of its regulars.

Sam's is a restaurant where the regulars reign supreme. And Sam's regulars are downtown business types, well-known to the establishment. It only takes reservations for six or more at lunch but will take reservations for dinner. The regulars, who all seem to know each other, simply walk in without reservations and hang out at Sam's small bar for a Bloody Mary or a straight-up martini. Later they're ushered into one of the curtained booths that hides them away from the occasional yelper or guidebook tourist.

While not a first string, varsity regular that suits up each day for my fix of fresh seafood, I have patronized Sam's for years on an occasional basis. Readers should know that Sam's is my kind of place—no nonsense food and drink, served in a no nonsense style. So when word got out that Sam's Grill had reopened I thought it would be a good time to reassess what was going on at that somewhat shabby corner of Bush Street and Belden Place.

But rather than make you wait longer for an evaluation let me state that things are just fine at Sam's Grill—meaning things are just about the same. The old tuxedoed waiters are still there (two of them have been there for more than 40 years), and the food has maintained that consistent excellence that drew me there in the first place.

The staff at Sam's Grill and Seafood Restaurant.
PHOTO: COURTESY OF PETER QUARTAROLI

Founded in 1867

A bit of history will help you position Sam's Grill in San Francisco restaurant lore. Tadich Grill dates its founding to 1849, the Old Clam House to 1861, Sam's Grill to 1867, Fior D' Italia 1886, and Schroeder's 1893. Sam's opened as an oyster saloon in San Francisco's California Market that stood where the Bank of America building is now. It was called M. B. Moraghan's at the time. Later, it was operated by Sam Zenovich. Its name was the Reception Café, but most patrons called it Sam's. Then it changed hands in 1937 when Frank Zeput bought it. He officially named it Sam's Grill and Seafood Restaurant. It moved to 374 Bush Street in 1946. Phil Lyons bought it in 2005. And now, as I said, a group of Sam's regulars have taken it over.

These days your host at Sam's is a personable young man named Peter Quartaroli who has become the proprietor and a general partner. Besides being a good front man for his restaurant, Peter is an actor and producer who has appeared in more than 30 film and TV projects—including playing a cop in the movie *Zodiac*. He has also produced six films and is currently brainstorming one based on a character from Sam's Grill. I'm looking forward to trying out for that part.

Simply Seafood

Since it reopened I've dined at Sam's with several buddies in whose palates I have considerable faith: James Melling, my North Beach chum whom I call the Gentleman Trencherman, Carl Nolte, the *Chronicle's* Native Son columnist, and dinners with a group headed by historian Kevin Starr and attorney John Briscoe.

Unless you are an unshakable total carnivore, an unremitting pasta-head, or a vegetarian, you go to Sam's for the seafood. That's why they call it Sam's Grill and Seafood Restaurant, we surmise. The menu is printed and dated each day since the restaurant gets daily delivery of fresh fish and the menu reflects that. So it's understandable that the line cooks at Sam's Grill have a sturdy embrace on the concept of the broiling, grilling or sautéing of fresh seafood. When I have dined there, my fish, scallops, prawns or whatever, almost always have been still sizzling on the plate as the tuxedoed waiter sets it down on the white tablecloth.

Before launching into an assessment of the menu, let me mention the crusty and sour sourdough bread, a special bake by Boudin, that greets you at your table along with the small crock of good salted butter.

Clam Chowder

Appetizers at Sam's are old school. The crab cocktail is a generous mound of Dungeness crab legs and body meat laced with a proper red, spicy dressing. The deep fried onion rings deserve applause—crisp and not greasy as they sometimes can be. I have enjoyed the Celery Victor salad originally created by chef Victor Hirtzler at the Hotel St. Francis, and the no nonsense Crab Louie, both of which remind me of my San Francisco roots.

The clam chowder is authoritative and well made. The mock turtle soup is an unusual offering and quite good—served only on Wednesdays. Another Sam's Grill goal is to try the Hangtown Fry, the oyster and bacon omelet that dates back to the Gold Rush. I'm a good eater but there are only so many days in a week for this research.

Fried Olympia Oysters

Probably the number one choice of diners at Sam's is the Petrale. I prefer it charcoal broiled and napped with a bit of brown butter and a squeeze of lemon. Other top choices for me are the boned Rex sole, halibut, and swordfish. All are well handled, presented simply and need no enhancing. I would also like to give a vote of confidence to the fried Olympia oysters. This is a favorite of mine. I dab a bit of tartar sauce on each bite and away I go.

As to side dishes—a requirement for my buddies and me—I go for the creamed spinach and the glorious, crispy hash browns.

The wine list at Sam's Grill is not extensive but it is serviceable.

————◆•◆————

CHAPTER 32

GREEN GODDESS DRESSING

Green Goddess salad dressing was created in 1923 by chef Philip Roemer at San Francisco's Palace Hotel. It was a tribute to actor George Arliss who was starring in a play at the Curran Theater called The Green Goddess. *Mayonnaise, sour cream, chervil, chives, anchovies, tarragon, lemon juice, salt and pepper. Today you can buy it bottled at your supermarket.*

THE GARDEN COURT
AT THE PALACE HOTEL

When I was a boy my parents took me occasionally to the Garden Court in the old Palace Hotel on Market Street. It was one of the grand dining experiences of my childhood. Nothing even came close.

But things change in case you haven't noticed. The old Palace Hotel is now the new Palace Hotel and I'm sure Sheraton management is trying hard to turn it back into the old one that all San Franciscans loved and believed to be part of their birthright.

In any case, the Garden Court remains today one of the grandest dining chambers anywhere in the world. It is simply magnificent. You may want to go there occasionally as I do, just to look at it—or even try it out.

When the Palace Hotel opened in 1875 the Grand Court in the center of the vast hotel served as a carriage entrance—a cobble-stoned, horse and buggy entryway. Later, when the hotel was rebuilt after the city's disastrous 1906 earthquake and fire, the Grand Court was transformed into the Garden Court, a magnificent dining room crowned by a stained glass dome and flanked by a double row of Ionic columns of Italian marble.

The Wow Factor

In the old days, dining in the Garden Court at the Palace was an ethereal experience, especially at luncheon when long beams of light slanted down from the stained glass roof several stories above. Adults were on their best behavior and wore their best clothes. Small boys distinguished themselves by not fidgeting and eating everything on their plates.

As a small boy I was spellbound when I sat in this grand room where a string quartet played Viennese waltzes. Conversational

The Garden Court at the Palace Hotel.
PHOTO: FRED LYON

murmurs drifted upward along with the muted clinks of fine silver on bone china. Surely choirs of angels intercepted these sweet sounds as they glanced off that heavenly ceiling. It was Rome's St. Peter's and New York's Grand Central Station—classic like the bold but delicate Green Goddess Salad and the Oysters Kirkpatrick I enjoyed there. Today, monosyllabically, we would take the easy way out and call this the wow factor.

Chef Philip Roemer and his Chicken Jerusalem

In those glory years—the 1940s—I can recall two Palace Hotel chefs. The first is Philip Roemer. I don't think I ever met him, but I do remember his Chicken Jerusalem. I still have a brittle newspaper clipping with the headline "Palace Hotel Chef Reveals Cuisine Secrets." There's a shot of Roemer with dark, heavy eyebrows, and on his head, a shallow toque. Then came the recipe. I've tried it. But don't expect a low-cal chicken dish. This one has lots of cream.

Chef Lucien Heyraud Had Flat Feet

Another chef from the old Palace was Lucien Heyraud. He was a great bear of a Frenchman and I do remember talking to him when he stopped by our table occasionally because my father knew him. Heyraud looked like a chef should look in those days. If you were casting a retro movie and sought an actor to play the part of a grand chef you could model him after Lucien Heyraud.

He was short, rotund, slightly stooped and had the chef's requisite flat feet. You could tell his feet were flat by the way he shuffled gingerly ahead. His feet hurt. He wore a high white toque, a double-breasted white jacket with cloth, claw buttons, and loose fitting black-and-white checked pants. This was long before the highly qualified men and women cooks with celebrity dark glasses, and headbands or baseball caps jammed backwards on their heads, holding forth in see-through kitchens today.

Back in the days I'm talking about chefs were "back of the house." They might be called into the dining room at the end of a dinner party to receive accolades from the hostess and a small sum tucked away in a creamy, pale blue envelope engraved with her initials on the flap. When called forth, the chef—probably cursing softly in French or German at the interruption—wiped his hands on the towel that always hung from his waist, well below what should have been his correct anatomical waistline, and shuffled into the dining room. That was Lucien Heyraud.

Heyraud's Celebratory Dinner

I have in hand an early menu for a dinner at the Palace Hotel that Heyraud prepared for the Chef's Association of the Pacific Coast back in the 1940s.

It opened with *Poire D'Avocat des Gourmet, Cour de Celeris* and *Olives de Californie* (sliced avocado vinaigrette, celery and olives), and *Consommé Confetti* (chicken consommé with finely diced carrots, green peppers and pimientos).

Then members and their ladies (chefs were all men in those days) became aware of the seriousness of Heyraud's art when they tucked into *Sacristains Diablo* (diced chicken in a sauce of stock, wine, vinegar, soft sweet butter kneaded into a paste with flour, and tomato puree, all encased in puff pastry).

This was followed by *Mousseline de Sol Granville* (a sole sautéed in butter and smothered in a sauce enriched with whipping cream), *Supreme de Faisan aux Mandarines* (pheasant with a sauce prepared of Cointreau and mandarin oranges), *Petit Pois Fin a la Francaise* (baby peas), and *Pointes D'Asperges Sauce Moutarde* (tips of asparagus with mustard sauce).

The meal wound up with *Fraises San Francisco* (fresh strawberries and cream) and a simple *Gateau des Chefs* (a decorated cake, this one probably with ice cream).

Amplitude overwhelmed the guests.

My father, a chef himself, attended that dinner. He lived to 93 but didn't dine in that fashion every day.

CHAPTER 33

DOWNTOWN DRESS-UP

When I was a boy in short pants my parents frequently took me downtown in San Francisco for lunch—usually to Bernstein's Fish Grotto on Powell Street. My mother wore a hat, sometimes with a veil, white or black gloves depending on the season, and a smart full-length coat. My father wore a snap-brim fedora, a suit with a white shirt and a necktie. I wore a necktie too. That's the way it was in those days. These days the downtown costume seems to be a hoodie, blue jeans and flip flops.

A TALE OF TWO HABERDASHERS

This is a tale of two haberdashers. One sells $5,000 suits to elite buyers out of a swanky, downtown San Francisco store. The other sells sport shirts, cotton socks, sweaters and such on the streets of North Beach out of a large black, airline, roll-on bag. I have patronized both.

Wilkes Bashford

Haberdasher number one is Wilkes Bashford, who died as I was writing this and whose downtown San Francisco store caters to former San Francisco Mayor Willie Brown, Jr. and swells of that type. I suppose I was once one of those swells. I had a charge account at Wilkes Bashford's store and bought my share of Brioni and Ermenegildo Zegna Italian suits there. There were also fancy shoes, Panama hats and very expensive German and Italian shirts.

Although Wilkes Bashford no longer owned the store that bears his exalted name (it was sold to Mitchells/Richards/Marshs of Westport, Connecticut several years ago), he was a dashing figure not only in the store but in San Francisco society. He was seen every Friday in the classy bistro Le Central on Bush Street, usually with his buddy "da mayor," Willie Brown—who favors the Wilkes Brioni and Zegna suits— and with now-gone *Chronicle* columnist Herb Caen.

Wilkes Bashford was a holdout for a style of living that some say is on the wane, others that it is coming back. I would like to see it come back. I'm tired of hoodies, blue jeans and flip-flops.

A Manhattan native, Wilkes Bashford moved to San Francisco in 1959. He worked for a while as a buyer in the old White House department store. When he opened his own store he sold menswear only. Later he added womenswear. Wilkes Bashford was an instantly recognizable San Francisco social figure. He was invited to all the A-list parties and cultural opening nights. A true gentleman.

Bernardo Quintana.
PHOTO: FROM THE AUTHOR'S COLLECTION

Bernardo Quintana

One recent day I stopped to chat with Bernardo Quintana, not only a North Beach haberdasher but an actor and philosopher. Bernie's an existentialist and deals in questions of social importance in the neighborhood. I find him a good sounding board, so I frequently stop him to talk and then wind up buying a couple of shirts out of his black bag.

Bernie is a native San Franciscan. He attended Polytechnic High School and played football there. A good looking guy of Mexican descent, Bernie became a male model and then an actor with a few good parts on TV.

Every time I see him he's at work on a film idea. He hooked me when he said that he wanted me to play the part of Walter Winchell in his upcoming movie. That day I bought a blue, fly fishing shirt, a sweater and a couple of pairs of white cotton socks. That's my usual costume and Bernie knows his customers.

CHAPTER 34

IN SEARCH OF THE PERFECT BLOODY MARY

Those of you who know me will appreciate my ongoing quest for the perfect Bloody Mary. I have journeyed far and wide in this task—to the Hemingway Bar at the Ritz Hotel in Paris and Harry's Bar in Venice, where legend has it this morning after eye-opener may have originated. Actually it was popularized in this country at the King Cole Bar in New York's St. Regis Hotel where it was called the Red Snapper. A good drink, but not in the same league as my favorite here in San Francisco. Bartenders at the late Ed Moose's Washington Square Bar & Grill had a serviceable Bloody Mary which I preferred mixed, shaken with ice, then poured through a sieve into a wine glass—the Moose way, we called it. And now, the guys and gals behind the bar at Original Joe's indulge me by serving my Bloody Mary the same way. One day at Gino and Carlo, instead of my de rigeur Campari and soda with a brandy float, it seemed like Bloody Mary time. Ron Minolli was behind the plank and I gave him a mandate to exercise his considerable experience. What I received in a short cocktail glass (with ice I should add), was the Perfect Bloody Mary. Quest ended. Here, in Ron's words, is how he does it: "Well, first, most bartenders screw up this fine drink by making it too watery. And second, they don't mix the ingredients into the tomato juice the way they should. Here's how I do it. Get yourself a 12-ounce glass and fill it with ice. Squeeze in the juice of two limes, four good shakes of salt, and three good shakes of pepper. Next comes about one half ounce of Worcestershire Sauce and a shake or two of Tabasco. Then, about a quarter teaspoon of horseradish right out of the jar. This is the time to add two ounces of a good vodka. Now here's the secret. Before you start pouring in the to-mato juice, mix thoroughly all the ingredients you have sensibly put into the glass. And only after these are all mixed do you add the tomato juice and mix that in thoroughly. See what we've done here? We have mixed and blended all the spices and the vodka into the Bloody Mary." Yes Ron, I see.

GINO AND CARLO:
THE QUINTESSENTIAL SALOON

I have a passion for saloons. And San Francisco is a good place to exercise that passion. One of my favorites is Gino and Carlo. It was established in 1942, is still family-owned and Italian, and proud of it. It's open 365 days a year from 6 a.m.–happy hour for those who work at night–to 2 a.m. You may be getting the idea that Gino and Carlo, on Green Street between Columbus Avenue and Upper Grant Avenue in North Beach, is not your usual San Francisco saloon. It's a sports bar with an attitude. It's a drinking establishment for what remains of the drinking establishment–a phrase I love and used earlier in this book. Janis Joplin liked to shoot pool at Gino and Carlo.

Frank Rossi, now retired, was one of the owners. He spent 42 years behind the bar. He still drops in occasionally, "to make sure the boys are doing everything right." Frank's son, Frank Rossi, Jr. is now one of those behind the bar–and he is doing everything right. And so is another son, Marco Rossi.

Ron Minolli, a part owner and bartender, who has been there for more than 30 years and began working in the bar when he was in college, has served a generation of newspaper reporters and columnists, police and fire workers, stock market people (who get up very early) and garbage crews that are up even earlier. And, of course, there are neighborhood regulars. I am one of those.

Gino and Carlo is a full-time saloon but not a full-time restaurant. On the first Thursday of every month it serves an Italian, family-style lunch for about a hundred lucky patrons. Salad, pasta, meat or fish, wine and bread. Thirty bucks. Denise Sabella (who died as I was writing this book) was a neighborhood roustabout, sometime bartender and cook. She prepared the family style meal. It's a helluva deal. But that's not the whole story on Gino and Carlo

Gino and Carlo barman, Ron Minolli, constructs one of his special Bloody Mary's while neighbor-hood Bloody Mary expert, James Melling, observes.
PHOTO: ERNEST BEYL

and Denise Sabella. Each year at Thanksgiving, Denise roasted several turkeys and served them with all the trimmings to those in the neighborhood without families to be with. All you needed was a few bucks to buy one drink and you were in for the Thanksgiving dinner. That tradition continues.

Thelonious Monk, Minton's Playhouse, 1947.
PHOTO: WILLIAM P. GOTTLIEB; LIBRARY OF CONGRESS; WIKIMEDIA COMMONS

CHAPTER 35

THELONIOUS MONK

I have an appetite for the angular, frequently dissonant, piano stylings of Thelonious Sphere Monk (his grandfather's name was Sphere Batts). An eccentric jazz piano genius, Monk was largely self-taught. When he first began playing piano in New York clubs, some in his audiences were baffled not only by the sounds that poured from the piano, but by his antics. A shy man, he didn't speak much, but while his sidemen were soloing he frequently jumped off the piano stool and did shuffling, whirling dances. These soon became part of his persona and were accepted by his fans and his fellow musicians. Although considered a major jazz artist, Monk was almost always in need of money, but in 1948—already with a considerable jazz reputation bolstering him—something occurred that altered his life. He was discovered by the Baroness Pannonica de Koenigswarter, a member of the powerful and immensely wealthy Rothschild banking family of Europe. A jazz enthusiast who had divorced her husband and abandoned their five children, in 1951 she moved to New York City where the jazz action was. She took a suite at the Stanhope Hotel on Fifth Avenue and began holding court for jazz musicians. She was promptly disinherited by the Rothschilds, but she had plenty of money. Jazz musicians, who were free to call on her at the Stanhope day or night, called her the Bebop Baroness. One day she heard a recording by a little-known jazz pianist named Thelonious Monk. After a while she became a Monk acolyte. She spent 28 years of her life devoted to Thelonious Monk and his music. She also was a fierce enthusiast of Charlie "Bird" Parker. The astounding jazz alto saxophonist died in her apartment and she was asked by the management of the Stanhope to move out. She moved into another New York hotel and later when Monk retired in the mid-1970s he moved into a house owned by the Bebop Baroness. Monk died there is 1982. During his long career Thelonious Monk spent a lot of time performing in San Francisco. He recorded a fine album at Fugazi Hall in North Beach. He was the second most recorded jazz composer after Duke Ellington. Monk composed more than 70 works, Ellington more than 1,000.

Beach Blanket Babylon's New Year's Eve finale, 2015.
PHOTO: RICK MARKOVICH

FUGAZI HALL: NORTH BEACH
SOCIAL CLUB

Fugazi Hall, known also as Club Fugazi, is a small theater in San Francisco's North Beach. It was financed by two local banks. One was the Columbus Savings and Loan Society, founded by John F. Fugazi in 1883. The other was *Banca Popolare Operaia Italiana,* founded in 1906.

Fugazi Hall was built in 1913 as a community center for the Italian community. It had a long life as a social club for Italian immigrants in the city. In the 1950s the Beat community took it over frequently for poetry readings. However, it is most famous as the theater for *Beach Blanket Babylon,* the long-running musical revue that features topical songs and dance acts that lampoon San Francisco and San Franciscans.

Fugazi Hall is located on Green Street, between Columbus Avenue and Powell Street. Also on this block is the Green Street Mortuary which serves mostly Asian families. The mortuary has become famous for its uniformed marching band that sends the deceased off to their maker by marching through the Italian neighborhood and Chinatown while playing Christian hymns. Today, the gravity of the Green Street Mortuary contrasts sharply with the silly exuberance of *Beach Blanket Babylon.*

And, as noted in the previous vignette, Thelonious Sphere Monk recorded a solo album at Fugazi Hall in 1959–"Thelonious Alone in San Francisco."

Veronica "Rocky" Cooper (Gary Cooper's wife), Ernest Hemingway, Mary Hemingway and Gary Cooper.
PHOTO: FROM THE AUTHOR'S COLLECTION

CHAPTER 36

HEMINGWAY'S ABALONE

Ernest Hemingway was a regular at the St. Francis Hotel, so regular that when he checked in the chef automatically prepared abalone from a personal Hemingway recipe. "Fry in oil, to which a little butter has been added, to a light brown like fried oysters. Oil must be sizzling before putting the abalone in. Time: A few minutes. Serve promptly with a little butter and lemon. Pop Ernest." In 1943 Hemingway took Ingrid Bergman to dinner in the Mural Room in the St. Francis to persuade her to take the leading role in the film of his 1940 novel For Whom the Bell Tolls. *He succeeded.*

THE ST. FRANCIS HOTEL:
HISTORY OF A GRANDE DAME

In 1840 Queen Victoria took tea at Claridge's in London with French Empress Eugenie. Claridge's is still seen as an extension of Buckingham Palace. In 1890 Auguste Escoffier fine-tuned his classic cuisine at the Ritz in Paris. In 1938 Adolph Hitler gave a speech (about peace) from the balcony of the Hotel Imperial in Vienna. Alexander Woolcott once marched nude through the lobby of the Grand Hotel du Cap Antibes, and Zelda Fitzgerald is said to have whipped off her undergarments in the same lobby.

Then there's the St. Francis here in San Francisco—now officially called the Westin St. Francis. Yes, exciting and sometimes saucy theatrics have also taken place in the St. Francis over the years, but let's not get ahead of our story.

The hotel has been an important part of the history of this raucous city since its doors first opened on March 21, 1904. In 1849 a somewhat primitive St. Francis Hotel was built in San Francisco at Clay and Dupont streets near the gold rush town's Portsmouth Plaza. It was destroyed by fire in 1853.

Just as an exuberant San Francisco ushered in the 20th century, trustees for the heirs of Charles Crocker, the railroad baron, invested $2.5 million and set about to create an establishment that would make San Francisco the "Paris of the West." After studying great hotels of Europe, including Claridge's and the Paris Ritz, as well as New York's Waldorf Astoria, San Francisco's St. Francis Hotel was announced with great fanfare.

Rising from the Ashes

The new St. Francis, planned as two steel braced towers, would be on Union Square, a rather quiet residential area not far from downtown. It opened with 250 rooms and soon became the center of San Francisco's cultural, social, and political life.

Then, of course, on April 18, 1906 the great earthquake and fire changed everything. The St. Francis, with her steel beams, was damaged by the earthquake but still stood. However, the subsequent fire gutted her. Within a few weeks a temporary replacement went up on Union Square. It was demolished to make room for the return of the real St. Francis that re-opened on December 1, 1907. San Francisco's elite returned to the re-created hotel whose china soon sported a phoenix as a symbol of its rising from the ashes. A third wing was added in 1908 and a fourth in 1913.

From that point on, the St. Francis never really looked back and one is tempted to say "and the rest is history," and of course, it is. In 1971 the hotel's 32-story Tower complex opened. Over the years she has been in-synch with the mood of the city most of the time. The enduring St. Francis has been the symbol of the city's power elite with an impenetrable cachet. Trying to imagine San Francisco without the St. Francis is much like trying to envision New York without Grand Central.

S, M, L, and XL

Those are the bare bones of the St. Francis story. We'll leave the year-by-year history to the annual reports. But let's put some meat on those bones and romp through 100 years of high drama and low comedy at the St. Francis.

Right from the start the St. Francis was the San Francisco haven for what its raw-boned westerners called society—high or otherwise. The most distinguished San Francisco families found the St. Francis just the place for weddings, birthdays, social chit chat, and one-upmanship. Monday luncheon in the hotel's Mural Room became an elaborate social ritual with "rules of engagement"—a seating location order as precise as the order of pieces on a chess board. And its queen—the most important chess piece as we know—was Eleanor Martin, doyen of a prominent clan of electric power capitalists, dynastically in the highest echelon of San Francisco society. If Eleanor Martin found in your favor you were graced with a table in a prominent Mural Room location. If not—Siberia.

When Eleanor Martin died in 1932, no society matron-in-training filled her shoes. In stepped a Swiss headwaiter named Ernest Gloor, who for the next quarter of a century ran the Mural Room with an iron hand. It wasn't until after World War II with its egalitarian upheavals that the social ranking practice disappeared. Along the way so did the Mural Room. Gloor, and Eleanor Martin before him, had ranked San Francisco society into sizes like T-shirts—S, M, L and XL. Today, San Francisco society likes to pretend that one size fits all.

Superstar Chef Victor Hirtzler

By all accounts Victor Hirtzler, chef de cuisine who opened the St. Francis in 1904, was a superstar. With his kitchen "whites" he wore a red fez and sported a goatee. Hirtzler was born in Alsace in the mid to late 19th century and was cooking by the time he was 13. Legend has it that he was a food taster for Russia's Tsar Nicholas II and later became chef for King Don Carlos of Portugal. A favorite Hirtzler story goes like this: In 1916 Hirtzler prepared a luncheon for Charles Evans Hughes who was running against Woodrow Wilson for president. The California vote would be crucial. A lavish San Francisco banquet for Hughes was arranged at the Commercial Club and the famed Victor Hirtzler from the St. Francis would prepare the meal. When Hughes was seated the waiters walked out on strike. We are told that Hughes was prepared to honor the strike but our man Victor convinced him otherwise. The next day handbills proclaimed Hughes to be non-union. On Election Day Wilson defeated Hughes by slightly more than 3,500 votes, approximately the number of union waiters in San Francisco.

Through the years the St. Francis has lived on the legend of Victor Hirtzler and many notable chefs have symbolically inherited his fez, including high-powered chef Michael Mina.

The Rich, the Famous, and the Infamous

Both high drama and low comedy have played out on the stage-like settings of the world's great hotels. The rich and famous, the infamous and just plain folks have performed leading roles against backdrops of gilded lobbies and mirrored bedchambers.

Many U.S. Presidents have either stayed in the St. Francis or attended major functions there. So have kings, queens, emperors and others, titled and entitled.

Japan's Emperor Hirohito stayed there in 1975. Once he had been considered Japan's Sun God and it was forbidden to raise your eyes to see him. But that was all in the past. Although he was accompanied by an entourage that included a grand chamberlain, master of ceremonies, imperial physician, pharmacist, and even a hair dresser, Hirohito's desires were simple. He wanted to discuss marine biology (an expert came up from Stanford) and to take a tour of the city.

When Queen Elizabeth II visited San Francisco in 1983 she stayed in the Presidential Suite of the St. Francis. On hand was President Ronald Reagan who stayed in the London Suite, named for the flamboyant, long-time manager Dan London. The Queen occupied one bedroom, Prince Philip the other. When the Royal couple checked out a hot water bottle with the Royal crest was found in the Queen's bed. It was not revealed if the Reagans occupied the same bedroom in their suite.

When Richard Nixon was President he stayed at the St. Francis. He needed 160 rooms for advisors, bodyguards, advance men, press aides, photographers, doctors, valets, and technicians. Nixon had a late night craving for milk and Oreo cookies. The milk was in the fridge. The hotel sent a bellman out to a 24-hour convenience store for the Oreo cookies.

A Shot Rang Out

In September 1975 President Gerald Ford attended a luncheon at the hotel. Later, accompanied by General Manager Bob Wilhelm, who was celebrating his first day on the job, Ford stepped out of the hotel by the Post Street entrance and was shot at by a middle-aged, self-styled radical, Sara Jane Moore. She missed. A disabled and discharged Vietnam marine, Oliver Sipple, grabbed her arm and prevented a second shot. In reporting the event the *San Francisco Chronicle* said that Sipple was gay. The "outing" caused a split with his family and much anguish. Later, in 1989, Sipple was discovered dead in his apartment in the San Francisco Tenderloin. Found there was a framed letter from the White House: "I want you to know how much I appreciated your selfless actions last Monday. The events were a shock to us all, but you acted quickly and without fear for your own safety. By doing so, you helped to avert danger to me and to others in the crowd. You have my heartfelt appreciation." The letter was signed President Gerald Ford.

MacArthur Turns Up

U.S. Navy Admirals Chester Nimitz and William Halsey planned the World War II attack on Okinawa in a St. Francis suite.

In 1951 when the Five Star General of the Army, Douglas MacArthur, was recalled from the Korean War by President Harry Truman, he flew to San Francisco and spent the night at the hotel before flying on to Washington D.C. to speak before Congress. More than 500,000 MacArthur fans gathered in front of the St. Francis to see the General.

Celebrities and Scandals

Pampering temperamental celebrities has always been a specialty of the St. Francis. Without a disapproving eye Ethel Barrymore's pet chimpanzee was looked after without question. Florenz Ziegfeld's ingénue wife, Anna Held, got 30 gallons of milk per day—for her bath. The unrestrained dancer Isadora Duncan checked in and shared her quarters with her pianist—that is, until his wife ordered him out. When Isadora checked out she discovered that her manager had disappeared with all her money. She borrowed to pay her hotel bill.

Charlie Chaplin, who was shooting some of his great silent films across the Bay in Niles Canyon, was introduced at the St. Francis to Edna Purviance who became his long-time lover.

But it was Roscoe "Fatty" Arbuckle whose name became forever linked to the St. Francis. On Labor Day of 1921, the hefty silent film star spent a scandalous night partying in his suite with friends. Among them was a model and would-be actress, Virginia Rappe who died mysteriously in suite 1221.

Later Arbuckle was accused of raping her and stood trial for manslaughter. The jury found him not guilty but his career was ruined. After a while the furor died down and Arbuckle tried leading an orchestra, and sang and danced a bit. He also directed a few films under the name Will B. Good.

High Drama and Low Comedy

In 1927 Al Jolson filmed much of the first "talkie," *The Jazz Singer*, near Union Square. In 1950 Jolson, who liked the St. Francis, checked in and was given suite 1221. While playing poker with his manager and his piano player, he died of a heart attack. Today, 1221 is the most requested suite at the St. Francis.

The 1920 Democratic National Convention was the first national political convention held on the West Coast. Delegates hung around the St. Francis which published a daily newsletter called *The St. Francis Lobbyist*. The first issue featured this message: "As Chief of Police of the City of San Francisco, permit me to extend to you the courtesy of committing any crime within reason while a guest of this community."

Big time newspaper writers like H.L. Mencken covered the convention which nominated Governor James Cox of Ohio. Cox was later defeated by Republican Warren G. Harding. Mencken, the *Baltimore Sun* columnist who obviously enjoyed his time in San Francisco, praised the city by writing: "What fetched me instantly (and thousands of other newcomers with me) was the subtle but unmistakable sense of escape from the United States. It (San Francisco) is no more American, in the sense that America has come to carry, than a wine festival in Spain or a carnival in Nice."

And so it goes at the St. Francis: high drama and low comedy—and the rest is history.

American Red Cross nurse Agnes von Kurowsky and Ernest Hemingway in Milan, Italy, 1918.

CHAPTER 37

AGNES VON KUROWSKY'S DEAR JOHN LETTER

Ernest Hemingway's nurse, Agnes von Kurowsky, who cared for him in a Milan hospital after he had been wounded in World War I, had a romantic relationship with the author—at least he thought she did until she wrote him the following letter.

Ernie, dear boy, I am writing this late at night after a long think by myself, & I am afraid it is going to hurt you, but I'm sure it won't harm you permanently. For quite a while before you left, I was trying to convince myself it was a real love affair, because, we always seemed to disagree, & then arguments always wore me out so that I finally gave in to keep you from doing something desperate. Now, after a couple of months away from you, I know that I am still very fond of you, but it is more as a mother than as a sweetheart. It's alright to say I'm a kid, but I'm not, & I'm getting less and less so every day. So Kid (still kid to me, & always will be) can you forgive me some day for unwittingly deceiving you? You know I'm not really bad, and don't mean to do you wrong, & now I realize it was my fault from the beginning that you cared for me, & regret it from the bottom of my heart. But, I am now and always will be too old, & that's the truth, and I can't get away from the fact that you're just a boy—a kid. I tried hard to make you understand a bit of what I was thinking on that trip from Padua to Milan, but you acted like a spoiled child, & I couldn't keep on hurting you. Now I only have the courage because I'm far away. Then, and believe me when I say this is sudden for me too—I expect to be married soon. And I hope and pray after you thought things out, you'll be able to forgive me & start a wonderful career & show what a man you really are. Ever admiringly & fondly, Your Friend, Aggie

THE TOP OF THE MARK

O ne day I was invited to a tea party. Now, I don't usually go to tea parties—not my cup of tea I am emboldened to add. I'm more of a saloonist than a teapartyist. But, since this particular tea party was going to be held at the Top of the Mark, 19 floors up in San Francisco's Mark Hopkins Hotel, I decided to attend and to engage in some serious reminiscence.

In 1946 I went to the Top of the Mark with my girlfriend the day before I shipped out for Okinawa as a private in the Marine Corp. In those days servicemen going overseas from San Francisco to the "Pacific Theater" considered it a rite of passage to have drinks at the Top of the Mark with their sweethearts—newly-found or steady—and look out at the Golden Gate. (Servicemen sometimes took their first dates across the street to the Venetian Room at the Fairmont Hotel where elaborate drinks were served with gardenias in them, and there was an indoor swimming pool with a floating raft on which a trio was playing Hawaiian music.)

Dear John

Three months after my Top of the Mark date with my girlfriend—after chasing down scared Japanese soldiers who had refused to surrender and were hiding out in the north end of the island and giving us the illusion of war—I heard my name shouted at mail call. On that day I got The Letter—the famous Dear John Letter. The girlfriend was getting married to some other guy from her high school class.

I got over it. When I returned from the Pacific I went back to the Mark Hopkins, took the elevator up to the Top of the Mark and had a couple of big ones.

A foggy day at the Top of the Mark.
PHOTO: ERNEST BEYL

The Mansions of Nob Hill

The history of the landmark Mark Hopkins Hotel on the crest of Nob Hill is another of those San Francisco Gold Rush tales we all love. Mark Hopkins was one of the founders of the Central Pacific Railroad that helped stitch trade and commerce from the East Coast out to the wild, Wild West. Hopkins, an opportunistic merchant, left New York City by ship in 1849 and sailed around Cape Horn to San Francisco. He became one of the so-called Big Four—Hopkins, Leland Stanford, Charles Crocker, and Collis Huntington. The Big Four became conspicuously wealthy beyond their dreams and built mansions on Nob Hill. The ornate Hopkins mansion survived its owner who died in 1878. The building made it through the 1906 earthquake but burned to the ground in the fire that followed it. And in 1926 mining engineer and hotel investor George D. Smith opened the Mark Hopkins Hotel. Famed San Francisco money man Lou Lurie bought it in 1962 and the InterContinental Hotels Group bought it in 1973. It now has landmark status being listed as one of the Historic Hotels of America by the National Trust for Historic Preservation. The hotel certainly provides historic perspective to the life of a certain callow youth who shipped out after sipping a few gin fizzes with his high school sweetheart.

View from near top of ramp down to first floor of the V.C. Morris Gift Shop, designed by Frank Lloyd Wright.
PHOTO: LIBRARY OF CONGRESS; WIKIMEDIA COMMONS

CHAPTER 38

FRANK LLOYD WRIGHT

"Only a city as beautiful as San Francisco could survive what you people are doing to it," said Frank Lloyd Wright, iconoclastic architect who died in 1959. Perhaps Wright's most celebrated building (it still survives) is known as Fallingwater in southeast Pennsylvania. It is now a National Historic Landmark. The architect is represented by only one building in San Francisco. It was built on Maiden Lane and was for many years the V.C. Morris Gift Shop built in 1943. Its spiral ramp was a precursor to his Guggenheim Museum in New York City built in 1959.

SAN FRANCISCO'S IDIOSYNCRATIC ARCHITECTURE

I have an appetite for old San Francisco buildings. Based on its modest size, the city has more than its share of blockbuster architecture: public and commercial buildings, and dwellings of considerable grace, beauty and historical interest to augment its world-class location of bay, hills and flatlands.

Through the years, San Francisco buildings have been grand or garish; stately or simple. They have ranged across architectural styles including Greek Revival, Italian Renaissance, Mission Revival, Victorian, Carpenter Gothic, and for lack of a better description, what we might call "Frontier, False Front, Movie Set, Row Houses." San Francisco has had them all. And these buildings have been designed by architects of vision like Arthur Page Brown, Willis Polk, Frederick Law Olmsted, Daniel Hudson Burnham, Timothy Pflueger, Bernard Maybeck, Frank Lloyd Wright, Richard Neutra, John Burgee, Philip Johnson, Mario Botta, and Rem Koolhaus, to name some of the big ones. Frank Gehry, perhaps the most famous architect in the world today, who did the Guggenheim Museum in Bilbao, did design a structure across the Bay, the Concord Pavilion, but to date there are no Gehry buildings in San Francisco.

What follows is not a San Francisco guidebook listing of popular standouts like City Hall, the Ferry Building, the Palace of Fine Arts, the Palace of the Legion of Honor, SF MOMA, the Conservatory of Flowers, the Transamerica Pyramid, and the Speckles' Mansion. Rather, this is an idiosyncratic, hodgepodge of largely unheralded sticks and stones, bricks, mortar, steel and glass that have caught the occasional fancy. Call them overlooked gems. Agree or not, these structures have contributed to the class and distinction of San Francisco.

Belli and his Historic Building

It seems a pity to begin this architectural potpourri with the Belli Building, but editorial good order calls for a chronological rundown. Today, that wonderful Barbary Coast building at 722 Montgomery Street is a battered hulk, closed to view from the street by a plywood barricade. The two story structure was erected in 1849 as a tobacco warehouse but became The Barbary Coast Melodeon. Lotta Crabtree, the Gold Rush-era singer and dancer, performed there. It was also the birthplace of Freemasonry in California. After a long period of neglect the flamboyant attorney Melvin Belli purchased the building in the 1960s and restored it to become his legal offices. It was a showplace brick structure with its wooden trim painted flat black. Boxes of red geraniums sat outside the tall, multi-paned windows facing the street. Upper windows were topped by cornices like raised eyebrows.

And, in fact, Melvin Belli and his building did raise eyebrows. His ground-floor office was nothing less than a Hollywood set decorator's dream of the ultimate Gold Rush saloon—part brothel social center with velvet hangings and tufted, overstuffed leather couches. A long, stand-up bar with a brass foot rail running its length was backed by a beveled mirror. Belli's law books were stacked on shelves that climbed to the ceiling from which hung clear glass chandeliers. Here Belli worked at an enormous partner's desk and looked out on Montgomery Street. San Francisco tourists and residents alike were free to look in. Except for the year-end holiday season, Belli stuck newspaper clippings about his legal and other triumphs on those windows facing out to the sidewalk at eye level. During year-end holidays, he did the same thing with Season's Greetings cards. So, while the Pisco Punches, which Belli favored as party drinks for politicians, newspaper editors and reporters, socialites, movie stars and assorted oddballs, were raised indoors in toasts to Belli, others—many others—looked in from the sidewalk. His wonderful building was severely damaged in the 1989 earthquake. There is no plan to renovate it.

Carpenter Gothic on Telegraph Hill

The East slope of Telegraph Hill has some of the oldest and most interesting dwellings in San Francisco. Here Greenwich and Filbert streets become steps. Originally wooden, now concrete, the steps assume the role of graded walkways. Both Greenwich and Filbert stretch from the summit of Telegraph Hill to Montgomery Street and then from Montgomery down to Sansome Street far below. Midway, the two are joined like the crosspiece on the letter H by Napier Lane, still a narrow wooden walkway with several old houses on both sides. Perhaps the most interesting structure on the slope is 228 Filbert Street, built by Phillip Brown from England. After spending time at sea Brown settled in San Francisco and started a stevedoring business. Wanting to be close to the waterfront that provided his livelihood he built his house on the Filbert Steps. The three-story building, described as being Carpenter Gothic in style, was completed in 1882. Brown lived there with his wife and seven children. The house remained in the Brown family until 1959. Today it is a reminder of early San Francisco. It was built by carpenters from simple plans available at the time. It is a classic, boxy wooden rectangle, topped by a scalloped gable and set in lush gardens designed and planted by Grace Marchant who lived at the corner of Filbert and Napier Lane.

Richardsonian Romanesque

McLaren Lodge, on the edge of Golden Gate Park at 501 Stanyan Street, is the headquarters for San Francisco's Recreation and Park Commission. When it was built in 1898, the large building of fitted sandstone with a tile roof was the home-office of John McLaren, the Scottish superintendent of the Park. McLaren, a master gardener, came to San Francisco in 1887 determined to plant a million trees in Northern California. By all accounts, he probably did. Golden Gate Park is McLaren's legacy. McLaren Lodge is an overlooked masterpiece in what is termed by architects as Richardsonian Romanesque, named for 19th century American architect Henry Hobson Richardson. The style is based on French and Spanish Romanesque architectural features.

Western Frontier, False Front, Movie Set, Row House

Not much is really known about the stark but stately building at 736 Bay Street. Its owner, Tom Brown, a retired Navy officer, inherited the building from his brother who purchased it and used it as his living and office space for his practice of psychiatry. It is a pre-1906 earthquake structure; just how pre-earthquake is open to conjecture. The three story wooden building is difficult to view in perspective. Bay Street is a heavy traffic thoroughfare and cars roar past at all hours. No time for architectural rubbernecking. Walking uphill westward along Bay one passes the building on the North side of the street; almost too close. You just can't back off for a good view of its simple rectangular charms.

Until someone like Pulitzer prize-winning architectural writer Allan Temko comes along to define 736 Bay Street for us, we will refer to it as a Western Frontier, False Front, Movie Set, Row House. A tall, vertical rectangle with a straight, horizontal, false front roof line, there is an appealing honesty about its forthright appearance. Painted smartly in a utilitarian sage green with no contrasting trim color, the building declares itself with no pretense toward decorative flourishes. A small garden leads the way to ground floor space. Adjacent is a wooden stairway that climbs to the second and third floors where narrow balconies overlook the street. It is difficult for this writer to underestimate the impact of this simple and graceful structure.

Coppola's Sentinel Building

First, let's get the name of this building right. It is not Columbus Tower as many think. It is the Sentinel Building. This nine-story, flatiron office building at 916 Columbus Avenue at the south end of the North Beach area, was begun in 1906 before the catastrophic earthquake and fire and was completed in 1907. It was built by San Francisco political boss Abe Ruef. Accused of graft, he did some time in San Quentin. The late Victorian, steel-framed structure is topped with a copper-clad dome and anchors a fine view corridor from Columbus Avenue to the North. The building fell into disrepair and was restored in 1958 by a

Western false-front house in San Francisco.
PHOTO: ERNEST BEYL

new owner and renamed the Columbus Tower. The Kingston Trio, that played the nearby hungry i, purchased the building in 1960 as its corporate headquarters and recorded albums in its basement as did the Grateful Dead. The tower building was re-sold in 1972 to Francis Ford Coppola, who revived the name Sentinel Building and moved in his film company, American Zoetrope. Today the ground floor is occupied by Coppola's bistro, Café Niebaum-Coppola. Part of the bistro is a retail wine operation, a branch of the movie giant's Napa Valley Niebaum-Coppola Estate Winery. Painted white after its restoration, it is now the color of creamed spinach.

The Humboldt Building

In 1905 the Humboldt Savings Bank embarked on plans to build a classic, beaux arts headquarters at 785 Market Street and engaged the architectural firm of Meyer and O'Brien. Before the building was well along, the earthquake and fire that ravaged San Francisco halted those plans. But within a year the steel frame of the new Humboldt Bank rose along a devastated Market Street. The 19-story, narrow shouldered, tower of granite, marble and tile over reinforced concrete, was completed in 1908. It was topped by an orange Faberge egg pretending to be a rococo dome. Today, this historic structure, with its improbable dome can be viewed by pedestrians strolling along Market Street as a reminder of turn-of-the-century San Francisco.

The Cannery and the Argonaut

The Cannery and the Argonaut Hotel should be considered as a single, cohesive unit and, as such, comprise one of the most interesting historic complexes in this city. At the time of the earthquake and fire, the California Fruit Canners Association operated a number of plants in the area that were destroyed. Following the earthquake and fire the association acquired a huge lot at the corner of Leavenworth and Beach streets and built a new brick cannery and warehouse. The cannery was completed in 1907 as a fruit and vegetable canning plant and occupied roughly half the lot. By 1909 it was the largest such operation in the world and operated under the name Calpak. Later it changed its brand name to Del Monte. Cannery operations ceased during the depression and the building functioned as a general warehouse until the early 1960s. It was slated for demolition but was purchased by Leonard Martin, an attorney who engaged the architect Joseph Esherick and instructed him not to tamper with the integrity and beauty of the old structure, but to turn it into a center for exclusive shops and restaurants. Esherick did a beautiful job of remodeling the old building, completing it in 1968 and Martin simply added a capital C to the name and the Cannery was launched on a new life.

Shortly after the old cannery was built, the brick Haslett Warehouse was erected on the other half of the big lot. It was once right on the edge of San Francisco Bay and ships unloaded their cargo directly into the building. Originally a train yard sat between the old cannery and the warehouse from which canned goods moved out to the rest of the country. When in the mid-1930s the canning and shipping operations shifted to the East Bay, William Randolph Hearst stored the disassembled stones from a Spanish monastery in part of the Haslett Warehouse. Later it became an eclectic office building called Wharfside. In 1978 the structure was transferred to the National Park Service and then in 1988 to the San Francisco National Historical Park. A few years later, the Haslett Warehouse opened as the 252-room Argonaut Hotel, operated by San Francisco-based Kimpton Hotel and Restaurant Group. It shares the ground floor with the San Francisco National Historical Park Visitors' Center.

The Pencil Building

In 1910 a tower was completed at 130 Bush Street that today is little known but certainly one of the most unique structures in San Francisco. Then it was the H. M. Heineman necktie, belt and suspender factory. It rose resolutely and with considerable grace to 10-stories and was topped with an elaborate rococo crown resembling nothing less than a giant pipe organ in a Gothic cathedral. The elegant Heineman Building towered confidently over its neighboring post-earthquake and fire structures. Today it's referred to as the Pencil Building since it is only 20 feet wide and 80 feet deep. The building is easy to miss since it is squeezed between the Adam Grant Building, 114 Sansome Street, also completed in 1910, and the Shell Building at 100 Bush Street, completed in 1929. Designed by the firm of MacDonald and Applegarth, 130 Bush Street is fronted by bowed windows, glazed terra cotta tiles and copper panels. No longer a factory, it is now ten floors of very narrow, very shallow office space. On the ground floor there is no lobby. Where would there be room for a lobby? Tenants and visitors enter directly into a tiny elevator and are disgorged on the proper floor directly into the offices.

Saints Peter and Paul Church

This Italian neo-Gothic Revival church with its twin steeples presides over one of the finest urban, outdoor public spaces in the U.S., Washington Square, the heart and soul of North Beach. It was originally designed by architects Frank Shea and John Lofquist in 1908, probably derived from the cathedral in the Italian town of Orvieto. When that effort bogged down, architect Charles Fantoni completed the job. An earlier Saints Peter and Paul church, overseen by the Salesian Order of St. John Bosco, was located at the corner of Filbert and Dupont streets (Grant Avenue). It was destroyed in the April 18, 1906 earthquake and fire and rebuilt by October of that year. Abe Ruef, the same Abe Ruef who built the Sentinel Building, owned property fronting Washington Square and sold it to the San Francisco Catholic Archdiocese. After a concerted fund drive the building was finally completed in 1924. Joe DiMaggio and his first wife were married in the church in 1939. The baseball legend and the movie legend Marilyn Monroe were married in San Francisco in 1954. Then they visited Saints Peter and Paul and stood on its steps for a well-orchestrated photo op.

The Crown Zellerbach Building

The classy Crown Zellerbach Building anchors lower Market Street with a sheer, glass-curtain tower reminiscent of New York's famed Lever House. That's logical since Skidmore, Owings and Merrill designed both. This slim and elegant, 20-story tower at One Bush Street, is offset by a sunken landscaped plaza of stone that includes a circular glass-walled rotunda. The scale of the 308-foot rectangular tower and the nearby, low circular rotunda is just right for the space. Described as Internationalist in architectural style, the Crown Zellerbach Building was completed in 1959. It was San Francisco's first glass-walled tower and in 1997 was given a special award by the American Institute of Architects, California Council. The building's utilities, elevators and stairways are located in a vertical, opaque cube and the adjacent office space is surrounded by a green-tinted glass wall, free of interior columns. Not a giant skyscraper by any means, the Crown Zellerbach Building seldom comes to mind as the architectural gem that it is.

A mixed architectural bag to be sure, but this jumble of unique buildings adds surprise and much charm to San Francisco.

CHAPTER 39

WHAT'S SO SPECIAL ABOUT JOE'S SPECIAL

What's so special about Joe's Special and what's its origin? I spoke to the indispensable Alessandro Baccari, Jr., retired San Francisco historian, whose knowledge of North Beach knows no bounds. This is what Baccari told me: "Joe's Special was introduced at New Joe's on Broadway by Joe Ingressia who ran the place. But the real origin of the dish was the old wholesale produce market which was where Embarcadero Center is now. The produce workers were up all night unloading vegetables from the San Joaquin and Salinas valleys. Around midnight they would drop into one of the small cafes that sprang up there and have a Midnight Special—eggs, a few vegetables like spinach or chard, a little ground meat and maybe a few hot peppers, all scrambled together. Joe Ingressia put it on the menu at New Joe's around 1930 and that was how Joe's Special was born." When I'm in a Joe's Special mood I go to Original Joe's in North Beach.

JOE'S BEGAT JOE'S, BEGAT JOE'S, BEGAT JOE'S

I was a child of the Depression, the one that began in 1929 and lasted more than ten years. But I wasn't necessarily depressed by the Depression. I chalk that up to a hard-working mother and father and, at least in part, to Original Joe's, which opened in 1937. Before you think this is a strange way to begin a serious restaurant review hear me out.

When I was just a sprout my family ate regularly at Original Joe's. It provided a good "square meal"—as they used to say—and not only was the food good, it was good value for the Depression dollar. Later, as a reporter for the *Chronicle,* I hustled over from Fifth and "Mish" to the Tenderloin, sat at the counter for a big breakfast, or sometimes dinner when I got off work.

Then, after a disastrous fire on Taylor Street several years ago, Original Joe's opened on my North Beach home turf—Union Street at Stockton, right across from Washington Square Park.

So, Original Joe's has been part of the fabric of my youth, adulthood and now beyond. I'm going through a mid-to-late-life food crisis. So, as soon as it opened in North Beach I ate lunch there at the counter several days in a row and followed that with frequent dinners in the comforting, deep red, retro booths just like the old place. They make me feel at home. I remembered some of the tuxedoed waiters, and my favorite Irish bartender, Michael Fraser, was behind the plank to serve me a "pop" of this or that. One might assume from my eagerness that I have a hasty palate—and I do.

The Patriarch Tony Rodin

But first a bit of history, courtesy of the young John Duggan, Jr., who with his father (also John Duggan), his mother Marie, and sister Elena, work their restaurant like good quarterbacks work an opposing defense. The founder of Original Joe's was Marie Duggan's father,

Tony Rodin, a Croatian from what was then Yugoslavia. Tony was a merchant seaman and in 1932 he jumped ship in San Francisco and wound up working at New Joe's in North Beach. That experience gave him an idea and in 1937 he founded Original Joe's. So Joe's begat Joe's and there you have it. But let's get on with what my hasty palate discovered.

The day it opened in North Beach I rushed in early and sat at the counter in front of the exhibition kitchen to see if I could channel the old Original Joe's ham and eggs. I could. As I remembered from the old days I was presented with a glorious, center-cut of chewy ham that almost covered my platter. And my eggs were perfectly scrambled. Everything was working.

A few days later I made another assault on the counter to try the omelet with ham, green peppers, onions, and cheddar cheese. It worked admirably for me. I was on a roll, so for my third counter visit I went for what the menu lists as "Joe's Famous Hamburger Sandwich with French Fries." Yes, it was as I remembered—a juicy hamburger steak-sized slab, nicely charred, with lots of onions wedged into two hollowed slabs of sourdough. It scratched the roof of my mouth just the way I liked it. It was pure nostalgia.

On a Friday evening when the place was packed—and it was packed every time I visited regardless of day or time—my wife Joan chose the filet of sole and I went for an old favorite, grilled calves liver with bacon and onions. We shared a side of sautéed spinach. Everything was outstanding—the sole, browned nicely and moist, my liver, pink on the inside, tender and juicy.

The Gentleman Trencherman

I stopped by for lunch one day with my friend James Melling, a North Beach gentlemen and trencherman of some distinction. A kitchen miscue brought James a plain omelet rather than the classic Denver omelet (the one with ham, green peppers, onions and cheddar cheese) he expected. Our waiter Nick (who remembered us from the Washington Square Bar & Grill) wanted to play catch-up and bring the proper omelet, but Gentlemen Jim would not have it. The omelet was just what it was, a good omelet. And that brings me to   one aspect of the plated offerings at Original Joe's that appeals to me mightily. What appears on your plate is not architecturally inspired. It doesn't climb like a downtown skyscraper. It looks like real food and it tastes like real food.

A few nights later with my wife and daughter we did some further research. Joan stuck with her conviction about the filet of sole. Daughter Laurel went for the smaller (10 oz.) New York steak, and I gave a vote of confidence to the prime rib (regular cut) served on Saturdays only. It was a perfect evening. As usual, service was prompt and carefully executed. The filet of sole lived up to Joan's expectations, the New York steak and the prime rib were beefy, pink and juicy.

A Vote of Confidence for the Fried Oysters

At another lunch my buddy Carl Nolte, columnist for the *Chronicle,* chose the Joe's Special. He proclaimed it "Just like old times" and I trust his judgment. The same day I opted for the fried oysters. From the Oregon Coast, the oysters were fried crispy in a light batter of cornmeal and flour and served with both tartar sauce and red cocktail sauce. As Nolte said "Just like old times."

Well, I'm sure you get the point here—retro and vintage Original Joe's, while not offering Great Depression pricing, gives fair value for the product delivered. That's Original Joe's legacy. One day John Duggan the elder said: "You can't run a legacy without the young people. You only get one chance to make a first impression."

Daughter Laurel brought it all back home: "I'm very into the vintage, retro vibes and something I enjoyed is that it managed to be very old-timey without being kitschy and contrived."

Original Joe's is impressive and brings a lot of panache and economic energy to North Beach.

CHAPTER 40

FROGTOWN USA

When Mark Twain lived in a cabin near Angels Camp in the Sierra foothills he heard a story about a group of miners who bet heavily on how far a frog could jump. He turned it into a story The Celebrated Jumping Frog of Calaveras County—*a classic today. Now, there is an annual Calaveras County Fair and Jumping Frog Jubilee each year in Angels Camp, sometimes called Frogtown USA. The world's record for the contest was achieved in 1986 when a stalwart frog named Rosie the Ribeter jumped 21 feet, 5 and ¼ inches.*

THE ENGLISH MAJOR AND THE COPYBOY

M any years ago, when I was fresh and tender, but a bit prickly like a young artichoke, I was a copyboy for the *San Francisco Chronicle*. Today, more than 50 years later, a bit tough and woody, I still miss those copyboy days.

One fine June morning, a Sunday in 1951, I received a bachelor's degree in English from Stanford at a ceremony on the Palo Alto campus. The next morning I reported for work as a copyboy for the *Chronicle* at Fifth and Mission streets in San Francisco. In the large, second floor "city room" as it was called—a jumble of battered desks, jangling telephones, gray cigarette smoke hanging in the stale air—I was turned over to a veteran copyboy with a history degree from Harvard. He taught me how to make "books" for the reporters. "Books" were long sheets of copy paper into which were folded sheets of letter-sized copy paper, alternated with carbon tissues. They formed a kind of paper sandwich. Copyboys folded and stacked the "books" and later the reporters rolled them into beat-up, clacking, Royal, manual typewriters and hammered out the news of the day. The "books" provided multiple, finger-smudged carbon copies. Making those "books" was the default task for the eight or so copyboys usually on duty during daytime working hours. At night, fewer copyboys, fewer "book" makers.

Copyboy Chores

The principal copyboy chore—the very essence of copyboyism—consisted of pacing between two rows of desks waiting for a reporter to yank a "book" from his typewriter, dangle it out into the aisle, and yell loudly—"Boy." When that happened, as it did every few minutes before the first edition deadline, the copyboy ran to the impatient reporter, snatched the "book" and ran (yes, ran) to the front of the large room, where he slapped it down on the "city desk" in front of city editor, Abe Mellinkoff and day editor, Carl Latham. They sat imperiously, side by side, in a vacuum of calm and order surrounded by a vortex of confusion.

Hard-Nosed Editors

Mellinkoff, short, dark, intense, and Latham, large, beefy, and avuncular, quickly edited the "copy" with thick black, number-two pencils, and then shuffled it off to another copyboy who rushed it several steps over to the half-circle "copy desk" where the "copy chief" sat in the "slot"—literally a slot in the large, half-circle desk. There it was dropped into a wire tray and then retrieved for further scrutiny by the "copy chief"—in my time a hard-nosed, patrician named Jim Benet. His father had been the noted poet William Rose Benet, which gave "copy chief" Benet a certain cache among his subordinate, hard-nosed copy editors. James Walker Benet had a fierce, proud aura that stemmed from his younger days when he joined the Abraham Lincoln Brigade and saw duty in Spain's Civil War. He was a *Chronicle* hero.

A Private Clubbiness

Recalling Mellinkoff, Latham, Benet, and others in the *Chronicle* "city room" reminds me of a conundrum, a mystery that I still think about these many years later. All the editors of the *Chronicle* at that time had an impenetrable inner composure that we copyboys never seemed to be able to crack. They were like oysters that extruded a pearl to keep copyboys from getting to the isolated grain of sand within their shell. Call it the how-to-do-it grain of sand. The veteran newsmen I talk about here had a kind of private clubbiness—polite but aloof. You were either on the inside like the editors and the reporters, or you were on the outside, simply copyboys. We were treated with courtesy, but we were not taught the elusive craft of daily newspaper journalism. This was not J-school. What we were able to learn on the job, we picked up by osmosis.

The Restaurant Run

Other important copyboy chores consisted of running into the adjacent "composing room" (where batteries of linotype machines clattered) to find galley proof print-outs of stories that we then rushed back to the "copy desk" for yet another look, for headline writing, and the infrequent assigning of a byline to a reporter who had done a good job. (Reporters never wrote headlines, nor added a byline to their stories.)

Seemingly equal in importance was running to nearby restaurants like Polo's or Original Joe's, over across Market Street, to get burgers on sourdough for the reporters. That of itself was a harrowing exercise. Words like rare, medium rare, medium, well-done, raw onion, grilled onions, no onions—all involved careful note taking or there was hell to pay when you got back to the "city room."

A Resemblance to Boot Camp

Copyboys did everything "on the run" like recruits in Marine Corps boot camp. And the resemblance to boot camp was not accidental. In those days editor-in-chief of the *Chronicle* was Paul C. Smith, who had a distinguished career as a marine during World War II. He had become editor of the paper in 1935. When the U.S. entered World War II, high-profile Smith received a commission as a Navy lieutenant commander and the top brass shipped him off to Washington. He endured that for a few months then resigned the commission and enlisted in the Marine Corps as a private. He was later re-commissioned as a U.S. Marine second lieutenant, saw combat in the Pacific, and was awarded the Silver Star. When he returned to the *Chronicle* at war's end, he loaded the paper's editorial staff with former marines. I was one of those, although a bit later in the peacetime Marine Corps.

Occasionally (not often), copyboys were allowed to insert a "book" into the rubber roller of an unused Royal, and struggle to write an obituary or to rewrite a handout about an upcoming Chamber of Commerce or Rotary Club luncheon speaker. No one told you how to write the story of the event or how much to write about it. If your story made the paper you were overjoyed. If it didn't, no one told you why it was "spiked" —"spiked" was the word for purgatory, from which stories almost never made it to the glories of newspaper heaven.

As a copyboy, if you didn't "make" reporter in about six months, you could forget about it. Your career in journalism—at least with the *Chronicle*—was about to be concluded. I don't recall that copyboys were ever fired. They just drifted off when they realized they weren't going to become reporters.

Suddenly Everything Became Clear

And that was the life of a copyboy. Oddly, I loved it. We were indeed all boys or young men then, most of us former marines, all college graduates. (There had been copygirls during World War II, but none by the time I worked for the paper.)

As I recall, copyboy work schedules were 8 am to 4 pm, 4 pm to midnight, and midnight to 8 am. If you worked a night shift you sometimes were allowed to answer the telephone at an empty desk near the night city editor.

People telephone newspapers at all hours and for all kinds of reasons. Some call with what they believe to be hot news tips. Others ask about the next day's weather. Many call in with all kinds of questions, out of curiosity or to settle bets or arguments.

One night when I was on duty the telephone rang and I picked it up and said "*Chronicle* city room," with a rising inflection to signify professional alertness.

"What was Joe DiMaggio's lifetime batting average?" the caller asked. Not an avid baseball fan, that was a difficult question for me.

"Call in tomorrow morning and ask for the sports department," I responded.

Later that same night I answered another call. This time a wobbly voice said "Hey, we're having a little discussion over here." ("Here" sounded like a bar.) "Who wrote that story about the jumping frog?"

"Samuel Clemens," I said.

"Who?"

"Mark Twain."

"Oh, yeah. Thanks."

Suddenly everything became clear: Those countless hours as an English Major. All that reading of everything from Ben Jonson to Ernest Hemingway. All those term papers. And now, all these hours making "books," getting burgers for the reporters, and running copy up to the city desk. Here I was, clearly utilizing my expensive education.

I did finally become a reporter but that's another story.

Performers Mary Ong, Fei Ying and Mae Dong in a dressing room at Forbidden City, 1942.
PHOTO: SAN FRANCISCO HISTORY CENTER, SAN FRANCISCO PUBLIC LIBRARY

CHAPTER 41

THE FORBIDDEN CITY

*San Francisco has always been a good nightlife city. It doesn't roll up the sidewalks after dark. Establishments where citizens so-inclined could enjoy the pleasures of the evening have always abounded here—right from the early Gold Rush times. Then there were melodeons and dance halls—showplaces for relaxation and excitement. And, understand that relaxation and excitement were not mutually exclusive then and aren't even to this day. Frisky lads didn't run out of gas as the clock advanced toward midnight. They frequented some of these nighttime social clubs. In the 1950s there was the Mexican nightclub Sinaloa on Powell Street in North Beach which offered flamenco. And from the 1930s until the 1950s there was Charlie Low's Forbidden City, a Chinese nightclub on the edges of Chinatown. Asian-American dancers, singers, and strippers were featured. Popular during World War II, a best-selling novel by C.Y. Yee—*Flower Drum Song—*took San Francisco's Forbidden City as its theme. In 1958 Rodgers and Hammerstein created a Broadway musical based on Yee's* Flower Drum Song. *Bimbo's 365 Club on Columbus Avenue in North Beach was a popular nightclub for many years. Now it is open only to private parties. San Franciscans will remember Bimbo's primarily for its nude girl in the fishbowl.*

MAXINE: THE NUDE GIRL IN
THE FISH BOWL

One day recently I had lunch at Original Joe's with Maxine Maas, 90 years old, great legs with trim ankles, and a face that reminded me of Ursula Andress, the Bond girl in the movie *Dr. No*. My buddy, Tommy Nunan, himself a fine judge of pulchritude, brought Maxine down from Napa so I could meet her. Why did Tommy think I would want to meet Maxine? Because she was the nude girl in the fish bowl at Bimbo's 365 Club. And if you don't know about the nude girl in the fish bowl at Bimbo's, you're new to this city or just haven't been paying attention to important bits of San Francisco's cultural history.

Hollywood A Powerful Attraction

I interviewed Maxine over lunch and I enjoyed her company. She began with a straight-up gin martini. And I commenced my day with a Bloody Mary, straight-up, shaken but not stirred, and poured into a wine glass.

Over drinks and the Joe's Special, Maxine told me that as a youngster she led a peripatetic life. At an early age she was dreaming about the movies and began running away from home. She wanted to go to Hollywood and be a star. "It was a powerful attraction," she told me.

Fallen Women Were in the Theater

Born in San Diego, her family moved to Oklahoma where her father began plugging for oil. He didn't find oil but he did find deposits of guano in bat caves and that led to his undoing. One day he slipped into a crevice and later died of his injuries. The family returned to San Diego and Maxine continued to run away from home. "All fallen women were in the theater," she told me. So she took voice lessons and worked in a modeling agency where the famous Dadaist Man Ray photographed her.

Patrons of Bimbo's 365 Club watching "the girl in the fish bowl".
PHOTO: SAN FRANCISCO HISTORY CENTER, SAN FRANCISCO PUBLIC LIBRARY

Maxine's Ten-Cents-A-Dance Job

Then for stability her mother brought her to the San Francisco Bay Area. Maxine promptly became a taxi dancer in Oakland while still in high school. But the job as a dime-a-dance girl in the Rose Room Ballroom came to an abrupt halt after several months. Her mother got her fired.

"I was making good money too. I made five cents a dance and the house got five cents. I liked to dance and my partners (mostly sailors) were nice and polite. No one got fresh with me. A pinch on the butt or an exaggerated bow and a kiss on the hand weren't unusual," she said. One day, on demand, the young Maxine marched into the boss's office and there was her mother. "My mother told Mrs. Schumann, the boss, 'Do you know how old this girl is?' I was 14. I got my coat, and my mother and I left and that was the end of my taxi dancing job," she said.

Maxine's Treasure Island Job

One job Maxine's mother approved of was to appear at the 1939-1940 World's Fair on Treasure Island. She appeared with Art Linkletter's Melodrama Theater as a chorus singer and dancer. So, once again Maxine was in show business and this time her costume was a nice, frilly pink dress. She wore grease paint on her face and sang Stephen Foster songs like "Oh Susanna." Between performances she hung out with the circus people.

Maxine's Palace Theater Job

When the World's Fair was over Maxine found another job (without her mother's knowledge) at the Old Palace Theater, a San Francisco burlesque house. There she became what was called a "parade girl." In a flesh-colored body stocking, a swim suit, and sequined, high-heel pumps that glittered, Maxine walked out on stage between acts blowing kisses to the audience. Over her shoulders she wore a sandwich board. On one side of the board was printed "APPLAUSE." The other side announced the next act.

That job didn't last either. Her mother got her fired. "It was a good job. I made $3.75 per performance," she said.

Her Date with Howard Hughes

"At one point I worked as an understudy for various parts in San Francisco's Curran Theater. The notorious Howard Hughes movie *The Outlaw,* starring Jane Russell, was playing in the same block at the time." One day on the set at the Curran, when she was the understudy for *Junior Miss,* Maxine said, "Howard Hughes walked in and pointed his finger at me. He took me to a nightclub called the Bal Tabarin. At the end of the evening we got into his limo, he took me back to the theater and let me out. That was my date with Howard Hughes."

Working Her Way through College

In 1940 she entered University of California in Berkeley majoring in dramatic arts. And while there, still hell bent on a show business

Maxine Maas today.
PHOTO: ERNEST BEYL

career, she got a job at Bimbo's 365 Club in San Francisco as the nude girl in the fish bowl. "I had to pay my bills," she recalls.

Bimbo's 365 Club was operated by an Italian immigrant from Tuscany named Agostino Giuntoli. His nickname was Bimbo (short for *bambino*—little boy in Italian). He opened Bimbo's on Market Street in 1931. The economic Depression was still rampant and Prohibition caused speakeasies to open all over the city. At Bimbo's there was a one-way mirror on the door that warned when police were about to raid the place for illegal alcohol. Even then the club featured the nude girl in the fish bowl. The first women to take that job were burlesque dancers. One of them who became famous in burlesque was named Tempest Storm.

Deep in the basement of the club was a catacomb of tunnels and a small room with a platform on which a woman reclined naked. A periscope of angled mirrors projected her image (about six inches long) into the nightclub above from what appeared to be an underwater grotto.

Gyrating on a Bench

By the time college girl Maxine got her job at Bimbo's, she gyrated on a backstage bench and that made it appear as if she was swimming in a glass fish bowl behind the bar. She let her hair down and wore a flesh-colored body stocking. Now she recalls that her physical dimensions in inches were 35-25-35, and she was a natural blonde.

There were three fishbowl girls at the time. Maxine worked the most popular nights—Friday, Saturday, and Sunday. She earned $7 a night.

"And that's how I put myself through college," she says now.

But Never a Headliner

Maxine married her husband Al in 1944 and he marched off to fight in World War II. He died in 1978. Maxine's show business drive did not slow down. She went to Chicago for a production of *Rosemarie*. When the show closed she took off for New York and worked at the Copacabana as a showgirl. And then she got a part in the Broadway show *Up in Central Park*—but not as a headliner. "I was never a headliner except at Bimbo's," she says ruefully.

Returning to the West Coast she went back to school and got a master's degree in social service from the University of San Francisco and moved to Contra Costa County where she worked for many years as a juvenile probation officer.

Then in 1987 she relocated to Napa where now she serves as a docent at the di Rosa Preserve, the art gallery founded by the late Rene di Rosa. "And that's my life," she concluded.

Maxine's Secret to Longevity

I had a final question for Maxine: "What's your secret to longevity?" I asked.

Here's her answer: "I used to say, one never gives up smoking, drinking, and entertaining men. But I'm not sure what I would say now, having given up smoking since all my men friends had to. My secret to longevity is a group of friends, young, old and in between, with diverse interests, that you love dearly and feel are important. And good genes might be helpful."

CHAPTER 42

NOTES FROM UNDERGROUND

One day not too long ago the remnants of San Francisco's Beat movement were all aflutter. An 18-page, 16,000-word letter from proto-Beat icon Neal Cassady to writer Jack Kerouac was discovered and slated to be auctioned—presumably to rake in big bucks. Known as the "Joan Anderson Letters" because much of it was devoted to relating Cassady's erotic adventures with her, it is said to have inspired Kerouac to write in a stream-of-consciousness style in his novel On the Road. *Last time I checked, the auction was on hold because of lawsuits by the Cassady and Kerouac estates, and the big letter is in a vault somewhere. Meanwhile, I made an interesting discovery in a box of old magazines in my closet. Back in the 1960s I had a buddy named John Bryan, an off-the-grid, late Beat and early hippie who wrote poetry and published a counterculture magazine called* Notes from Underground. *What I found in my closet was a copy of the magazine, volume one, published in 1964. When I browsed through it, I made a startling discovery. Bryan had published a 13,000-word excerpt from the Joan Anderson Letters.* Notes from Underground *also published a lengthy reply by Kerouac. No, I'm not going to give you 13,000 of Cassady's words here. But rather a few comments from Kerouac's reply. Here they are: "Just a word now about your wonderful 16,000-word letter about Joan Anderson and Cherry Mary. I thought it ranked among the best things ever written in America…. You gather together all the best styles of Joyce, Celine, Dusty (Dostoevsky) and Proust…. It can't possibly be sparse and halting like Hemingway, because it hides nothing, the material is painfully necessary…. Hurry to New York so we can plan and all take off in a big flying boat '32 Chandler across crazy land…. I got to work now on script so I can pay Uncle Sam his bloody tax & landlord's bloody old rent…Jack."*

THE REPORTER AND THE IRISH SETTER

When I think back on it now, I was not a very good reporter. Nevertheless, in the early fifties, after nearly six months as a copyboy, I became a reporter for the *San Francisco Chronicle*. I was as proud as a chef who was just awarded his first Michelin star.

At first, for several days, I re-wrote handouts—press releases—about this and that. A few of them turned up in the paper's first edition but were dropped later.

Then one morning as I sat at my reporter's desk in the *Chronicle* "city room," as it was called, swilling down coffee (as all reporters are programmed to do), and staring at my old Royal typewriter, city editor Abe Mellinkoff called my name and said I would accompany photographer Joe Rosenthal on a story.

Joe Rosenthal and Iwo Jima

Joe Rosenthal! The guy who shot the photo of U.S. Marines raising the flag on Iwo Jima. To say that I (a former marine) was excited would be a ridiculous understatement.

Joe and I got into his beat-up car and drove out to the Sunset District. The story was that an Irish Setter had given birth to 12 pups. Unusual? No, incredible, we were told! We found the house, were admitted and met the proud mother. While I made page after page of notes, Joe lined up the pups in a low bureau drawer and posed mama off to one side. She smiled, thinking of her achievement, and Joe shot the photo. When we returned to the *Chronicle*, I wrote a 500-word story, turned it in and waited for the first edition—and what I hoped would be a byline. When the paper arrived in the city room I grabbed a copy. There it was on page one—three columns, above the fold—Joe's photo of the smiling mother and the 12 pups peeking out of the drawer. Below was a photo caption. It told the story in about 20 words—distilled from my long, doggy essay.

And that began my short but lustrous career as a *San Francisco Chronicle* reporter.

An Exclusive Bunch

The only byline I ever got at the *Chronicle* was on a story about a San Francisco flower show. It ran page one in the first edition, then later disappeared inside the paper. Eventually, over the next year or two, I did get few good stories to cover and write—numerous building fires, and one story, a mysterious death, later ruled a suicide. Those were the golden years for me.

The times I speak of here were the early fifties. There was a sense of adventure about working for the paper. We had great reporters, several who went on to big careers elsewhere, and great photographers—like Joe Rosenthal.

Boilermakers and Smoothies

As *Chronicle* reporters we felt we were an exclusive bunch. A tight fraternity of writers who were having fun doing what we were doing. Reporters having fun, what's wrong with that?

In those days almost all reporters smoked. With cigarettes dangling from the corners of our mouths we looked cool. We looked like reporters. And in those days almost all of us drank. That's what reporters did then. We drank beer—frequently with a bourbon chaser. And we drank scotch—maybe with a little water, but not too much, and on occasion, we drank boilermakers—a glass of beer with a shot glass of whisky dropped into it. That is what we drank in those days.

These days—I am told by qualified observers—things are a bit different. Reporters drink smoothies, or craft cocktails decorated with a sprig of kale. If I am wrong about this someone should please advise me for the sake of historical perspective.

In my time, we *Chronicle* types had our own bar, Hanno's, behind the *Chronicle* building in an alley called Minna Street. After deadline, Hanno's in the Alley (its official name) was jammed with *Chronicle* reporters, photographers, composing room workers, and newspaper truck drivers.

Hanno's in the Alley

Escaping to Hanno's *before* deadline was another matter entirely. But it was possible. It was an art form, and only the brave among us engaged in it. From his or her city room desk (some women reporters were active in this sport as well), the reporter got up and walked down the hall to the rest rooms, made quick work of that visit, and then raced down a convenient staircase, out of the building and over to Hanno's in the Alley. If accomplished with alacrity, it was possible to have a belt—maybe even two—and get back to your desk without city editor Abe Mellinkoff or day editor, Carl Latham, even realizing you were out of sight.

I do remember a notable time when Latham wanted a certain reporter to take a telephone call to write a story from another reporter out on his beat. There was a direct line from the city desk to Hanno's. Latham simply picked up the phone, got Hanno's on the line, and yelled at the bartender to send the reporter back to the paper immediately. The reporter rushed back, took the telephoned story and wrote it in time for the first edition.

Hanno's in the Alley closed in 1975. Apparently that was when we newspaper types stopped drinking.

There are many fine reporters working for the *Chronicle* now—but that's a back story for another time. But there were many great reporters during my time, and they deserve mention. There was:

Kevin Wallace—A *Chronicle* feature writer who went on to work for *The New Yorker*.

—*Chronicle* rewrite man, the fastest typewriter in the West. Monte was adept at leaving the building and winding up at Hanno's in the Alley.

Pierre Salinger (yes, that Pierre Salinger)—He once got himself arrested and locked up in jail under the pseudonym Emil Glick, then wrote about the experience for the *Chronicle*.

Carolyn Anspacher—We used to call women reporters sob sisters. Carolyn Anspacher was a sob sister, but also a damned good reporter.

She covered the Patty Hearst trial, and some of the other major news stories of our time.

Herb Caen—You remember him, or you should.

Stanton Delaplane—Stan was my all-time favorite reporter. He could write fewer words and say more than any reporter I can recall. I try to emulate him but I can never get it right.

And that's the way it was in the old days when I was a young, very wet behind the ears, reporter—interviewing Irish Setters.

———•◦•———

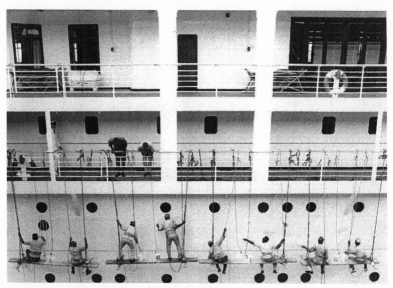

Goanese sailors painting the side of a P&O passenger ship.
PHOTO: FROM THE AUTHOR'S COLLECTION

CHAPTER 43

PORT OUT STARBOARD HOME

Have you ever wondered how the word "posh"—meaning high quality or elegant service—came into being? More than a century ago the first steamships of the Peninsular and Oriental Steam Navigation Company (the famed P&O, began steamer service from England to India. This was before the opening of the Suez Canal, and passengers traveled overland from the Mediterranean across the desert by camel to the Red Sea where they transferred to waiting steamers. As a courtesy, dignitaries were assigned the cooler cabins on the shady or port side of the ship going out to India, and the shady or starboard side going home to England. Their tickets were accordingly stamped P.O.S.H.—port out starboard home. For many years the grand old steamships of the P&O called on San Francisco from Australia—Himalaya, Arcadia, Iberia, and Chusan—but by that time P.O.S.H. had disappeared. The Pacific was cooler.

JIM MARSHALL AND HIS LEICAS

It was hard to be neutral about Jim Marshall. Most of us who came into contact with him either admired him for his obvious talent, or disliked him for his brash, often arrogant and combative manner. I was an admirer.

Many years ago I published a travel magazine called POSH. One day in 1966 a young man walked into my office without knocking and demanded to talk to the editor. He was nervous and intense and had two Leica, 35-millimeter cameras hanging around his neck. He said he was a photographer who had just arrived in San Francisco from New York and was looking for assignments. I didn't know if I liked him or not at that point but I liked his Leicas. And, I had an assignment. Someone had talked me into covering the Scottish Games in Santa Rosa, just a few miles north of San Francisco.

Tossing the Caber

Highlight of the Santa Rosa Scottish Games event was the caber toss. This sport, which dates back to the 16th century, was a favorite sport of King Henry VIII. In those days it was called "Ye tossing of the bar." The sport was originated by woodsmen who in their spare time tossed trees they had cut, and bet on who could toss them farther. The caber is tossed by running forward and then tossing the tree end over end.

That's what I sent Jim Marshall to cover. A week later he came into my office with a series of 35-millimeter color slides that were terrific. I published them and gave him a fee of $500—a good fee at the time. So that was how I met Jim Marshall and how we became friends.

After that I saw Jim Marshall only occasionally, but I remained aware of him because he was on his way to becoming the premier rock 'n' roll photographer.

Rock 'n' Roll and Jazz Photographer

It is safe to say that Jim Marshall photographed all major rock 'n' roll artists and was a fixture at every major rock 'n' roll event. He photographed Janis Joplin, Jimi Hendrix, Bob Dylan, Eric Clapton, the Rolling Stones, and so it went. His photos have appeared on the covers of more than 500 record albums. He was the chief photographer at Woodstock. When the Beatles played their final concert in San Francisco's Candlestick Park in 1966 he was the only photographer allowed backstage. He shot the famous Monterey Pop Festival and caught Jimi Hendrix on stage setting fire to his guitar. He was also a presence at major jazz events and photographed such stars as Thelonious Monk and Miles Davis.

Jim Marshall and Bill Graham Were a Match

Jim Marshall was mercurial and single-minded about his art. He had access to the personalities he photographed. They understood and appreciated his bull-dozing manner (perhaps much like their own) and his lack of fawning bullshit. A close friend of impresario Bill Graham, who matched him in chutzpah, Marshall was allowed a free run of Graham's Fillmore Auditorium in San Francisco and other venues he controlled.

The North Beach Color Shots

At one point during our casual friendship, I ran into Marshall at Enrico's Coffee House on Broadway. Over a drink he asked me what I was up to. I was doing some free-lance writing at the time and told him I wanted to do a story on North Beach. He said he had some 35-millimeter color-slides of North Beach activity that I might be able to use. Later he gave me a stack of Kodachromes that included a shot of Carol Doda dancing topless on the top of a white piano at the Condor Club. Another slide he gave me was a night shot of traffic along Broadway. Still others were of hippies on Upper Grant Avenue.

I never got around to doing the story. And whenever I ran into Marshall I told him I wanted to return his slides. He repeatedly told me to keep them, so I filed them away. Then in 2010 Jim Marshall died. I wonder what ever happened to his Leicas.

CHAPTER 44

DUKE ELLINGTON
LOVES YOU MADLY

Many years ago Duke Ellington and his Orchestra appeared in San Francisco at Basin Street West in North Beach. I knew Ellington from the Monterey Jazz Festival where I served for a time as publicity director. Between sets at Basin Street West I was admitted into the inner sanctum—Ellington's dressing room. He was holding court in his underwear, topped by a silk robe. Many admiring women were in attendance. To each he gave a kiss on both cheeks and proclaimed "I love you madly." Then he sat down at a small table with some sheet music spread out on it. It was the score for his concert of sacred music which he would later perform at Grace Cathedral.

Duke Ellington at the Hurricane Club. New York, N.Y., May 1943.
PHOTO: WIKIMEDIA COMMONS

MOVIEMAKING IN SAN FRANCISCO: A LOVE AFFAIR WITH HOLLYWOOD

San Francisco narrowly missed out on becoming the film capital of the world. Perhaps it's just as well. The city has enough narcissism and other "isms" without being "Hollywood by the Bay." Nevertheless, San Francisco, in fact most of the Northern California Bay Area, has had a long love affair with the movies.

Motion pictures were invented in 1878 down on the Stanford farm in Palo Alto. The first public motion picture exhibition took place in 1880 in San Francisco. The first complete movie studio on the Pacific Coast, 1906, was not in Southern California, it was in San Francisco. The classic Western with the strong, silent cowboy hero was first developed in 1907 across San Francisco Bay in Niles Canyon. Movies in color were developed across the Golden Gate in Marin County in 1918. The first "talkie," *The Jazz Singer*, was filmed near Union Square in 1927.

All true. None of these "firsts" happened in Southern California. So, in moviemaking parlance, let's cut to the chase.

The Zoopraziscope

In the 1870s railroad baron and former California Governor Leland Stanford made an intriguing wager with a friend that ultimately led to what we know today as movies. Stanford bet $25,000 that at full gallop all four of a horse's hooves are off the ground at the same time. All he had to do was prove it. In 1878 on Stanford's Palo Alto estate, an English-born photographer Eadweard Muybridge rigged a series of 24 cameras and set them to release their shutters in sequence when one of Stanford's thoroughbreds, Sallie Gardner, galloped by. The experiment proved two things. First, Stanford was correct in his assumption about galloping horses. But it was the second discovery that led to what we know today as Hollywood: motion could be reproduced in a realistic fashion. Then Muybridge, with financial aid from an enthusiastic

Stanford, constructed a primitive, sequential photo projector called the zoopraziscope. On May 4, 1880 Muybridge presented the first public movie screening. It was held at the San Francisco Art Association Exhibition Hall, on Pine Street between Montgomery and Kearny and was called *Illustrated Photographs in Motion*. Admission was 50 cents. The show featured the thoroughbred Sallie Gardner and a gymnast named William Lawton. Sallie was the precursor to Lassie; Lawton to Arnold Schwarzenegger.

The Nickelodeons

A few years later Thomas Alva Edison invented a more sophisticated and practical motion picture camera and projector, and in 1893, at the Chicago World's Fair, spectators were charged a nickel to view Edison's lab assistant sneezing. Then in 1895 in Paris the French brothers, Lewis and Auguste Lumiere, with their own version of motion pictures, exhibited a projection of a baby being fed, and a train coming into a railroad station. In 1903 along came the *Great Train Robbery*, produced and directed by a former Edison cameraman Edwin S. Porter. The film ran about ten minutes and it had a story—a quantum leap forward for movies. To see it cost a nickel and it played in small halls that were becoming known as nickelodeons. That was the start of the great silent films that continue to intrigue filmgoers today.

Broncho Billy

In 1907 Gilbert M. Anderson, a largely unsuccessful stage actor, teamed with George K. Spoor, a motion picture exhibitor and distributor, to form the Chicago-based Essanay Film Manufacturing Company. The name Essanay was selected from the initials of their last names. Anderson soon became a single-reel film producer and director. Not satisfied with the quality of the actors, he began performing in his own films. He called himself Broncho Billy and became the forerunner of that most enduring motion picture hero—the stoic loner, the brave, sometimes shy, cowboy who fights evil with his six-guns, chases off the bad guys, saves the town, rescues the heroine, then mounts up and rides into the sunset. The classic western movie was born and Broncho Billy Anderson preceded a long line of western heroes: William S. Hart, Tom Mix, John Wayne, Gary Cooper, Clint Eastwood, and almost every other male movie star in film history.

Niles Canyon

Essanay shot most of its early, single reel films in Chicago. As Broncho Billy, Anderson developed his cowboy western genre, and soon was shooting in Colorado, New Mexico, and Southern California. Searching for the ideal western location, he moved north, shot his movies in various Northern California locations and then found his way to Niles Canyon, now part of Fremont in the East Bay. Within a few years Essanay in Niles Canyon had a complete film studio. As Broncho Billy, Anderson made hundreds of western "flickers" in Niles Canyon, but cowboy films were not the only short movies that were shot there. Slapstick was popular with nickelodeon audiences, and Ben Turpin, who had joined Anderson in Niles Canyon as a carpenter, became a comedian. Turpin turned a physical challenge, crossed eyes, into a comic asset. Later he joined Mack Sennett, whose Keystone Cops pioneered the wonderful slapstick silent films.

Others who appeared in films in Niles Canyon or other San Francisco area sites include Charlie Chaplin, Buster Keaton, Wallace Beery, Mary Pickford, and Mabel Normand.

Charlie Chaplin

Charlie Chaplin shot many of the scenes for five of his great silent films in or near Niles Canyon—*A Night Out, The Champion, A Jitney Elopement, In the Park,* and *The Tramp.* Certainly the most famous of these was *The Tramp* in 1915. It featured the unforgettable Chaplin character balanced delicately between whimsy and pathos: a bedraggled little man in a derby hat, tight cutaway coat, baggy pants, over-sized shoes with upturned toes, carrying a cane. Chaplin later explained *The Tramp* to Mack Sennett: "You know this fellow is many-sided, a tramp, a gentleman, a poet, a dreamer, a lonely fellow, always hopeful of romance and adventure."

Charlie Chaplin in The Tramp.
PHOTO: WIKIMEDIA COMMONS

In one early scene he enters a hotel lobby and stumbles over a lady's foot. He turns to her and raises his hat apologetically. Then he stumbles over a cuspidor. He turns to the cuspidor and raises his hat to it as well. The Museum of Modern Art in New York City has in its Film Stills Archive a defining photograph of Chaplin as *The Tramp*, his back to the camera; as he walks down a lonely road in Niles Canyon.

The Miles Brothers

Ambitious and wanting a piece of the motion picture action, in 1902 three San Francisco brothers Harry, Herbert, and Earl Miles organized a company to rent films to exhibitors. This was a revolutionary idea at a time when exhibitors purchased movies directly from the manufacturers. In addition to their rental business they formed The Miles Brothers Motion Picture Company. Soon they were making simple, single-reel travel films. Then, in 1905, planning to add fictional story lines to their films, the brothers built a complete film studio in San Francisco on Mission Street. Bad timing! April 18, 1906 changed everything. The catastrophic 1906 San Francisco earthquake and fire stopped motion picture making in Northern California for several years. Meanwhile, Southern California became dominant in filmmaking.

The California Motion Picture Company

In 1912 San Franciscan Herbert Payne, heir to a Comstock mining fortune who identified himself as a "clubman," founded The California Motion Picture Company just north of San Francisco in San Rafael. Payne capitalized the company with one million dollars (big money at the time) and became president. He allied himself with George E. Middleton, from a prominent San Francisco family who operated an automobile agency on Van Ness Avenue. Middleton would become executive producer. Alex Beyfuss, an advertising executive, was the company's chief accountant.

Although The California Motion Picture Company began making short films promoting the Middleton auto agency, by 1913 it was talking about going "big time" with full-length features. Middleton met a seductive, Latin musical comedy star, Beatriz Michelena, who was featured celebrity at the San Francisco Automobile Show in 1913. He married her and the fledgling film company had its star. It billed her as "The California Prima Donna" and in 1914 *Salomy Jane*, from a story by Bret Harte, was released in a burst of publicity. The film was, as they say, a box office smash. After that "The California Prima Donna" starred in almost every CMPC film. Middleton turned out to be a good director and Michelena a fine actress, albeit in a bravura, musical comedy fashion.

The Southland Beckoned

But it was just not to be. The Southland was rising. Hollywood film magnates like Adolph Zukor, William Fox, Carl Laemmle, and Jesse Lasky, who was born in San Francisco, not only made movies but controlled distribution outlets as well. Payne, Middleton, Michelena, and Beyfuss were left without sufficient theaters in which to show their films. The last CMPC film was *Flame of Hellgate*. The beauteous Beatriz played a dance-hall girl. But that was the end. The company closed down in 1917. Middleton and Michelena divorced. He went back to the automobile business. She went back to the stage for a while and spent her final years in Spain. Although details are sketchy, film historian Geoffrey Bell in his book *The Golden Gate and the Silver Screen* (Fairleigh Dickinson University Press, 1984), states that Payne and Beyfuss, "both, in time, were reported suicides."

Even though Southern California and the major studios with their chains of exhibitors were in the ascendancy in the early 1900s, the San Francisco Bay Area continued as a center of filmmaking activity. All through the years of the silent films there were studios here. Not only The California Motion Picture Company in San Rafael and Essanay in Niles Canyon which finally shut down in 1916, but also the Leon Douglass Natural Color Studio that produced some of the very early color motion pictures, and Vim Motion Picture Company in Alameda and others.

Erich von Stroheim

The imperious director and actor Erich von Stroheim made one of his great films, *Greed*, in San Francisco in 1923. He took the novel *McTeague*, written by San Franciscan Frank Norris in 1899, and developed his own screenplay. A stickler for authenticity, von Stroheim found a two story, 19th century building at the corner of Hayes and Laguna streets and used it as the principal location for what critics agree was the director's masterpiece. The mercurial von Stroheim, hell bent for realism, made his actors live in the rooms he used as the setting for much of the film. The building at Hayes and Laguna gained fame. It was reported by historian William M. Drew that in the late 1960s and early 1970s it was a brothel. *Greed* was seven hours in length. The autocratic director shortened it to four hours. After it had been further reduced against his will to 100 minutes it was finally exhibited. When asked by the show business trade publication *Variety* how it would be possible to screen a movie almost eight hours in length on one evening, he replied "That is a detail I hadn't time to bother about."

The Jazz Singer

Al Jolson—the son of a cantor—who ran away from home to join a circus, became a black-faced minstrel and then a New York stage legend. In *The Jazz Singer*, much of it shot in San Francisco around Union Square, Jolson ad libbed a line, "You ain't heard nothin' yet." It was true: from *The Jazz Singer* onward film audiences "heard" more and more.

How many movies have been shot, at least in part, in or around San Francisco over the years? Who's counting? But here are a few good ones on my personal short list. *The Maltese Falcon* (1941), *All about Eve* (1950), *Pal Joey* (1957), *Vertigo* (1958), *The Graduate* (1967), *Bullitt* (1968), *Dirty Harry* (1971), *What's Up, Doc?* (1972), *American Graffiti* (1973), *Birdman of Alcatraz* (1979), *Basic Instinct* (1992), *Mrs. Doubtfire* (1993), and *Blue Jasmine* (2013).

Hollywood Became Hollywood

So, why isn't San Francisco "Hollywood by the Bay"? What went wrong? Or, depending upon your viewpoint, what went right? Pioneers like D. W. Griffith, Mack Sennett, and Cecil B. DeMille favored Southern California for their filmmaking. Yes, the weather was good for outdoor shooting and local booster groups did much to encourage filmmakers. A major consideration was that the Los Angeles area was close to Mexico. Lawyers in the East were diligent about tracking down infringements against the Thomas Edison motion picture camera and projector patents. From the Los Angeles area the movie people could easily skip over the border to Mexico for a while. Then the San Francisco earthquake and fire of 1906 put the skids to Northern California's ambitious moviemaking—at least for several years.

So how did Hollywood get to be Hollywood? In 1887 Horace and Daeida Wilcox, who had migrated to Southern California from Kansas a few years earlier, bought 160 acres of fig and apricot orchards and planned to build a house there and subdivide the rest. Mrs. Wilcox planted English holly bushes by her house and named the place Hollywood. In a few years the movie people began arriving. D. W. Griffith was the first. By 1908, an actor turned motion picture director, Griffith had 288 films to his credit with the Biograph Company of New York. In 1910 he rented facilities in the small, sleepy village of Hollywood. Mack Sennett, a Griffith disciple, soon was producing his famous Keystone Comedies nearby with Charlie Chaplin. Cecil B. DeMille, a stage actor of modest ability who had never directed a film, joined the pioneers. It was the start of what would become mythic Hollywood, the world's film capital. By 1915 film companies in or near Hollywood included Fox, Goldwyn, Metro, Paramount, United Artists, Universal, and Warner Brothers. San Francisco had been out-maneuvered, out-smarted and out-gunned with some help from an earthquake and fire.

However, over the years, there was never a time when San Francisco was not a mecca for ambitious filmmakers wanting to produce films here, use the area as a film location, or for visiting movie stars up from Hollywood just wanting to dine out or hang out.

The area abounds with movie societies, organizations and events: the Pacific Film Archive in Berkeley, the Bay Area Film Alliance in San Francisco, the San Francisco International Film Festival, the San Francisco International Lesbian and Gay Film Festival, the San Francisco Silent Film Festival, the San Francisco Jewish Film Festival, and others.

Today, while Hollywood cossets actors who want to become politicians and politicians who are acting, San Francisco offers—well, whatever San Francisco offers. The San Francisco Film Commission, overseen by City Hall, has a program to encourage filmmakers to come to shoot here. It has had considerable success, and benefits the city in fees and the hiring of local talent and production personnel. Woody Allen's *Blue Jasmine* starring Cate Blanchett, who won an Academy Award for her role in the picture, worked here for more than a month. Many moviemakers and movie stars live and work in the area. Perhaps those producers, directors, actors and technicians living here and only occasionally journeying to Southern California have the best of both worlds. They can immerse themselves in the Hollywood magic broth when and if they choose to. If they don't want to, they don't. Among these are George Lucas, Francis Ford Coppola, the late Saul Zaentz, Phil Kaufman, John Korty, Sean Penn, Robert Redford (we are told he has a residence in Marin County), and the late Robin Williams.

Although shooting films in San Francisco has dropped off in recent years, these days a week doesn't go by—so it seems—without a movie star sighting in San Francisco, a carefully choreographed car chase, a virtual bridge collapse or a rogue detective trying to make someone's day.

———————

CHAPTER 45

THE SHEARING SOUND

In Jack Kerouac's classic novel On the Road, *there is a scene in which an unannounced George Shearing drops into a crowded nightclub. He is recognized as the jazz artist he is and encouraged to play the piano. He does so for more than an hour. When he leaves someone says "There ain't nothing left after that." For jazz enthusiasts, that's the way it was. I first heard Shearing in a long-gone San Francisco nightclub, the Blackhawk. At one point he chose to play that old World War I chestnut "Roses of Picardy." A saccharine tune at best, but I became a Shearing devotee. There was nothing left after that.*

REMEMBERING ORNETTE COLEMAN

A s I was writing this, word came that Ornette Coleman had died at 85. He was an iconic figure in jazz. I was fortunate in that I met him through Jimmy Lyons, founder and general manager of the Monterey Jazz Festival. I first heard Ornette Coleman at the 1959 Monterey event. He played a white plastic alto saxophone. It had a strange, "plastic" sound, not like a brass instrument with its more rounded tone. Ornette's music at that time was baffling, strange to my ears. He played his song "Lonely Woman," and I thought it sounded like a lonely woman. It was bluesy, dissonant and atonal, with shifting tempos, or maybe with no tempo at all.

The last time I heard Ornette was a few years ago, again at the Monterey Jazz Festival. That time his music didn't sound so strange. Ornette Coleman hadn't changed but my ears had.

I knew Ornette and would see him occasionally in New York or when he was on the West Coast. Many years ago he dropped into my tiny office in the Belli Building in North Beach. He regarded me as a good music publicist and he knew that I loved his music. Ornette knew that his music was revolutionary, but he believed in it and wanted to have more and larger audiences. He wanted me to arrange a concert for him at the San Francisco Opera House. I agreed to give it a try and I tried hard. I contacted the opera movers and shakers but I couldn't bring it off. Today that chore would be easy. We caught up with Ornette's music.

CHAPTER 46

CONSIDER THE OYSTER

"He was a bold man that first ate an oyster,"

–Jonathon Swift

"I will not eat oysters. I want my food dead—not wounded."

–Woody Allen

"I never was much of an oyster eater, nor can I relish them'in naturalibus' as some do perhaps with bread and butter and so forth to make them palatable."

–William Makepeace Thackeray

"Before I was born my mother was in great agony of spirit and in a tragic situation. She could take no food except iced oysters and champagne. If people ask me when I began to dance, I reply' in my mother's womb, probably as a result of the oysters and champagne—the food of Aphrodite.'"

–Isadora Duncan

"You needn't tell me that a man who doesn't love oysters and asparagus and good wines has got a soul, or a stomach either. He's simply got the instinct for being unhappy."

–Saki (pen name for Hector Hughes Munro)

"As I ate the oysters with their strong taste of the sea and their faint metallic taste that the cold white wine washed away, leaving only the sea taste and the succulent texture, and as I drank their cold liquid from each shell and washed it down with the crisp taste of the wine, I lost the empty feeling and began to be happy and to make plans."

—Ernest Hemingway

"A loaf of bread, the walrus said,
Is what we chiefly need;
Pepper and vinegar besides
Are very good indeed—
Now if you're ready, Oysters dear,
We can begin to feed."

-Lewis Carroll

SWAN OYSTER DEPOT

True classics are old hat for San Franciscans. Classic places and pleasures are part of the city's folklore and its guidebooks. As San Franciscans we assume these classics will always be here for us. But they can slip away at the blink of a complacent eye. When they do they are mourned for a while, but then the newest craze, mall, theme restaurant or theme park, creeps into our consciousness.

The landmark, sidewalk clock in front of the old Columbus Avenue jewelry store, R. Matteucci & Co., is gone, knocked over by an errant delivery truck. Gone too are the original cobblestones on Commercial Street, Barnaby Conrad's intimate Broadway club, El Matador, the elegant I Magnin's fashion house across from Union Square, and Jack's restaurant, to name former classics some of us still remember.

But there are a few treasured institutions left. They exist in a time warp, and is anything more satisfying than a good time warp? The Tadich Grill qualifies. So do the Green Street Mortuary Marching Band, Lawrence Ferlinghetti's bookstore, City Lights and that throwback to a more satisfying era, Swan Oyster Depot. Certainly this is not a comprehensive list of San Francisco's best of this and that. The reader may add other personal classics—as long as Swan Oyster Depot makes the cut.

The Sanciminos

Ah Swan. That tiny temple dedicated to the glories of *frutta di mare* dates back to 1912 when four Danish brothers opened a small, narrow shop where, those inclined, sat at a white marble counter and slurped oysters. It was located at 1517 Polk Street right off California Avenue. They named it Swan Oyster Depot because in Scandinavian countries the swan traditionally has been a symbol of good luck and prosperity.

But it was an Italian immigrant family, the Sanciminos, that brought to life those glory years of Swan Oyster Depot. This Sicilian family of fishermen came to San Francisco from the small village of Sciacca, on Sicily's south coast. As did many Sicilians in those pre, turn-of-the-century times, four Sancimino brothers immigrated to the United States in the 1880s. They struck out West to San Francisco and joined other Italian countrymen on Fisherman's Wharf where they plied their fishing skills. In 1890 their younger brother, Vincent, 10 years of age at the time, joined them and began shining shoes on Market Street. By the time Vincent was 12 he was working on Fisherman's Wharf as well. The youngster gutted and cleaned fish, mended nets, tended the crab boilers. In a few years he took his place as a fisherman beside his older brothers and spent long, hard days fishing in San Francisco Bay and up along the Northern California coast. He set crab pots, caught salmon and halibut by hook and line, and bottom fish with drag nets.

Salvatore Became a Fisherman

When the great earthquake and fire struck the city in 1906 Vincent, along with many, headed for the open spaces in Golden Gate Park. There he saw a young woman of Sicilian descent named Maria at an emergency soup kitchen. "I'm going to marry you," he said. And he did. The couple had six children, two boys and four girls. And it was the oldest boy, Salvatore, who later set the Sancimino stage for what was to become that San Francisco classic, Swan Oyster Depot.

Salvatore Sancimino was born in 1919, did the obligatory shining of shoes for small change as a kid, attended Galileo High School and graduated in 1937. He then began life in earnest, as the saying went, as a runner, chasing around town on errands, for the Bank of Italy, and doing other odd jobs.

Early in World War II he joined the Seabees and was shipped out to the South Pacific. On a Navy LST sailing back to San Francisco in 1946 when the war was over, he won $8,000.00 playing craps. With that stake he bought his father a new, maroon Packard Coupe and his mother a handsome console radio. He banked the rest and when he was discharged from the Seabees, went to work for a wholesale fish company. Two years later, with the rest of his winnings, he purchased Swan Oyster

Salvatore Sancimino cracking crab at Swan Oyster Depot.
PHOTO: FRED LYON

Depot with three cousins. He bought them out a few years later. Under Salvatore's direction, Swan became a fresh fish market as well as a popular stop where San Franciscans could sit at the counter for a little something to keep hunger at bay.

While going through his Seabee discharge procedures, Salvatore, a cocky, young Italian American with a wide grin, had met an attractive lieutenant in the Army Nursing Corps named Rose. "I'm going to marry you," he said echoing the brash style of his father, Vincent. They did marry, moved into a flat on Taylor Street in Italian North Beach and began their own family that grew to six sons and a daughter.

The Sancimino Brothers

Today, the Sancimino brothers operate Swan Oyster Depot, where they once worked as kids for their father, who died in 1989 at the age of 69.

Walk into Swan Oyster Depot today and you will usually find some of the brothers, frequently joined by their own offspring, behind the counter, boning salmon, cracking crab, shucking oysters, slicing sourdough, serving chowder or filling dozens of orders for home delivery that come in by telephone.

The eldest brother, Vincent, became an attorney and practiced law for nine years before rejoining his brothers in a flash of family spirit. Steve, whom Salvatore designated as manager to succeed him, is married and has two boys and a girl. John was married and had two boys and a girl. Tom is married with two girls. Jim is single. Phil is single and spent two-and-a-half years in the Navy. Except for Vincent who attended Riordan High School before going on to study law at San Francisco Law School, all the brothers attended St. Ignatius High School and played football there.

Drop in for Dungeness Crab

They are a close family in their off-duty hours too. They enjoy sports and are proud of the fact that they all have played rugby together for a local team. All live in San Francisco except Steve, who lives nearby in Novato. They spend Easter, Christmas and other holidays together. Back in 1989 five of the six swam San Francisco Bay in the annual Dolphin Club swim from Fort Point to Lime Rock on the Marin County shore. They set the world record for the most siblings to swim in the event. The lone hold- out was Vincent who says he doesn't like the water.

Today, Swan Oyster Depot displays a dazzling, piscatorial textbook array of fresh fish and shellfish. It is delivered at six in the morning from purveyors, many of whom have supplied Swan's since the beginning. The 18-stool, white marble, counter is still there, topped with all the necessities—large bowls of oyster crackers, wedges of lemon, paper napkins, salt and pepper, grated horseradish and Tabasco. More than 30 other types of hot sauce are available for the committed connoisseur. A soda bottle with a single rose bud provides decoration every few feet. It is at this simple counter, in this freewheeling, confraternity, where those so inclined can enjoy a bowl of clam chowder, or their choice of dozens of shellfish cocktails or salads. Devotees drop by regularly during the Dungeness crab season for clam chowder and a beer, while waiting for one of the brothers to clean and crack a fine, sweet crab to be enjoyed later with a bottle of Sauvignon Blanc; a San Francisco ritual sustenance.

Clam Juice is a Secret Ingredient

One day recently a young couple sat at the counter. The young man, a Swan regular, ordered a bowl of clam chowder. "Yes Sir," responds brother Phil. "Know what the secret ingredient is in our clam chowder?" he asks.

"Clams," the young man responds as expected. Phil chuckles and says "What can I get you, Miss?" The lady would have a crab cocktail.

"Know what the true secret ingredient is in our red cocktail sauce?" he asks her. She shakes her head in an amused negative.

"Clam juice," he says. And indeed it is true. A spoonful of clam juice is added to the red cocktail sauce, a practice instituted by Salvatore, who got it from his father, who got it from....

Vincent discusses calamari salad, a popular item at Swan. "The recipe is 2,300 years old," he cracks. As rumbles of incredulity creep along the counter, he tells his story:

Swan Oyster Depot is a happy place to dine.
PHOTO: FRED LYON

"Back then there was a Greek coin with the imprint of a squid on one side and a stalk of celery on the other. Although the coin was legal tender, it was also an advertising medium and pushed local products. So our recipe came down through oral tradition. We got it from our grandmother who got it from her grandmother. We marinate the calamari in olive oil and wine vinegar. Then we add chopped celery, parsley and garlic and a little anchovy paste. Twenty-three-hundred years old," he adds slyly.

Old-World, Italian, Family Style

Swan Oyster Depot still operates at its original site on Polk Street. It is a San Francisco institution with few counterparts anywhere. Nearly three generations of San Franciscans have recognized its greatness.

The Sanciminos have brought a comfortable, old-world-Italian, family-style to Swan Oyster Depot. Today, anyone who walks in for a piece of fresh halibut or that elegant local sole called petrale, a cracked crab or a few slices of locally-smoked salmon, becomes "family" and is treated as such.

Vincent, who refers to himself as the Sancimino "Custodian of Memories," explains this. "We were always very close. We were a pack of wild kids and our father was strict with us. We were brought up with the philosophy that you must respect your family. He said 'To earn respect, you must give respect.'"

Brother Jim picks up the thread of the story: "Our father never laid a hand on us, but he would give us the stare—a cold fishy stare," he says, pleased with the fishy metaphor. "That stare meant we were in big trouble."

Early and strict family training has obviously paid off. Today the Sancimino brothers, indeed the entire shop, would appear to have been sealed in Saran Wrap back in the forties—in gentler, more polite and salubrious times—and unfolded today for our pleasure. May there never be a swan song for this San Francisco classic.

CHAPTER 47

CHARLES MINGUS AND
HIS BULLWHIP

In 1965 mercurial jazz bassist Charles Mingus played San Francisco's Jazz Workshop in North Beach. Mingus was in a mood. Between original pieces like "Fables of Faubus" and "Goodbye Porkpie Hat," he picked up his leather bullwhip and cracked it intermittently out over the heads of the worshipful but astonished audience. I was there.

KEYSTONE KORNER

One day I walked up Vallejo Street in North Beach. I was on my way to Central Station. I wanted to ask the cops about something I was planning to write about the old neighborhood. But being an Aries with a short attention span, I began thinking about other things. I passed Little Garden, a Chinese restaurant on Vallejo and the other things I started thinking about were a long-gone jazz club called Keystone Korner, and the jazz artists who played there back in the 1970s. So I dropped into Little Garden for pot stickers and to commune with the jazz ghosts.

Filthy McNasty

The first ghost who made an appearance was the great, hard bop pianist Horace Silver who died awhile back. In my mind's ear I could hear his jumpy, funky tune "Filthy McNasty." I knew Horace slightly because wherever he performed—if I happened to be within striking distance— you could find me listening to the Horace Silver Quintet. He finally got to recognize me in the audience. I not only heard Horace Silver at the Village Gate in New York's Greenwich Village and at the Monterey Jazz Festival, where I talked to him backstage, but I dropped in one night to hear him at Keystone Korner. He played some of his great stuff—"Song for my Father" (about his Cape Verde Islands, Afro-Portuguese father), "Sister Sadie" and "The Preacher." Between sets, he walked by my table, acknowledged me as a fan, sat down and I bought him a drink. I told him how much I enjoyed his music and he asked me what my favorite Horace Silver tune was. I replied "Filthy McNasty." He said he would play it in the next set. And he did—dedicating it to "my friend Filthy McErnie."

Freddie Freeloader

Ghost number two was Miles Davis.

One night I went to Keystone Korner to hear the mercurial Miles.

Miles Davis in Honolulu, 1988.
PHOTO: COURTESY OF RON HUDSON

Miles was not in a good mood that night. Was he ever in a good mood? Not in my presence, and I heard him play many times. He was a wonderful jazz artist but the word *prickly* was invented for him. Between sets at Keystone Korner I approached the man timidly and requested politely that in his next set could he please play "Freddie Freeloader"—from his great 1959 album *Kind of Blue.*

"Get lost," he said in his gravelly voice, and turned his back on me.

Over those pot stickers at Little Garden I thought I heard Miles playing "Freddie Freeloader," and just like last time I heard Miles say "get lost"—so I did.

———•◦•———

Maria Callas as Violetta in La Traviata, *1958.*
PHOTO: WIKIMEDIA COMMONS

CHAPTER 48

MARIA CALLAS AT HER FINEST

Following an audition for a role in a San Francisco Opera production, Gaetano Merola, general director of the world-acclaimed opera company for 30 seasons, told Maria Callas "You are young, Maria. Go and make your career in Italy and then I'll sign you up." Her reply was "After I make my career in Italy I will no longer need you." She never did sing with the San Francisco Opera. Years later in 1957, she was due to open the San Francisco Opera season. In the midst of cloying, celebrity adoration by social doyen Elsa Maxwell, and Greek shipping magnet Aristotle Onassis and others, she cancelled four days before the opening. At that point, the San Francisco Opera general director, Kurt Herbert Adler, became incensed and cancelled all of her appearances.

Ernest Beyl

FROM GIRLIE SHOWS TO OPERA

In the early days of San Francisco not all residents played the banjo and patronized the girlie shows. Doubtless there were Gold Rush miners and merchants who whistled Mozart's *Allegro* from *Eine Kleine Nachtmusik* or hummed Verdi's *Brindisi* from *La Traviata*.

While the performing arts were dominated by brothels and honky-tonks, it didn't take long for the largely male population of the small frontier town to begin patronizing productions of more classic offerings. By 1851 grand opera was being performed in San Francisco as theaters and opera houses sprang up, seemingly overnight. The first opera heard in San Francisco was Bellini's *Sonnambula* in 1851. By the 1906 earthquake and fire more than 5,000 grand opera performances had been presented in 26 San Francisco theaters. Touring companies included fast-growing San Francisco on their schedules. One, whose impresario was Maurice Grau, under contract to New York's Metropolitan Opera Company, played San Francisco on the eve of April 17, 1906. The Opera was Bizet's *Carmen*. The star was Enrico Caruso who sang the role of Don Jose. When the earthquake struck and the fire raged the next morning, Caruso, who had been staying at the Palace Hotel on Market Street, left San Francisco and never returned.

In the 1850s the art of the dance was represented by Lola Montez who did her famed spider dance (the spider was believed to be crawling about beneath her costume) and somewhat later by the free form, free thinking Isadora Duncan.

It is also recorded that in 1881 there existed a San Francisco Philharmonic Society and it presented a well-received series of concerts offering pops of the day and the occasional symphonic work by Mozart or Handel. Behind the baton was Gustav Henrich. The Philharmonic moved ahead in fits and starts until that famed April

Maestro Kurt Herbert Adler conducting the San Francisco Opera.
PHOTO: PHOTOGRAPHER UNKNOWN; PHOTO COURTESY OF SAN FRANCISCO OPERA ARCHIVES

1906 disaster and it wasn't until 1911 that symphonic music gained a foothold once more.

Such are the healthy roots of San Francisco's world-famed performing arts institutions of today. Today the San Francisco Opera is one of the world's premiere companies. It is the second oldest opera company in the U.S., second only to New York's Metropolitan which was founded in 1883. It is also the second largest, just behind the Met.

Proprietor Joe Mastrelli in Molinari.
PHOTO: AUTHOR'S COLLECTION

CHAPTER 49

THE SALAMI CHRONICLES

Molinari, San Francisco's classic, North Beach delicatessen, is the repository of literally dozens of cured delicatessen meats and from these its counter staff creates classic sandwiches on hard sourdough rolls. The glossary of these deli meats includes:

Coppa—*dry cured, Italian pork that comes in a sweet or hot variety.*

Cotechino—*finely ground pork, flavored with salt and spices, it is boiled before serving.*

Galantina—*a chopped ham luncheon meat flavored with pistachio nuts, garlic and a bit of Marsala wine.*

Mortadella—*finely ground cured pork, with some bits of pork fat and pistachio nuts.*

Pancetta—*Italian bacon made from pork belly, spiced with black pepper and salt cured.*

Pepperoni—*a small, slightly smoky sausage, made from cured pork and beef.*

Prosciutto—*Italian ham, hung and cured from several months to a couple of years.*

Salami—*pork and-or beef flavored with garlic, minced fat, white pepper and other spices, vinegar and wine. The salami is then hung in its casing to cure.*

Soppressata—*made from pig's head, tongue, and stomach.*

Zampino—*another finely chopped pork luncheon meat with a bit of veal for added flavor.*

MOLINARI: FROM ANTIPASTO TO ZAMPINO

Perhaps no other institution represents the heady essence of San Francisco's North Beach better than Molinari, the Italian delicatessen. It dates back to 1896 and has always been at the same hallowed site at the corner of Columbus and Vallejo.

Like s full-figured, bel canto diva, supremely confident in her ability to shatter a wineglass with her high C, it would not by amiss to suggest that Molinari reigns proudly as the quintessential symbol of North Beach.

The Molinaris and the Masttrellis

High profile, and usually so crowded that it's necessary to grab a numbered, paper tally, to be relinquished when your number is finally called. Molinari is the legacy of two Italian families—the Molinaris and the Mastrellis—both of Italy's Piedmonte region, high on the map's Italian-booted thigh. In the lineage of both families, can be found a great number of butchers, and sausage makers. The Molinari's immigrated to San Francisco in the mid-1800s and opened a sausage factory. In 1896 they opened the delicatessen at 373 Columbus Avenue, heart of the Italian community. Alfred Mastrelli came to the city in 1908, married a local Italian-American woman and gravitated to the specialty food business, eventually becoming a partner in another delicatessen. The Mastrellis joined the Molinaris and the two families made deli history. Side note: Joe DiMaggio included instructions in his will that his memorial service at nearby Saints Peter and Paul Church on Washington Square be catered by Molinari.

CHAPTER 50

SAN FRANCISCO OPEN YOUR GOLDEN GATE

San Francisco, open your Golden Gate
You let no stranger wait outside your door.
San Francisco, here is your wanderin' one
Saying I'll wander no more.
Other places only make me love you best.
Tell me you're the heart of all the golden west.
San Francisco, welcome me home again
I'm coming home to go roaming no more.

–Jeanette MacDonald
in the 1936 movie *San Francisco*

Ernest Beyl

A SYMPHONY FOR SAN FRANCISCO

In 1911, San Francisco had sufficiently recovered its equilibrium after the earthquake and fire, and a symphony orchestra was on the drawing boards. In December of that year the San Francisco Symphony gave its first concert. Henry Hadley, one of the foremost American composers of the time, was music director. There were 62 musicians in the orchestra—61 were male; the exception was the harpist. The orchestra received glowing reviews. Hadley left San Francisco in 1915 and the podium was turned over to Alfred Hertz, a German well acquainted with Wagner and Brahms who were represented on many of his programs. Hertz was no stranger to San Francisco. Earlier in 1906, he had conducted the orchestra for Caruso's performance in *Carmen*. When asked later to describe the earthquake, Hertz said it sounded "something comparable to the *mezzo forte* roll on a cymbal or gong."

Le Sacre du Printemps

Much later the famed French conductor Pierre Monteux came to San Francisco amidst great fanfare. Monteux had been the conductor of Igor Stravinsky's *Le Sacre du Printemps* for its uproarious Paris debut in 1913. Vaslev Nijinsky had choreographed the dance to Stravinsky's music for Sergei Diaghilev's Ballet Russe performance. The audience went wild—the Rite of Spring with young maidens sacrificed to the sun god, and all that. The music was described by one writer of the time as "Spring seen from the inside with its violence, its spasms and its fissions." That notoriety played well in San Francisco, a city that still recalled the glorious days of Isadora Duncan who, it was said, had influenced Nijinsky when she danced with him in Paris. In any event, San Francisco loved Pierre Monteux. He added the professionalism of a first-rate musical artist and a whiff of French sophistication with the *Le Sacre du Printemps* scandal. It wasn't

Patrons dancing in the lobby of the San Francisco Symphony.
PHOTO: FRED LYON

until 1939 that Monteux conducted the San Francisco Symphony in *Le Sacre du Printemps*. No scandal this time. The seasoned San Francisco audience had done its homework and wildly applauded the once-racy work. Invited by Monteux, Stravinsky himself conducted the San Francisco Symphony several times. In January 1942, amidst the patriotic fervor following Pearl Harbor, he led the symphony in his own orchestrated version of the *Star Spangled Banner*.

Frisco's Frenchman

Monteux's musical credentials were considerable. He had studied at the Paris Conservatory. He was a renowned violist. He had conducted for the New York's Metropolitan Opera for two seasons and for the Boston Symphony Orchestra from 1919 to 1924. Not only was he a consummate musician and student of the classics but he was a courtly, Gallic charmer. He had San Francisco music lovers vying for his attention at dinner parties and civic events. He was the perfect, central-casting version of the French maestro—mustachioed, roly-poly, jolly, he even had a French poodle named Fifi. When introduced to supper club singer Hildegarde who went by that one name only, he referred to her as "Miss Garde." Herb Caen, who reported the Hildegarde story as a three dot item, referred to Monteux as "Frisco's Frenchman." Whether or not you liked symphonic music, Pierre Monteux was your maestro.

Michael Tilson Thomas

Several other conductors followed. Michael Tilson Thomas assumed his role as the San Francisco Symphony's eleventh music director. Tilson Thomas had a strong relationship with the San Francisco Symphony dating back to 1974 when he conducted the orchestra in Mahler's *Symphony No. 9*. These Michael Tilson Thomas years have been exciting ones for the Symphony. Landmark recordings have been made, several Grammy Awards have been received, TV specials have been praised, tours have been highly successful. Under the baton of Tilson Thomas, who is still conductor as of this writing, the orchestra has ranged from time-tested, classic European works to purely American modernist productions. Honors have been heaped on the orchestra, its musical director, and on the leadership of its supporters and sponsors.

CHAPTER 51

CAPP'S CORNER:
IN CASE OF EMERGENCY

When San Francisco experienced what would later be called the Loma Prieta Earthquake in 1989 just as the cross-bay World Series was about to start between the Oakland Athletics and the San Francisco Giants, I was at home on Telegraph Hill preparing to watch the game. My building shook violently but there was no real damage to my apartment. After an uneasy night, the next morning I walked down to Capp's Corner at Powell and Green streets. It was open and a bunch of us had Bloody Marys and told earthquake stories. On the wall above the door at Capp's Corner was a large sign that read:

EMERGENCY INSTRUCTIONS:

1. **GRAB YOUR COAT AND GET YOUR HAT**

2. **LEAVE YOUR WORRIES ON THE DOORSTEP**

3. **JUST DIRECT YOUR FEET TO THE SUNNY SIDE OF THE STREET**

And that began my love affair with the now-closed joint, Capp's Corner.

THE SAUERKRAUT KID

Schroeder's, one of the oldest San Francisco restaurants—it was established in 1893—has reopened after undergoing some sensitive renovations. They were sensitive because you don't want to mess too much with a good thing. And Schroeder's was—and still is—a very good thing. So the Sauerkraut Kid decided to check it out.

As you may have guessed, your author is the Sauerkraut Kid. That's the nickname my father gave me when he began taking me to Schroeder's in 1940 or thereabouts. I think I was about 12. Even as a kid I liked sauerkraut. But I liked it most with large hunks of pork loin or with one of the sausages or *wursts* like *Bratwurst*. Sometimes, when I wasn't the Sauerkraut Kid, my Dad called me the *Wurst* Kid. He thought that was funny.

The Best of the Wursts

There are a lot of *wursts*—not all of these are served at Schroeder's—so if you are not a *wurst* person you may want to turn the page right now. We are about to get esoteric.

Consider: *Augbergerwurst, Bauernwurst, Blutwurst, Bockwurst, Bratwurst, Gehrinwurst, Kalbsgekrosewurst, Kartoffelwurst, Konigswurst, Knackwurst, Knoblauchwurst, Mettwurst, Nurnburgerwurst, Polnischwurst, Rindfleischkohwurst, Rotwurst, Weisswurst or Zungenwurst*—all strong-flavored, full of character and designed for hearty eaters.

My father and I had a thing about restaurants. We frequented the Cliff House for New England-style clam chowder, Original Joes (the old one on Taylor) for beef stew or spaghetti and meatballs, and on special occasions, the Garden Court of the Palace Hotel for the elaborate Palace Court Salad. I still remember it: artichoke hearts, tomatoes, shredded lettuce, hardboiled eggs, Dungeness crab and either Louie or the famous Green Goddess Dressing.

When we went to the Garden Court we dressed up because it was a fancy place, and my mother was always with us.

Schroeder's was a Guy Joint

When we went to Schroeder's my mother didn't join us because women were not allowed then. It was a guy joint until 1970. Not realizing we were insensitive males—this was considerably before insensitive maleness—we happily went to Schroeder's, 240 Front Street—that's where it's still located—for sauerkraut, *wurst* of course, *weiner schnitzel* and copious steins of German beer. At least my father had copious steins of beer. Our white-aproned waiter poured me a stein of Coca-Cola. The stein, with a lid on it, made my day.

Other Old Time San Francisco Restaurants

As I said, Schroeder's was established in 1893 making it one of the oldest restaurants in San Francisco. Other old-timers, you will recall are Tadich Grill, 240 California Street, which dates its founding to 1849 when it started out as a street stand. Then there's the Old Clam House, 299 Bayshore Boulevard, which opened in 1861, Sam's Grill, 344 Bush Street, 1867, and Fior D' Italia, 2237 Mason Street, 1886.

German Beer and Sauerkraut

Here's a fast history of Schroeder's: Henry and John Schroeder, whose father had come to San Francisco from the Prussian Provence of Hanover in 1861, first opened their restaurant at 1346 Market Street between First and Second. It was destroyed in the great earthquake and fire of 1906. A few years later it reopened at 117 Front Street. Then in 1921 the Schroeders sold it to Max Kniesche, also from Prussia, and in 1959 Kniesche moved it to the present 240 Front Street location. In 1997 Stefan and Jana Filipcik bought the historic spot and more recently it was sold to Andy Chun and Jan Wiginton who also operate the Press Club in the Financial District. The new "German-inspired" cuisine is under the direction of Chef Manfred Wrembel who is of German descent. And that should do it for this history lesson.

My father—an Alsatian who knew a thing or two about German food—isn't with us anymore and neither is the old Schroeder's. But the new Schroeder's attracted me and I raised a cold glass of a powerful, nearly black, *Schneider Aventinus Weizenbock* (a German lager), to my father. Then I checked out the bratwurst and sauerkraut, both house made and both excellent. The sauerkraut was crunchy and mellow, not limp and sour. My companion and I decided to share, which was wise. She ordered potato pancakes. They were topped with a bit of smoked trout, crème fraiche, capers and threads of mild horseradish. It was a new take on potato pancakes but she enjoyed it.

Here are a few last words on sauerkraut from the Sauerkraut Kid. If you don't like it—and I realize it has its detractors—I think I know why. It's sour. Sauerkraut needs to be rinsed with cold water and drained several times before it is prepared. There are many simple sauerkraut recipes. So cook up some with a few hot dogs if you can't find a proper *wurst*. Pour a stein of German beer and propose a toast to the old, and the new, Schroeder's. *Prost!*

CHAPTER 52

A CHINATOWN JOOK JOINT

One of the oldest restaurants in San Francisco's Chinatown— Sam Wo—took great pride in featuring "the rudest waiter in the world." His name was Edsel Ford Fung—at least he said it was. Sam Wo was founded in 1912. The original site was on Washington Street in a narrow three story structure. Over the years it catered to San Franciscans and tourists alike. In the fifties it was popular with the Beats and was open until 3 a.m. Diners entered through the kitchen and took a narrow winding staircase up to rooms on the second or third floors. Orders were delivered from the kitchen by dumbwaiter. Food orders were basic Chinese—won ton soup, jook (a rice porridge also known as congee), a few noodle dishes and what-have-you. Sam Wo closed in 2012 for various health and safety violations, but reopened on Clay Street in Chinatown. The menu was upgraded as were the prices. The new place even has a dumbwaiter to deliver food. What made the old place so popular? Two elements—the dumbwaiter delivery in the narrow building, and the rude waiter whose welcoming line was usually "Sit down and shut up."

EDSEL FORD FUNG AND ZEPPELIN WONG

E dsel Ford Fung, who died in 1984, was the son of the owner of Sam Wo, the Chinatown restaurant well-known for having the rudest waiter in the world. Edsel Ford Fung was that waiter. His name was really Edsel Fung but adopting the name Edsel Ford was too good to pass up. You will recall that the Ford Motor Company came out with a dog of an automobile in 1957 and named it the Edsel after the son and only child of Henry Ford. Yes, that Henry Ford who developed the Ford Motor Company and built the Model-T Ford about which Henry said "You can have it in any color you want—as long as it's black." Before settling on the name Edsel for the automobile, the company asked poet Marianne Moore to come up with a name. She did—Utopian Turtletop.

But back to our notable waiter, his deportment and his famous one-liners: If a customer took too long perusing the food-spotted menu, Edsel Ford Fung would cry out "What is this, a library?" He was also famous for insisting that customers clean their own tables and for making passes at women customers.

Now, on to my friend Zeppelin Wong—this San Francisco lawyer's first name really is Zeppelin. You can check his birth certificate.

In 1929 the German dirigible, Graf Zeppelin, became the first lighter-than-air craft to circle the globe. On August 25 it made several dramatic passes over San Francisco. The Wong family who lived in Chinatown witnessed this. A week later, September 1, a male baby was born and its mother named him Zeppelin Wai Wong. The young man went on to attend Stanford University and become a lawyer. He also owned a restaurant but was never rude to customers.

CHAPTER 53

SAINT JOHN COLTRANE

Jazz giant John Coltrane, known for his almost mind-altering tenor saxophone "sheets of sound," was once asked by a journalist in Japan what he would like to be in five years. Coltrane replied "A saint." And that's just what happened. In 1964 he recorded "A Love Supreme" while he was studying Christian and various Eastern religions. The music became more and more spiritual and avant-garde—"Ascension," "Om," and "Meditations." He became addicted to heroin, quit cold turkey and died of a liver ailment in 1967. Following his death, his deification took place in a storefront church in San Francisco's Fillmore district. It was called The John Will-I-am Coltrane African Orthodox Church. John Coltrane is considered a patron saint. The last time he played in San Francisco was in 1966 at the Jazz Workshop in North Beach. In 2014 on the 50th anniversary of his landmark recording "A Love Supreme," SFJAZZ, the city's cultural gift to this indigenous art form, held a week-long, John Coltrane symposium to discuss the importance of the artist and perform his works.

Charles Lloyd.
PHOTO: FROM THE COLLECTION OF CHARLES LLOYD AND DOROTHY DARR

REACHING FOR THE STARS
WITH CHARLES LLOYD

I first met Charles Lloyd in the 1960s. Columbia records A&R man, George Avakian, got us together when I was the publicity director for the Monterey Jazz Festival. I didn't realize it at that first meeting at the San Francisco nightclub El Matador, that the tall, skinny, bespectacled saxophonist and flutist would become a dominant figure in my appreciation of the musical culture of my time. But that's what happened. And over a period of 50 years, Charles and I moved from being casual acquaintances to being close friends.

Lloyd, of mixed ancestry that includes African, American Indian, Mongolian and Irish, was born in Memphis and absorbed the sounds of the city—gospel, blues and jazz—and hung out with famous inhabitants like pianist Phineas Newborn Jr., and trumpet player Booker Little. Through Booker Little he met and was able to play with fellow saxophonist Frank Strozier and pianist Harold Maben. As a youngster Lloyd was already playing his horn as a sideman for Bobby "Blue" Bland, Howlin' Wolf and B.B. King.

A Young Man with a Bartok Bent

He had a wide range of musical interests even then and followed so-called classical music avidly. One passion was the music of Hungarian composer, Bela Bartok. That set Lloyd off on musical tracks that have lasted to this day. Bartok was a seeker whose music could be stormy, sentimental and thematic, with tonal or atonal whispers, shrieks and roars. To me that is also a description of the current state of Charles Lloyd's music. But I'm leaping ahead here.

In 1956 Lloyd departed Memphis for Los Angeles and enrolled in the University of Southern California to study for a master's degree in music which he gained in 1960. One of his professors was Halsey Stevens, a leading authority on the music of Bartok.

Playing with the radical Jazz Performers

But while studying Bartok by day, Lloyd was schooling himself by night in on-the-job training with some of the most radical jazz performers of the day—Ornette Coleman, Don Cherry, Billy Higgins, Eric Dolphy, and Scott LaFaro. He also played for a while in the Gerald Wilson band and in 1960 became musical director for an adventurous Chico Hamilton band. Soon he was composing and arranging some of Hamilton's best recorded work. "Passing Through" and "Man from Two Worlds" on Impulse are considered classics today.

In 1964 Lloyd joined the Cannonball Adderley Sextet for a couple of years and then struck out on his own and was signed by Columbia. Two of his albums were highly significant—"Of Course, Of Course" and "Discovery." They displayed a confident, young musician, leading his own small band in music that was perhaps ahead of its time. But it was Lloyd's next brainstorm that went on to make jazz history. He formed a quartet with pianist Keith Jarrett, drummer Jack DeJohnette, and bassist Cecil McBee.

Charles Lloyd the Dream Weaver

It was then that the Columbia A&R man George Avakian opened my ears and turned me on to the Charles Lloyd sound and thereby gave me a new musical direction. I was smitten by the groups' initial recording "Dream Weaver." To me Lloyd was a dream weaver, sinuously getting into my head. But it was "Forest Flower: Live at Monterey" that rocketed Lloyd on a trajectory that broke new ground. It was the first jazz album to sell more than a million copies. I got on board big time.

Soon the Charles Lloyd Quartet was playing Bill Graham's famed Fillmore Auditorium and Chet Helms's Avalon Ballroom in San Francisco. Lloyd, Jarrett, DeJohnette and McBee (later Ron McClure), and their acoustic, avant-garde improvisation—with Lloyd's saxophone grinding and screeching one minute, and smooth and insinuating the next—had crossed over. It was psychedelic with a jazz twist. He began appearing on rock venue bills with Jimi Hendrix, the Grateful Dead,

Jefferson Airplane, Janis Joplin and her band Big Brother and the Holding Company, and Paul Butterfield and his Blues Band.

Charles and Janis at the Avalon

By this time I was actively promoting the Charles Lloyd Quartet and following it like a rock groupie. I even went to New York to hear the group play Town Hall. And I turned on my two young sons—Mike, then 14 and Jeff, 12—on to Charles Lloyd. Mike later became a recording sound engineer. Jeff plays jazz, blues, rock, and even classic guitar.

One San Francisco night back in those heady times, I took my youngsters to the Avalon Ballroom. The Charles Lloyd Quartet was on the bill. We were admitted to the so-called Green Room backstage to hang out with my idol. Lloyd was gracious and welcomed my sons. Just before he was to go onstage he said he was thirsty and wanted a glass of water. I turned and asked a young woman standing behind me if she would mind getting Charles a glass of water. No problem. She returned in a moment. It was Janis Joplin. Her band Big Brother and the Holding Company was also on the bill that night. No one found it a bit unusual that an acoustic jazz group was on the same bill as a blues-rock band. And Janis Joplin didn't find it strange to get a glass of water for a fellow artist.

The Big Sur Years

Charles Lloyd took a break early in the 1970s, stopped performing on a regular basis, and moved to Big Sur as many other artists had before him: Robinson Jeffers, Henry Miller, and Lawrence Ferlinghetti. It was a long break—about ten years—and Charles only rarely came out of hibernation to join studio gigs with such diverse groups as the Beach Boys, Canned Heat, and the Doors. He resurfaced in the early 80s performing even more strongly than before.

The Spiritual Mystic

Charles Lloyd is a very spiritual man. He is enlightened and I view him as an enchanted mystic, a sort of shaman. In my judgment, he fronts the best, small jazz ensemble working today. It features a rotating group of top musicians who find working with Lloyd to be invigorating and challenging. Towering musical artists themselves, like pianists Jason Moran and Gerald Clayton, drummer Eric Harland, and bassist Reuben Rogers, or some combination of those excellent musicians. The point is, Charles Lloyd has such stature as a musical giant that he attracts major performers, much in the fashion of Woody Allen, who attracts some of the leading actors of our time.

Wild Man Dance Suite

Lloyd maintains a grueling schedule. He is constantly on the move because he is constantly in demand. He performs at concerts and festivals not only in the U.S., but also abroad. As I write this, his 2015 touring schedule reads like the timetable for some mad, peripatetic travel writer. Certainly a highlight of Lloyd's 2015 tour was his performance of "Wild Man Dance Suite" in the New York Metropolitan Museum's Temple of Dendur. The "Wild Man Dance Suite" is a thematic, sometimes mournful, sometimes savage, sometimes lyrical tour de force in Lloyd's spiritual oeuvre. For the work, Charles employed a sextet format that included Sokratis Sinopoulos on the lyra and Miklos Lukacs on cymbalom—not your usual instrumentation for a jazz sextet.

The Charles Lloyd Legacy

The 2015 leaping and bounding around the world also included the New Orleans Jazz Festival (Lloyd has never forgotten his Memphis roots), and dates in Umbria, Ghent, Cologne, Augsburg, Lodz, St. Moritz, Bordeaux, Baku (Azerbaija)—and his hometown Memphis. He spent his 77th birthday, March 15, performing at the 80th anniversary of New York's seminal jazz club, the Village Vanguard.

What is the Charles Lloyd legacy? His work anticipated so-called world music, the fusion movement and the rock/jazz hybrid bands. He set the stage for other jazz artists (including Miles Davis) to stretch the limits of jazz to the breaking point with psychedelic musings. And finally, Charles Lloyd's music swings for the heavens in a mystical manner. In a sense he is a mystic. His spiritual aesthetic, a result of transcendental meditation, and his calm demeanor, bursts open in an almost cosmic fashion. It is wild abandon, contrasted with tight ensemble work.

One day here in San Francisco my son Jeff and I had lunch with Charles and his wife, Dorothy Darr. Later he asked us to visit his quarters at the Fairmont Hotel so he could play us excerpts from recent concerts. At one point he turned up the volume on the computer and played a bit of the recreated "Forest Flower" from his 2014 performance at the Monterey Jazz Festival. Charles looked at us with a quizzical look—as much as saying "Well?"

Jeff looked at him and said "You were reaching for the stars."

Jazz is a free-fall art form to which certain artists abandon themselves. Once in a while one of these artists hits an updraft and soars to the stars. Charles Lloyd is such an artist—always reaching for the stars. And frequently colliding with them.

CHAPTER 54

M.F.K. FISHER AND THE ART OF EATING

Almost everyone who writes about food wishes they could write like M.F.K. Fisher, the voluptuary of prose, a sensualist once described by John Updike as "a poet of the appetites." Here is my favorite M.F.K. Fisher quote: "First we eat, then we do everything else." She died in 1992.

NARSAI DAVID'S SAN FRANCISCO CULINARY PERSPECTIVE: TODAY AND IN THE FUTURE

Several years ago I conceived the idea of writing about what I called "Unlikely Heroes and Heroines in the Gastronomic Trenches." I published several essays in the *Marina Times* under that headline and readers seemed to like the series. Some of those unlikely heroes and heroines were *The New Yorker* writers Calvin Trillin and A. J. Liebling, *New York Times* trencherman Johnny Apple who traveled the world dining at his favorite restaurants then writing about the experiences, celebrated St. Francis Hotel celebrity chef Victor Hirtzler, Gertrude Stein's buddy and lover Alice B. Toklas, Gael Greene, the restaurant critic I called "The Insatiable Gourmet," and an African-American freed slave, Mrs. Abby Fisher, who journeyed west to San Francisco after the Civil War and became a prominent cook, caterer, and cookbook author.

Now I'm raising the flag to another gastronomic hero. He is David, who went from soda jerk to caterer for rock stars (including the Rolling Stones), to chef-restaurateur and gourmet guru who played a leading role in the evolution of California Cuisine. His imprint on the San Francisco Bay Area dining scene has been significant and exceptional.

Assyrian Refugees

Narsai was a son of Assyrian immigrants. His father, Michael Khanno David, was born in a mountain village in Southeast Turkey, his mother, Shulamith Sayad, in Northwest Iran. Their families were refugees escaping from Turkey and Iran to avoid the persecution of Christians during World War I. It was referred to as the Ottoman Genocide. Narsai's father was born in 1888 and immigrated to the U.S. in 1912 when he was 24 years old. His mother immigrated in 1918 when she was 13. She was born in 1905.

"The Assyrians were a minority people with no country of their own," Narsai recalls.   Both families settled in the American Midwest where there were many Assyrian immigrants. Narsai's parents met socially and later married. Narsai was born in South Bend, Indiana, just a short distance from Chicago where they soon moved. Narsai's father worked in his uncle's Oriental rug business there. When Narsai was eleven years old the family moved to Turlock, California, a Central Valley community where many Assyrians had settled in a search for a region reminding them of their homeland—where they could grow grapes and walnuts and enjoy the warm weather.

Narsai the Soda Jerk

Young Narsai David grew up with a good appetite. He loved food and its preparation. Many years later he said, "If my mother had had a daughter, there's a good chance I would never have ended up in the food business, because the daughter would have been in the kitchen helping my mother. But she had three sons and we all helped her and all grew to love preparing our meals."

As a youth Narsai also worked in the agricultural fields around Turlock harvesting onions. "It was stoop-labor and it was very hard work, but I loved the onions—those big red ones." In his senior high school year he avoided the stoop-labor of the fields by working as a cooks' helper in a drive-in restaurant. He found that more to his liking. Then when he left home at 16 and moved to Berkeley to enter the University of California, he applied for part-time work as a fry cook at a nearby drive-in restaurant. He was hired—but as a soda jerk.

The Potluck Restaurant

After a couple of years as a math major, Narsai left the University and looked for work. He did brief stints in plastic manufacturing and in the printing business. Then he sought a job in a restaurant. The food business had become a passion with him and he found a post as relief bartender in the Potluck Restaurant in Berkeley. The Potluck was started

Narsai David.
PHOTO: COURTESY OF NARSAI DAVID

by Ed Brown in 1954 at the foot of University Avenue next to the Southern Pacific railroad station. It was the first truly French style bistro in
Berkeley. Diners literally took "potluck" as the menu changed constantly.
It moved to Channing and San Pablo in 1958, with a full menu and wine
list. But Narsai's restaurant career was interrupted by six month active
duty in the U.S. Army Reserve. When he got out of the service he went
back to the Potluck and was offered the job as the restaurant's manager.
Narsai's involvement with the Potluck turned out to be a defining
experience for him. "It changed the course of my life," he said recently.

The Potluck started what it called its Monday Night Dinners.
"Each Monday we featured the cuisine from a different country—
France, Italy, Germany and so on. Our Monday Night Dinners caused
a sensation among diners in Berkeley—students and young people
especially. Everything was fresh and seasonal. We designed our meals
around what was available. Most of our ingredients were sourced
locally and we even began foraging. I can remember harvesting fresh
mussels in the wild," Narsai told me.

A Forerunner of California Cuisine

He went on: "The Potluck has been gone many years now, but I
think we should remember it as a forerunner to what eventually be-

came known as California Cuisine. Three things stand out in my mind as distinctions about the Potluck. First, we were providing really tasty food and very fair prices with some European simplicity and flair. Second was our development of a California wine list at a time when French wines dominated the market. And third, for our Monday Night Dinners, we went to tremendous effort to emulate the best cuisine from the country we chose to highlight. And everything was fresh. I don't mean fresh-frozen. I mean fresh," Narsai said.

In 1970 Narsai left the Potluck Restaurant and started putting together his own business. Catering came first because he was able to rent space in a commercial kitchen.

Narsai David and Bill Graham

At first Narsai's catering business was quite informal. One of his first clients was a young Jewish refugee from Europe, Wulf Granjonca, who had taken the name named Bill Graham. The young man was hired by Ronnie Davis to help promote the San Francisco Mime Troupe, a group that performed political satire in San Francisco parks at no cost to the crowds that flocked to its events. Graham decided to hold a fund raiser for the frequently-broke Mime Troupe. It would be a rock 'n' roll concert, and healthy-living Graham asked Narsai to provide old-fashioned bushels of apples that the young concert-goers could pick up free and munch on during the show.

Soon Narsai was in charge of all of Graham's catering for the artists who were backstage at the Fillmore Auditorium and Winterland waiting to perform—including, for example, the Rolling Stones.

"That was the beginning," Narsai recalls. But after a while, he was catering not only for Bill Graham, but parties for people like Janis Joplin. Then along came full banquet catering for Charles Hitch, president for the University of California, Tom Clausen, president of the Bank of America, and others from academic and corporate America. "But Bill Graham occupied a lot of my attention and I did major events for him in San Francisco and elsewhere," Narsai remembers.

The Band, with Bob Dylan and guests, during "I Shall Be Released."
PHOTO: DAVID GANS; FLICKR.COM//54178245@N00

The Band and the Last Waltz

"I think the biggest job I did for Bill was to cater 3000 Thanksgiving turkey dinners for the final performance of the famous group called The Band. It was a dance at Winterland in San Francisco and was billed as 'The Last Waltz'—one of the most famous rock concerts in history. Bill insisted on whole, fresh turkeys, roasted and carved for the kids to eat. We gave them complete Thanksgiving turkey dinners—turkey, stuffing, cranberry sauce, sweet potatoes, the whole works. What a thrill that was."

Narsai's Restaurant

Then in 1972 Narsai the caterer added to his list of accomplishments and became a restaurateur. He opened Narsai's in the East Bay community of Kensington. Quickly it became a leading gastronomic center for those who craved fine and unusual dining. Its simple but hospitable dining room—built around a giant redwood cask—was something new in the area and so was the food Narsai and his staff prepared. Centerpiece for the restaurant's fame was its Monday Night Dinners that offered a fixed menu and featured dishes from various cuisines that had captured Narsai's imagination. It was a tip of Narsai's hat to the Potluck. The Monday Night Dinners at Narsai's became famous. Reservations were in great demand. These unusual dinners were accompanied by wines from Narsai's 1,500-bottle cellar that the *New York Times* described as one of the ten best collections of wine in the world.

Then in 1978 he opened Narsai's Market, next to the restaurant, for his own line of specialty food items that included a unique French-spined baguette called *Epine* as one of the regular bread items, as well as croissants and desserts. During this time Narsai kept his catering business alive. He continued providing service to Bill Graham, for example, but also catered various special events, one for the British Royal Family on a San Francisco visit.

Narsai closed his restaurant in 1985, not because of lack of business or his lack of interest in hospitality or food service, but because he was becoming swamped with new fields to conquer. He soon excelled in a media career that over the years included a radio show in San Francisco called "The KCBS Kitchen," a TV spot as resident chef on KPIX-TV, then later on KTVU-TV, weekly guest chef on "Over Easy," hosted by Hugh Downs and Mary Martin on PBS, and a PBS series "Cook Off America" that highlighted regional cuisine around the country. He wrote a column for the *San Francisco Chronicle* called "California Cuisine" and became the San Francisco Macy's department store "Culinary Expert" and hosted cooking demonstrations every Saturday. He took time to write a couple of books—*Monday Night at Narsai's*, and *The Menu: A Guide to the Top 200 Restaurants in the San Francisco Bay Area*. In July 2016 he was named to the San Francisco Radio Hall of Fame.

Narsai on Cooking and Dining Trends and Styles

In a recent, far-reaching discussion Narsai commented at length on present cooking and dining trends and styles. His remarks are pertinent and thought provoking.

The Arts and Crafts of Chefs Today: "The degree to which chefs are behaving now is fascinating. Some of it, I'm excited about. But I have to say, some of it is getting a little bit over the top. I find myself thinking—but do I want to eat it? Yes, it's wonderful that you are nourishing my soul and it's wonderful that it (my plated food) looks elegant enough to make a permanent painting that you could put on the wall. But at this moment I'm anxious to get this food into my mouth. When I see, time and again, photos in the press of a chef using a pair of tweezers to put a couple of leaves of microgreen in a particular position, it seem his entire job in the kitchen is to garnish with tweezers, I worry that we have gone too far. Do I want the next generation of chefs to behave like artists painting a picture? We need to recognize the difference between what an artist does and what a chef does. An artist makes a painting or a sculpture and it's completed and that's his statement. But the chef is preparing something transitory and is serving it at the table to feed you. It's not just for you to look at. It may be a little too precious and this worries me."

Chefs Burdened by Tradition: "I like to separate chefs into two camps—those burdened by tradition as to how food should be prepared, and those open to fresh ideas. Let me give you an example: You don't find too many French chefs who will use ginger in their everyday cooking. I'm talking about fresh ginger, not the powdered kind which more traditional chefs are using. But here in California many of chefs have been influenced by the cuisines of Pacific Islanders and by the Japanese. And they find fresh ginger, not just a spice but a component. There is an openness that chefs in California display and that is a good thing."

Revolutionary Cuisines for the Sake of Revolution: These days there's a lot of talk and excitement about so-called revolutionary cuisines. There are some mad-scientist chefs who are using liquid nitrogen as a method to freeze something and change its physical characteristic. Yes, there are some exciting things these guys do. But I question how nourishing and deeply satisfying this food is. And, isn't that what eating is all about—to be nourishing and satisfying?"

Narsai in Relaxation

These days Narsai David, 80-years-old as I write this, is enjoying producing fine Napa Valley, Narsai David Estates wines, and involving himself with charitable projects—an activity he has pursued most of his life. For years he's been active as a benefactor of the Berkeley Repertory Theater. He's enjoying fine meals, travel and companionship with Veni, his wife of 52 years, and helping his son Daniel, whose Kensington-based Grizzly Peak Press has published the book you are now reading. Narsai in repose is almost as active as when he was a top San Francisco Bay Area restaurateur.

Narsai and California Cuisine

So what will be the Narsai David legacy? In a series of conversations conducted in 2011-2012 by now-retired Vic Geraci, food and wine historian for the Oral History Center, The Bancroft Library, University of California, Berkeley 2013. Narsai was quoted on the subject of California Cuisine:

"I think—Alice Waters, Jeremiah Tower, Joyce Goldstein, Paul Bertolli, Deborah Madison and others—(and, this writer adds Narsai David) deservedly get credit for what is now known around the world as California Cuisine. Its nexus was Berkeley, that free-spirited, open-to-all ideas, university town.

"As I recall, the phrase 'California Cuisine' was first used by Caroline Bates in *Gourmet Magazine.* I discussed this once with Alice Waters and Joyce Goldstein at Chez Panisse. None of us had any idea of what was California Cuisine. We were just using the ingredients that we wanted to use and we put together things that were fun. What we developed—and Alice became a major figure in this when she opened Chez Panisse in Berkeley in 1971—depended a lot of our geographic location. We were centered between the greatest wine growing areas in the country—Napa, Sonoma and Mendocino to the North, Livermore to the East, and the Santa Clara Valley and the Monterey area to the South—and with an audience wide open to new ideas," Narsai recalls.

No one realized at the time that they were starting a food revolution with its emphasis on fresh, locally grown and foraged foods, prepared simply.

The San Francisco Bay Area takes the pleasures of the table very seriously. And no one takes these pleasures more seriously than Narsai David.

———•••———

CHAPTER 55

THE WORLD'S BEST SANDWICH

When I was a kid I created a sandwich that I believed then to be the best in the world. After all these years I still stick to that assessment. This is not a fancy sandwich—a flakey croissant, perhaps, stuffed with foie gras, baby lettuces and maybe a dash of balsamic vinegar, nor a mile high Dagwood for those of you who remember the Blondie comic strip. This is a no nonsense sandwich. I think the British statesman, Lord John Montagu, the 4th Earl of Sandwich, who is credited with inventing the genre in the 1700s, would like this one. So, here it is—the world's best sandwich. First, get two slices of white, foamy commercial bread. When I was a kid I discovered that a popular baker's brand called Wonder Bread was best for my sandwich. Now, smear one side of both slices of that bread with mayonnaise right from the jar. You don't have to get fancy and make your own mayonnaise for this. Best Foods or Hellman's or whatever works for you is just fine. Now you need a large, ripe tomato. I mean large and I mean ripe. Avoid those pale pink, hard-as-a-rock bocce balls frequently being passed off as tomatoes. Get your tomatoes from a good farmer's market or from your mother's garden. That's what I did when I was a hungry youth. Slice that big red baby into four, maybe six, round hunks.

Now put half the sliced tomato on one side of the bread and half on the other—right over the mayonnaise. Salt and pepper the tomato and be lavish about it. Now you are ready for the onion. Locate a large, white or yellow or purple onion—a good heavy one that will make a thick slice of about the same size as the bread and tomato slices. The onion slice should be about one eighth to one quarter of an inch thick. Place that onion slice between the two tomato-topped pieces of bread so you have a slice of bread, slice of tomato, slice of onion, slice of tomato and finally a slice of bread. Place this sandwich on a large round plate. A platter works even better. Handle the sandwich carefully. You don't want a lot of your mayonnaise to squirt out. Now get a stool from your kitchen, a thick towel and a roll of paper towels—an entire roll please. You're going to need it. Take all of the above out into your backyard or your driveway or your sidewalk. Sit on the stool. Spread the towel over your lap. Place the roll of paper towels at your feet. Place the plate or platter with your tomato-onion sandwich across your towel-covered knees. Pick up your sandwich gently in both fists. Prop your elbows on your spread knees. Lean forward and open your mouth as wide as you can. Insert the sandwich and bite. That's all there is to it. You will find that mayonnaise and tomato juice will drip down your arms. That's okay. Enough of this will get into your mouth. I should have reminded you to wear a T-shirt.

HARD TIMES BUT GOOD TIMES

Boom and bust is not unknown to San Franciscans. The bursting of the Dot Com bubble in 2000 was a shock to me. I suppose it shouldn't have been. Remember those Super Bowl ads that featured upstart companies with funny names, seemingly without products? And, of course, there are those who are predicting the present tech bubble to burst. But my job here is not to predict but to recall. Today I'd like to recall hard times, but good times here in San Francisco during the Great Depression of the 1930s. This is what I remember or was told by family members.

Black Tuesday 1929

I was born in Fresno in 1928. My mother, father and I moved to San Francisco—with me in a basket—later that same year. We made the trip in my father's 1922 Willy's Knight Country Club Phaeton, a very fancy car. My father bought it used, but he never admitted how much he paid for it. He had a good job in the kitchen of a Fresno hotel. Later, through a chef named Victor Hirtzler from his hometown, Strasbourg in Alsace, my father got a job as a cook in San Francisco's St. Francis Hotel.

A year later, with my father firmly ensconced as a cook at the St. Francis, my family was already starting to think about the year-end holidays—Thanksgiving turkey with all the trimmings, food to serve friends, gifts to give, a Christmas tree. Optimism abounded. It was a time of easy credit and installment buying. Then on Black Tuesday, October 29, 1929, the Stock Market crashed and sent everything spinning downward. Banks closed, credit dried up. (In 1931 a scholarly book came out with the title: *Can Governments Cure Unemployment?* We are still asking that question aren't we?)

The exuberant hurly burly that was San Francisco stuttered to a crawl. It seemed everyone was out of work. My father however retained his job. He sold the fancy Phaeton—"for peanuts" he told me many years later.

Life on the Cheap

We lived in a rented flat out on Turk Street, almost to the Pacific Ocean. Across the street were sand dunes. In a few years I had a paper route. I delivered the old *San Francisco Examiner*. Then a bit later I also sold donuts door-to-door. That was tough. My family ate a lot of donuts.

Actually, we ate quite well in those days. There was not much meat. Fish was cheap. We ate a lot of soup—split pea, lentil, vegetable soup. Occasionally we went out to dinner, usually to Original Joe's that opened in the Tenderloin in 1937. You could get what we then called "a good square meal" for a buck or two. Sometimes we ate at Lucca's the Italian, family-style place at Powell and Francisco in North Beach. It had a sign—"All you can eat for 50 Cents."

Out of Work

Yes, there were periods when my Dad was out of work. But the family hung together and looked forward to better times. There was work to be had if you didn't mind heights. Construction began on the San Francisco-Oakland Bay Bridge in 1933. That bridge was completed in 1936. The Golden Gate Bridge was begun in 1933 and completed in 1937.

Some artists got jobs through the Public Works of Art Project, a federal government "New Deal" program. They painted frescoed murals on the interior of Coit Tower which was completed in 1933. Another federal program putting people back to work was called the W.P.A. (Works Projects Administration).

As a kid, I didn't really know we were in hard times. I wasn't necessarily depressed by the Depression. But I could always tell when my father had lost his job even though it wasn't discussed with me. He loved to swim and, if during weekdays, he took me by streetcar out to Land's End at Point Lobos to swim at nearby Sutro Baths, the massive, glass-enclosed Victorian amusement center that featured several heated saltwater tanks—my father was out of work.

The All American Boy

Although prohibition ended in 1933, my mother and father—not big drinkers—didn't take advantage of it. Hanging out in bars wasn't their thing. But there was other entertainment. We played Monopoly and got a jolt from dealing with the play money.

And we listened to our radio, a large wooden table top model that ran on vacuum tubes and resembled the doorway of a medieval cathedral. We gathered around it and listened to serials The Romance of Helen Trent ("…the real life drama of Helen Trent, who, when life mocks her, breaks her hopes, dashes her against the rocks of despair, fights back bravely…"), or Jack Armstrong, the All-American Boy. Other radio favorites in those lean days were Jack Benny, Fibber McGee and Molly and One Man's Family, a story about a well-off family who lived in Seacliff overlooking the Golden Gate—a different world from my Turk Street world.

Time on My Hands

A popular Tin Pan Alley tune of the day was "Time On My Hands," sung by Rudy Vallee. In 1936 Bing Crosby gave us "Pennies from Heaven." Other optimistic songs were "Happy Days Are Here Again" and "We're in the Money."

We also went to movies: adults a quarter, kids ten cents. We saw screwball comedies, light romances, and Busby Berkeley dance movies with Fred Astaire and Ginger Rogers—classics I still enjoy. Others were *King Kong* about the giant ape that kidnapped actress Fay Wray to have his way with her and scaled the Empire State Building (construction had begun in 1930. It miraculously opened a little more than a year later). Feel-good films during the Great Depression were *You Can't Take It With You* (we didn't have it anyway) and later, in 1939, *The Wizard of Oz* with Judy Garland.

Baseball was great entertainment, cost little and banished worries for a while. We went to Pacific Coast League baseball games. Bleacher seats at Seals Stadium, Sixteenth and Bryant, were fifty cents for adults and ten cents for kids.

I had two autographed baseballs—one with signatures of players with the Oakland Oaks, and one with the autographs of Seals' manager "Lefty" O'Doul and Joe DiMaggio. Years later, I was relieved of the responsibility of owning these treasures, when a friend of a friend swiped them.

"Lefty" O'Doul, a San Francisco native, born in "Butchertown" south of Market, had been a star for the Yankees and later for the Giants in the "Majors." He became manager of the Seals in 1937. Joe DiMaggio played for him. Occasionally my Father and I took the ferry across the Bay and a streetcar to Emeryville where the Oakland Oaks played. I had my favorites there too—first baseman, Dolph Camilli; outfielder, Smead Jolley; and the pitcher Ralph Buxton. Then, as now, there was a fierce cross-bay rivalry.

The Great Depression lasted until 1939 when World War II started kicking everything into high gear again. But the WW2 years in San Francisco is another Back Story for another time. As I said earlier in these memories of growing up in the years of the Great Depression— they were hard times but good times.

———•◦•———

CHAPTER 55

U.S. PATENT NUMBER 139121

Jacob W. Davis, of Reno, Nevada, Assignor to himself and Levi Strauss & Company, of San Francisco, California. Improvement in Fastening Pocket-Openings: To all whom it may concern Be it known that I, JACOB W. DAVIS, of Reno, county of Washoe and State of Nevada , have invented an Improvement in Fastening seams; and do hereby declare the following description and accompanying drawing are sufficient to enable a person skilled in the art or science to which it most nearly appertains to make and use my said invention or improvement without further invention or experiment. My invention relates to a fastening for pocket-openings, whereby; the sewed seams are prevented from ripping or starting from frequent pressure or strain thereon; and it consists in the employment of a metal rivet or eyelet at each edge of the pocket-opening, to prevent the ripping of the seam at those points. The rivet or eyelet is so fastened in the seam as to bind the two parts of cloth which the seam unites together, so that it shall prevent the strain or pressure from coming upon the thread with which the seam is sewed.... .

LEVI STRAUSS AND THE PANTS THAT CHANGED THE WAY THE WORLD DRESSES

I can't say I'm much of a world traveler anymore—travel is no fun these days—but everywhere in the world I've been just about everyone was wearing blue jeans. I've seen them on the Great Wall of China, at the Hermitage in St. Petersburg, and along the Inca Trail above the Urubamba River in Peru.

Why is this? What is it about blue jeans—some distressed with holes in the knees, and worn proudly by the hip, the hipsters, the hip hoppers, and just plain folks? Blue jeans are the ubiquitous fashion statement, much like the little black dress and the boxer briefs. But, unlike the little black dress and the boxer briefs, blue jeans are unisex and universal. Doubtless, when we colonize Mars, blue jeans will be the space uniform.

The Bavarian Immigrant

Levi Strauss was born in Buttenheim, Bavaria in 1829. When he was 17 he and his sisters immigrated to New York where two older brothers owned a wholesale dry goods business. Levi learned the trade and in 1853, filled with tales of the California Gold Rush, he made his way to San Francisco. He founded his own wholesale dry goods business and also represented the family's New York firm. That was the beginning of Levi Strauss & Co. It sold clothing, blankets, handkerchiefs, and other items to small general stores in the American West.

Jacob W. Davis and his Rivets

In 1872 or thereabouts, Jacob W. Davis, a tailor in Reno, Nevada, wrote to Levi Strauss with a proposition. Jacob Davis had invented a way of relieving stress on the pockets of what were then known as waist overalls. One day the wife of a local laborer in Reno asked the tailor to make a pair of pants for her husband that would not fall apart

San Francisco Gold Rush miners wore Levi's.
PHOTO: LEVI STRAUSS & CO. ARCHIVES

from use. Davis came up with the idea of placing metal rivets at points of stress like the pocket corners and the bottom of the fly. The riveted pants were a success. So Jacob Davis began applying the rivets to the strain points and he felt sure he could get a U.S. patent on the concept. He needed a partner and asked Levi Strauss to join him in the venture. Levi Strauss was enthusiastic about the idea and the pair applied for the patent and got it. The year was 1873 and that's how Levi's blue jeans were born, almost 150 years ago.

The Crotch Rivet

Here are a few more significant dates in the Levi's saga. 1886—the two horse logo is first branded onto the leather patch of the jeans. 1902—Levi Strauss dies at 73 and newspapers describe him as a merchant and philanthropist. 1906—the San Francisco earthquake and fire destroys Levi Strauss & Co. headquarters and a new one is built on San Francisco's Battery Street. 1936—the iconic small red tab is placed on the right back pocket and the word "Levi's" is stitched on the tab. 1960—the Company replaces the word "overalls" with "jeans" on all labels. 1941—the Levi's crotch rivet is removed. The story goes like this: Levi's-clad cowboys crouching close to a campfire on cold nights received a painful shock when the crotch rivet heated and burned their private parts. That's the story anyway.

CHAPTER 56

CAN THE OLD SAN FRANCISCO WITH ITS MIDDLE CLASS VALUES CO-EXIST WITH THE NEW SAN FRANCISCO AND THE NEW SAN FRANCISCANS?

"If we want things to stay as they are, things will have to change."

–Giuseppi di Lampedusa
in his novel The Leopard

SEEKERS OF THE GOOD LIFE:
SAN FRANCISCO NOW AND THEN

Recently I had lunch with Carl Nolte who writes the Native Son column for the *San Francisco Chronicle*. Carl is a young whippersnapper compared to me, but we find common ground when we talk about the history of our city. We decided to don neckties and sports coats and go downtown to Sam's Grill which had reopened after an unsettling time when we thought it might be gone forever.

Carl decided to give the Alaskan cod a vote of confidence and proclaimed it well deserved, flaky and flavorful. I opted for the fried oysters and some creamed spinach. They were excellent.

From our choice of restaurants you might surmise that Carl and I put value on the traditional. We do. And after lunch, with our neckties still firmly in place, we got to reminiscing over a second glass of sauvignon blanc—just two old San Franciscans thinking about "then" and "now" in their favorite city.

Carl posed a question: Can the old-time San Francisco with its middle class values (where he and I grew up) co-exist with the new San Francisco and the new San Franciscans? He answered his own question in the affirmative but said it would be a balancing act. I agreed. We parted, loosening our neckties.

Since the Sam's Grill lunch with Carl I've been reflecting on our conversation and have developed the following Back Story on the "then" and "now" of San Francisco.

The Instant City

Right from its early days the raw-boned, fog-bound town called San Francisco had a high degree of sophistication that belied its edge-of-the-continent isolation. The Gold Rush in 1849, the discovery of Nevada's Comstock Lode of silver in 1857, and the completion of the Transcontinental Railroad in 1869 had turned this tiny village into an instant city. Suddenly San Francisco became a western metropolis with worldly tastes and enthusiasms.

Early San Francisco was rambunctious and disorderly. It was overrun with a motley crowd of adventurers—both men and women—from all over the world. Along with the gold seekers, get-rich-quick ruffians and con-artists, came merchants, farmers, clerks, clergy, bankers, doctors, poets, prostitutes, lawyers, sailors, socialites, salesmen, speculators, and just plain seekers of the good life. Some just liked the climate and wanted to live in the European-styled instant city by the Golden Gate. By 1875 the population of San Francisco was 190,000. In 1900 it was 350,000.

Paris of the Pacific

Obviously, all of these independent mavericks wanted to get rich, but they shared other desires as well. They sought good food and drink and good entertainment. Those who did not occupy tents or jerry-built wooden shanties lived in boarding houses and hotels which sprang up all over town. And suddenly there were restaurants to feed them. San Francisco became a city that eats out. Diners had money in their jeans and expected the best. That's what they got. Early San Francisco chefs tended to be Frenchmen from what were already fine restaurants on the country's East Coast. Some said San Francisco was on its way to becoming the Paris of the Pacific.

Not only were there skilled chefs here but the raw materials for their art was plentiful—oysters, crab and many kinds of fish were to be found in the bay and nearby rivers. Game roamed the adjacent wilderness. Valleys to the North and South provided vegetables and fruit. The Hungarian Count Agostin Haraszthy brought European wine grape cuttings here from France in 1861. But even earlier knowledgeable San Franciscans were drinking French wines that came around the Horn by sailing ship, or a bit later by transcontinental rail.

The Poodle Dog

One of the first San Francisco restaurants was the Poodle Dog that opened in 1849. The restaurant's true name was *Poulet d'Or* ("Golden

Chicken") but it is widely believed that unschooled miners corrupted the name thinking it sounded like "poodle dog." Soon the owners adopted the corruption and even installed a white poodle. But if many denizens of the instant city did not understand the French language, they did understand the language of French cuisine.

And there were other reliable temples of gastronomy in those days. Perhaps the most famous was Delmonico's which was serving elegant French food here in 1850. (The original Delmonico's opened in New York in 1837.) Other San Francisco old-timers are Tadich Grill that dates back to 1849, Jack's that opened in 1864. Sam's Grill (the inspiration for this Back Story) opened in 1867. The Cliff House (1863), Old Clam House (1861), the Palace Hotel with its incredible, stained glass-enclosed Garden Court (1875), Schroeder's (1893), Fior d' Italia (1893).

The San Francisco Good Life

The mining camps in the Sierra foothills were the Silicon Valley startups of the time. And while life panning gold could be rigorous, the miners dined on top quality foodstuff from San Francisco. Oysters, fish, game and vegetables arrived by riverboat up the Sacramento and American rivers and then overland by oxen-pulled wagons.

Booze was plentiful, and so was entertainment, both raucous and refined. Many of the top entertainers of the time journeyed to the camps to perform. Famed Shakespearean actor Edwin Booth and child singer-dancer Lotta Crabtree played the camps and were paid handsomely.

There were gold miners who had staked claims and were doing well and preferred to live in comfortable San Francisco. They journeyed to and from the gold fields in what today would be Google buses—horse and buggy or by river steamboat to San Francisco Bay.

Many miners, merchants and professionals the gold rush attracted later became part of the San Francisco community where they could not only participate in the good life—but get their laundry done. They involved themselves in civic affairs and paid big bucks (or a lot of gold nuggets) to build McMansions.

Those not politically oriented set up shop as doctors, lawyers or merchants. Some did what Silicon Valley "techies" do today—they got into politics. One miner, Andrew Jackson Bryant, made a poke and later became mayor.

And that's the way it was.

Has San Francisco Changed?

These days San Francisco's new citizens—whether they're so-called "techies" or some other types of end-of-the-rainbow seekers—are not unlike those who followed their dreams west in those early days. For every rough-neck miner and adventurer there were smart, creative, self-motivated, self-starters: Merchants like Levi Strauss who changed the way the world dresses. Businessmen like railroad barons Collis P. Huntington, Mark Hopkins, Leland Stanford, and Charles Crocker. Bankers like A.P. Giannini who financed San Francisco after the 1906 earthquake and fire. Publishers like Sam Brannan who ran San Francisco's first newspaper. And Charles James Brenham, a ship's captain who ferried miners from San Francisco to Sacramento.

Now, just as they did then, ambitious folks come here for the food, entertainment, the good life, and to get rich. Has San Francisco changed so much? No, I don't think so. Can this diverse group coexist? Yes, I do think so.

ACKNOWLEDGMENTS: SOURCES AND INSPIRATIONS

I had a lot of help with *San Francisco Appetites and Afterthoughts.* I did research in the pages of many books (hard copies, I should add). I also used the internet as we all do, and I relied on many people who gave freely of their time.

First, here is a list of books I found enlightening and useful in writing the book.

A Cook's Tour of San Francisco by Doris Muscatine (Charles Scribner's Sons, 1963)

Americans and the California Dream: 1850-1915 by Dr. Kevin Starr (Peregrine Smith, Inc., 1981)

The Annals of San Francisco by Frank Soule, John H. Gihon, and James Nisbet (Berkeley Hills Books, 1999)

The Barbary Coast, by Herbert Asbury (Alfred A. Knopf, 1933)

Bohemia: Where Art, Angst, Love, and Strong Coffee Meet by Herbert Gold (Axios Press, 1993)

Celebrating the Duke: and Louis, Billie, Bird, Carmen, Miles, Dizzy and Other Heroes by Ralph J. Gleason (Da Capo Press, 1995)

Cool Gray City of Love: 49 Views of San Francisco by Gary Kamiya (Bloomsbury USA, 2013)

Dizzy, Duke, the Count and Me: The Story of the Monterey Jazz Festival by Jimmy Lyons—with Ira Kamin (The *San Francisco Examiner* Division of the Hearst Corporation, 1978)

Entertainment in the Old West by Jeremy Agnew (McFarland & Company, Inc., 2011)

High Spirits: The Legacy Bars of San Francisco by J.K. Dineen (Heyday, 2015)

The History of Jazz by Ted Gioia (Oxford University Press, 1997)

Imperial San Francisco: Urban Power, Earthly Ruin by Gray Brechin (University of California Press, 1999)

The Madams of San Francisco by Curt Gentry (Doubleday & Company, Inc., 1964)

The Monterey Jazz Festival: Forty Legendary Years by William Miner (Angel City Press, 1997)

The Parade's Gone by Kevin Brownlow (University of California Press, 1968)

The Portable Beat Reader edited by Ann Charters (Penguin Books, 1992)

Tadich Grill: The Story of San Francisco's Oldest Restaurant, with Recipes by John Briscoe (Ten Speed Press, 2002)

Verdi at the Golden Gate: Opera and San Francisco in the Gold Rush Years by George Martin (University of California Press, 1993)

And here are the people who have been instrumental in the formulation of this book:

Joan Beyl—My wife Joan deserves to be first on this list. Not only does she read everything I write, but she edits and proofreads it. This is an enormous task and I appreciate it and love her for it. I didn't let her read these acknowledgments. She would have edited this awkward encomium.

Laurel Beyl—My daughter Laurel has a good editorial head on her shoulders and has tempered her enthusiasm for her Dad's writing with some sound advice. I trust her judgment.

Jeff Beyl—My son Jeff, a writer himself, has encouraged me in this book. His comments are important and Jeff knows how to encourage without being fawning.

Sara Brownell—Then there is my gal-pal Sara. She handled design and layout of my first book and of this one as well. She also serves as my photo editor. She's the best.

Bruce Bellingham—Bruce is a writer with a passion for San Francisco that matches my own and is always ready with a quip and a promise. He brightens my days.

Daniel David—My Grizzly Peak Press Publisher. Daniel gave me a chance when I didn't even know I had a book in me.

Lawrence Ferlinghetti—Lawrence inspires me. I count him a friend and a major influence on my writing life.

Steve Clickard—Steve is a constant source of inspiration to me. Steve sits next to me at the Monterey Jazz Festival and knows more about jazz than anyone I know.

Rick Carroll—I am always engaged by highly-charged, optimistic people. Rick cheers me on. He has done so with this book. He's like a hot, supercharged Porsche.

Carl Nolte—Carl writes the "Native Son" column for the *San Francisco Chronicle*. I try out ideas on him. If he gives "thumbs up" I go for it—"thumbs down," I forget it.

I must also mention my comrades at the *Marina Times*. That San Francisco publication has been publishing my essays and columns for several years. Publisher **Earl Adkins** is a tolerant man who gives me a lot of editorial leeway. Editor-in-Chief **Susan Dyer Reynolds** is wonderfully supportive as are Executive Editor **John Zipperer** and Managing Editor **Lynette Majer.**

Finally, I call your attention to the photos in this book. The limitations of the book's size doesn't do them service. Many of them are magnificent, salon photos, which if viewed in much greater size would be thrilling. For example, the Fred Lyon photo of the Garden Court at the Palace Hotel which appears on page 182 is a collector's item. So too are some of the photos of various jazz artists from the Ron Hudson collection.

There are more books I should probably mention and certainly more individuals who have helped me. Perhaps I can get to them in my third book.

ABOUT THE AUTHOR

Ernest Beyl is a San Francisco writer who has long had a love affair with his city. His first book—*Sketches from a North Beach Journal*—was a series of word portraits of larger-than-life characters from the Gold Rush to the present that have given San Francisco so much excitement and panache. It was published in 2015 and was widely acclaimed. This second book—*San Francisco Appetites and Afterthoughts: In search of the Good Life by the Golden Gate*—picks up on themes he explored earlier and takes the position that not all appetites are about food. This new book delves into the author's special passions for jazz, blues, rock 'n' roll, San Francisco poetry and prose, books and bookstores, architecture, Panama hats, saloons, bartenders, nightclubs, and the history and traditions in his city by the Golden Gate.

When not researching and writing what he plans as a continuing series of books with San Francisco as a background, Beyl writes a monthly column for the *Marina Times*. "This allows me to engage readers on many subjects that strike my fancy—including the ones in *San Francisco Appetites and Afterthoughts*."

Almost a native San Franciscan—he was born in Fresno, California but his family moved to his adopted city when he was an infant—he now lives on Telegraph Hill and explores nearby North Beach and other city neighborhoods "In search of the Good Life by the Golden Gate."

Ernest Beyl is married to Joan Lawson Beyl and has a son and daughter.

INDEX